DAVID G BAILEY's debut publication in fantasy adventure novel aimed at and beyon (2022) returned to a world more recognisab voices the lives of four sisters over more th childhood. A husband of a Roper sister takes centre stage in *Them Feltwell Boys* (2023). With the same gritty realism and sometimes dark humour found in its predecessor, this follows Ray Roden's crude attempts at teenage love in counterpoint to his cynical womanising as an adult. *The Sunny Side of the House* (2024) is a first venture into non-fiction in another projected series, *When Life Gives You Strawberries – Memories of a Fenland Boy.* The origin story of *Seventeen* appears within the clear-eyed narrative of a 1960s boyhood in East Anglia, where both David's contemporary novels are partly set. He currently lives in the Midlands.

To read more of and about David's work, including a quarterly newsletter and new content daily comprising extracts from diaries and other writing over more than fifty years, visit his website www.davidgbailey.com.

Also by David G Bailey

Young adult fantasy football adventure

Seventeen: or the Blood City Tommy O'Reilly Benefit Tour

Contemporary adult fiction

Them Roper Girls

Them Feltwell Boys

The Sunny Side of the House

When Life Gives You Strawberries
– Memories of a Fenland Boy (I)

DAVID G BAILEY

SilverWood

Published in 2024 by SilverWood Books

SilverWood Books Ltd
14 Small Street, Bristol, BS1 1DE, United Kingdom
www.silverwoodbooks.co.uk

ISBN 978-1-80042-282-7 (paperback)
ISBN 978-1-80042-283-4 (hardback)

British Library Cataloguing in Publication Data
A CIP catalogue record for this book is
available from the British Library

Page design and typesetting by SilverWood Books

For Damien, Joe and Amy

and

To family: wherever and however you find it, you know it.

Author's Note and Acknowledgements

This is my first volume of memories to be published, from earlier incarnations with working titles like *Before the Diaries Kick In* and *Yoof*. It has proved a much more collaborative process than I envisaged when I wrote those drafts, with only myself to please.

I tried to discharge the duty of care to family and friends wherever possible by showing them in advance their mentions. I then omitted the odd memory I know to be true on the principle of sparing upset to others and their own families. I refrained from shedding light on some sensitive matters I learned of only as an adult. I hope it is clear in the text where I am speaking from first-hand experience and where (as often) based on the input of others. In thanking all those who have contributed to inform and enrich the text, including its copyeditor my fellow Wisbech Old Grammarian Ivan Butler, I naturally take responsibility for any errors or lapses of taste that could have been avoided in my presentation.

I have taken no firm line but individual decisions on whether to show people's full names or (rarely) substitute generic ones. The absence of a surname does not mean I have forgotten it any more than its presence means the person is no longer above ground.

These are personal recollections rather than any attempt at social history, but I did find of great interest, and help in returning to the village of my boyhood, publications by local historian William P (Bill) Smith including *Outwell in a Nutshell* and *Outwell Pictorial*. The contemporary annual magazines of Wisbech Grammar School were another valuable source.

My reading list of how-to books on non-fiction of this kind was postponed in favour of examples of the art such as Tolstoy's *Childhood, Boyhood, Youth* and Edward Storey's *Fen Boy First*. I have enjoyed handsome presentations by Allan Gambles (*My Back Pages*) and Colin Gough (*A Goodly Heritage*), both friends attentive and encouraging readers of my work, as well as featuring in many volumes of my life. Edited extracts from this one have appeared in The

Cafe Writers of Rugby's (www.rugbycafewriters.com) *A Story for Every Day of Autumn* and *A Story for Every Day of Spring*. I heartily recommend these compilations, along with two more from them whose titles you can probably guess.

While this book deals with uncomfortable realities including physical and mental illness and domestic violence, I take the view that its publication cannot hurt the dear departed. If they live on, I trust it will be with enough understanding to accept whatever I am up to down here, where some readers may find certain language and scenes offensive or upsetting.

All the best, David.

Contents

Illustrations

THE SUNNY SIDE OF THE HOUSE

Bailey and Hills Family Tree 1923-1970

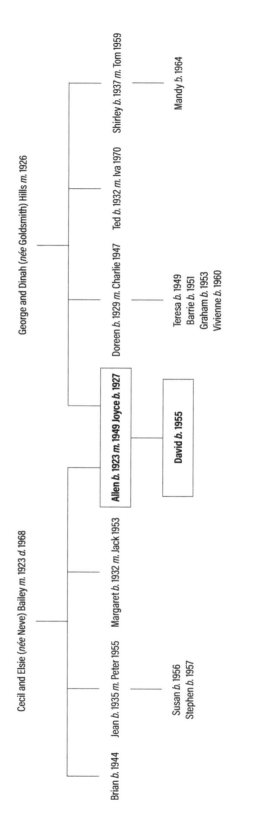

George and Dinah (*née* Goldsmith) Hills *m.* 1926

Cecil and Elsie (*née* Neve) Bailey *m.* 1923 *d.* 1968

Shirley *b.* 1937 *m.* Tom 1959

Mandy *b.* 1964

Ted *b.* 1932 *m.* Iva 1970

Doreen *b.* 1929 *m.* Charlie 1947

Teresa *b.* 1949
Barrie *b.* 1951
Graham *b.* 1953
Vivienne *b.* 1960

Allen *b.* 1923 *m.* 1949 Joyce *b.* 1927

David *b.* 1955

Margaret *b.* 1932 *m.* Jack 1953

Jean *b.* 1935 *m.* Peter 1955

Brian *b.* 1944

Susan *b.* 1956
Stephen *b.* 1957

Wedding of Joyce Hills and Allen Bailey, 15 October 1949

(L to R) Cecil Bailey, Elsie Bailey, Shirley Hills, Eric Scott, Margaret Bailey behind Betty Goldsmith, Allen Bailey, Joyce Hills, Doreen Rowell, George Hills, Jean Bailey behind Brian Bailey, Dinah Hills, Ted Hills, Charlie Rowell

Chapter One

The Hag and the Head

'So you're a yeller-belly then?'

It would be unseemly for a man already long past his prime to grab and pummel one twenty years older. Since we were in the upstairs bar of a Northampton pub, not a black-and-white Western, gunplay was no more of an option. I'd given John the opening, admitting that although I proudly call myself an East Anglian, I was born in Lincoln. Knowing nothing of his Suffolk, I hoped the all-purpose put-down for country folk would serve for reply: 'Better than being a sheep-shagger.'

Despite spending my early years there from birth in 1955, I had not heard of the term 'yellow-belly' applying to citizens of Lincolnshire. Perhaps in that context it has nothing to do with cowardice. Perhaps it no longer means much in any context to anyone under fifty.

As I plot a walk around my homeland I am thinking of the perimeter of Cambridgeshire (or Isle of Ely in less energetic moods). I would not have to make a big detour to visit Sutton Bridge, where my dad and mum, Allen and Joyce, made their first marital home.

'The Bridge' lies just off the A17 between Sleaford and King's Lynn, much closer to the latter. Some five miles inland from the Wash, it is no higher than other parts of the Fens. Land reclamation and drainage are important. On Dad's wedding certificate under 'Father's Occupation' appears 'excavator driver'. On mine it would read 'dragline driver'.

I am not inclined to trace family beyond those I knew personally, which takes me no further than Dad's parents. They were Nana and Grandad Bailey when Mum mentioned them. Because I never heard her address either by a

Christian name, I didn't know for years that they were Cecil Allen, born on 8 December 1901, and Charlotte Elsie (called Elsie) on 22 November 1904.

Allen Edward Bailey was their first child, born on 9 August 1923, less than nine months after the wedding I understand. Births beginning with Allen's grandad Albert in 1868 were recorded inside the back cover of the family's Holy Bible. After the birth and death of Cecil, a brother to Allen, within three months during 1927, there followed Margaret (1932), Jean (1935) and Brian a war child in 1944.

I don't recall Dad ever telling me anything about his parents. Why would he? I had not the slightest interest in their history, not until it was too late to satisfy it. What I do have is constructed from memories of adult conversations, no doubt as partial and distorted as Mum's direct recollection of her in-laws, which also gave me some material.

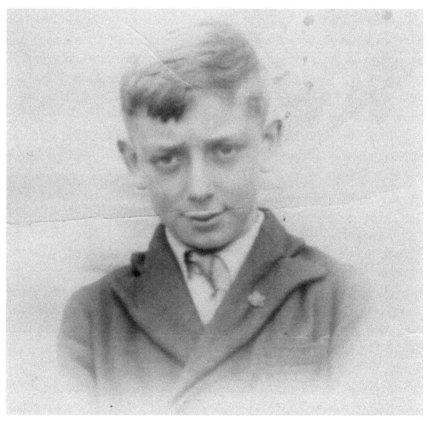

Young Allen

Cecil's mum yanked him out of the Great War army recruiting line: 'You've got one of my boys, you're not having this one.' He worked at Leesons garage before getting involved in excavation, apart from casual labour, like many other men in the Bridge, on its docks when the opportunity was there. He was always a grafter, in later life cycling over twenty-five miles each way daily to jobs in Swaffham.

Grandad had an allotment of a couple of acres. I remember sheltering from the sun in a shed on its headland, reading a slim paperback. My copy of Roger Lancelyn Green's *The Tale of Troy*, a three-shilling Puffin book, is inscribed 'To David, From Mum and Dad, July 1964'.

The land kept Grandad Bailey occupied throughout his life, helped feed the family. It fed him less conventionally; Dad said that on occasion his father's heartburn was so severe he would eat earth against it. Dad also remembered him reading the Bible from cover to cover, making no such claim for himself on the equally bulky *Life of Our Blessed Lord and Saviour Jesus Christ and Lives of the Apostles*. He had it for his seventh birthday.

The only further evidence of Grandad's reading is *The Last of the Mohicans*. In its flyleaf inscription dated 18 December 1950, after Cecil's full address appears the injunction:

If this book should dare to roam,
Box its ears and send it home

Mum and Dad began married life in his parents' council house, 58 Railway Lane. I get the impression the arrangement was not a roaring success. By the time I came along they had their own home at 42 Princes Street, on a newer council estate almost a mile away across the main road through the village. We had an indoor flushing toilet there, as against the outside wooden board over an open cesspit at Grandad's. I dreaded having to use that, but there was no alternative.

I picture Grandad sitting massively in an armchair in the single downstairs room beyond the kitchen and scullery. Hands on knees, wearing several layers of brown clothing, a jacket and tie, a cloth cap. It was surely a Sunday for him to be so confined. I think of Nana Bailey in dark clothes too, white-haired, pale sharp features under tortoiseshell glasses. Apart from bringing up her own children and looking after us grandkids, Nana worked on the land and at Lockwoods canning factory.

The food I recall from my grandparents' house is jam sandwiches Nana would make for us to eat outside, a bonus if the jam was strawberry or raspberry. The food everyone recalls from Sutton Bridge up to the mid-sixties is 'Cashy' Cawthorn's fish and chips (few are left to recall his given name of Arthur). In his shop at the top of Railway Lane I would greet and be greeted by one of the assistants as Captain Pugwash.

Outside the tiny yard, where the shithouse bulked and stank, was a small patch of grass shared by Grandad and two or three neighbours. On this was a swing, where my cousin Susan – some six months my junior – taught me to blow bubbles with gum and I taught her to whistle. I remember a long walk the two of us had along the nearby railway track. We got as far as a place called Whistle Stop before deciding we had better turn back.

Further beyond various outbuildings was unkempt grassland where we would play games of soldiers, based on war films rather than the first-hand experience our fathers did not share with us. In one I volunteered to be the soldier who is always eating.

Throughout my first years and beyond primary school, the constellation of Grandad Bailey's family was fixed. His elder daughter Margaret, moon-faced with heavy glasses speaking to the poor eyesight shared by several of the family, lived a couple of hundred yards further out from the village in a prefab shared with her husband Jack, from Long Sutton and torpedoed in the war. Childless, both worked on the land. Mum spoke proudly of how Dad helped them talk to the council to secure better housing, which went unvisited by me.

Aunt Jean was much prettier and livelier than her sister. She married a farmer who was still in the army doing National Service on their big day. It was coincidence they already shared a surname, not an example of Fenland inbreeding. Uncle Peter was tall and lean. I once heard Dad speak admiringly of his strength, able to carry a hundredweight sack of potatoes under each arm.

Peter's father owned the land they worked, away from the Bridge but not by more than twenty miles, in one of the Walpoles. Sue came along, maybe not quite nine months after one name became one, always to me a beautiful, brown-eyed girl. I never had the same closeness with her brother Stephen, perhaps because Uncle Peter would set us to wrestle each other when we visited their home. All the adults were watching and there was no physical damage done. I took no credit in pinning my younger and slighter cousin who, even at that tender age, had to take off his glasses to fight.

20

Uncle Brian lived at home with his parents. I remember him sitting in front of the telly in their living room; otherwise, apart from being christened in the same 17 June 1956 ceremony when I was a baby and he was eleven, we had little contact during my childhood. Although in age closer to us, his nephews and niece, than to some of his siblings, Brian was not boyish or playful. He left school at fifteen to work at Goddard's, a local company involved in building as well as undertaking. I don't blame him for not wanting to play with us kids when he was already doing a man's job.

With no recollection of the upstairs in Railway Lane, I don't know how crowded it was with Mum and Dad living there – not excessively so perhaps, at least physically. In Princes Street I had my own bedroom as an only child (from here on read 'spoilt bastard' whenever I slip in that phrase), with a third apart from the one my parents shared.

Early playmates in other houses on Princes Street were Brian Gilham and David Tingey. Malcolm Easy lived across the road, while my best friend once I was allowed to venture more than a couple of doors away became Steve O'Reilly, in another street. Memories, before starting school or just after, are fragmentary: giving Malc too much of a start in a race, then slowing to a halt in a pretence we were not running against each other at all; playing in Brian's back yard, becoming uneasy or frightened for some reason by the presence of an older boy, saying I would go home to fetch something and not returning; shocked at the lack of formality at Kevin Crane's birthday party, when after tea people would leave only to come back later; fishing sticklebacks out of a creek between our houses with Steve, with whom I also often played indoors, at my home or his.

Are children nowadays encouraged, as we were practically obliged, to address their parents' friends as 'Uncle' or 'Aunt'? The neighbours immediately to our left were Uncle Ken and Aunt Molly. He was a somewhat scary-looking character in jeans and crew cut, the same hairstyle imposed on his three sons – Martyn was closest in age to me, a bit younger. Aunt Molly was buxom and kind, their daughter an impossibly remote creature. So too was Geraldine, only child of Uncle John and Aunt June, who moved away to St Ives near Huntingdon. John's claim to fame was once taking all Mum's washing off the line to preserve it from a downpour, while leaving his own wife's out.

Closer to John and June than Ken and Molly, Mum and Dad's best friends were Aunt Maud and Uncle Norman Chappell. Their oldest son, Brian, was so far above my age that he was also 'Uncle Brian' (which gave me two of them). Christine, David and Geoffrey descended in order of age to within a year or two of me, then Lesley was a year or so younger. I had no time for her, for that reason and her gender, though outward civilities had to be maintained. She was at our back door one day as I was eating chips at the kitchen table.

'I like chips,' she intoned in a formula that only varied by noun.

'Yeah, so do I,' with no adults around I sniggered to Steve, not sharing.

Within a couple of streets in opposite directions were Aunts Beryl and Beulah. These did have a family connection, as cousins to Dad. Beulah I hardly knew, while Aunt Beryl was no more than the harassed mother of my tough cousins.

Roy and Barry were older than I, Michael a little younger. Age differences matter a lot to kids, down to months, especially if there is a separation of a school year. I would never have dreamed of challenging his brothers but wasn't going to take any shit from Micky. There were a few physical scuffles with him, the only conclusive result when he out-machoed me without striking a blow.

We were with at least one other boy, in a place where we shouldn't have been, perhaps a lumber yard. As a man came hollering at us, we ran along what turned out to be a kind of dry-land pier, the only escape route a drop into thick grass. Micky and the other boy took it, beckoning me down to join them. I couldn't. I dared not jump.

I don't know how big the leap was – several times our own height is all my mind's eye reports. I don't recall anything of the telling-off from the yardman, nor any ribbing from Micky when I next saw him a few minutes or few days later. I do recall a deep sense of shame at my cowardice when I turned to face the man and his music.

Those second cousins were regarded as wild by Mum, who did not have the liveliest sense of adventure for me. We were allowed to roam as far as our legs would take us, the only outright prohibition – for which I was secretly grateful – that I must not go with the other boys to play at a swimming hole by the river. Again, I don't recall any sense of drawing their scorn; it was not a regular haunt, and excuses were easily made. Being unable to swim was not one of them – none of us could do that.

I was generally a biddable child, albeit with an angry and stubborn streak on occasion. Mum was washing me from a bowl on the living-room table one night, telling me how some kids my age had been attacked by older ones.

'I'd have hit the fuckers back,' I bragged.

I suppose she exchanged looks with Dad, who was probably trying his best not to grin.

'David, I want you to promise me you'll never use language like that again.'

I made the promise; kept it too, a surprisingly long time.

Sutton Bridge was small enough that you could rely on any mischief being reported to your parents. Another courtesy uncle from down our road (Johnny, wife Ethel, two daughters older than me, possibly twins) had to swerve on the main street to avoid me running under his car. He went up no end in my estimation when the tale didn't reach home.

Even the most protective parents felt able to leave their children out playing unsupervised, without worrying unduly about harm caused to or by them. Roaming the rough around the golf course looking for balls we had no use for; pelting stones at hundreds of rats milling unperturbed around wasteland behind the playing field; knocking on the front door of the terraced house near Aunt Beulah's where a witch lived: these were adventures for us. Then again, we were only five years old.

From my earliest days I was pleased to be outside the house, or to have friends round, as a way of avoiding the tensions and outright rows between Mum and Dad. In my early teens I had a taste for horror comics, Hammer films and the paperback series edited by Herbert Van Thal, which ran to at least *The 23rd Pan Book of Horror Stories*. In one comic I read of a handsome couple arriving at their honeymoon destination. Alone at last in their suite, he is smartly suited and necktied, clean-cut and clean-shaven; she is lovely in her wedding finery. Rather than withdraw to prepare herself for bed, she offers him the chance to watch her disrobe.

The bride is not shy. The beautiful young woman reveals herself slowly, frame by frame, to be a hideous crone gloating at having tricked her new husband. He is unfazed, the topper to the story (though of less impact on me than the woman's transformation) coming as he removes his own head to stow it, grinning still, under his arm. Years later, when I thought of writing a memoir or fictionalised account of my parents' marriage, the title I toyed with was 'The Hag and the Head'.

Chapter Two

Mum and Dad

Bailey family at seaside
(L to R) Cecil with Jean on lap, Elsie with Margaret, Allen

Grandad Bailey reportedly refused to let his oldest child go to grammar school, although he passed the scholarship. According to Mum, Allen said his dad would rather have money to sit in a pub than spend on his education, which might have helped him get an office job later on.

'I don't remember hearing of Grandad being a drinker. He didn't go out much, did he?'

'I never really saw that either,' she conceded, 'but *his* father owned a pub in the Bridge, I can't remember the name, on the road to Long Sutton. He was a nice old boy, living in a home when we got married. We used to have him round to Sunday tea. That was before you were born,' she added when I said I had no memory of him.

I found the address at which Allen's grandad Albert Bailey was awarded a pension: Salutation Inn, Sutton Bridge. His son Albert Edward, Cecil's older brother, joined the Royal Fusiliers aged seventeen in December 1914 and was sent to France. The first job he scheduled for his eventual return was to kill father Albert if he was still hitting their mother. Sapper Albert Edward Bailey died on the Somme on 13 April 2018. The pension Albert drew was as his dependant.

Mum spoke of Allen taking fierce beatings from his dad, Cecil. Whether these were more outside the norm than Allen leaving school as soon as possible is impossible to know, but his younger siblings confirmed he was hit, as they were not. Cecil's grandchildren had softer memories of him, though he still knew how to make himself respected if not feared. As to the drinking, well he did grow up in a pub, his landlord father reputedly a violent drunk. When in his fifties as a grandad though, Cecil is remembered as always returning from his Sunday pint on time for dinner. Sometimes people can break the cycle, change for the better. Perhaps the great-grandad Bailey I never knew had also changed, become that 'nice old boy'.

On the matter of education, there was usually a cost to put a child in grammar school until the 1944 Education Act, on the other side of which Allen's sister Jean would attend Spalding High School. I never heard Dad comment on either the hidings or schooling he received, yet knew he hoped better for me.

At fifteen, Allen was apprenticed as a grocer's boy, the second part in a two-and-sixpenny deed of indenture where his father (the Guardian) was the first part and the 'INTERNATIONAL TEA COMPANY'S STORES LIMITED', headquartered at Mitre Square in the City of London, the Company of the third part. Over three years from 9 January 1939 he would 'learn the art trade and business of a Grocer and Provision merchant'. Percentage wage increases of 50% after the first year and 33.3% from the second do not look as impressive in monetary terms: the starting point was ten shillings, rising from fifteen to twenty, which in 1941 would be one pound a week.

I don't know whether such an apprenticeship would have been prized compared to those for other trades (sparkies or chippies, say), or more a catch-as-catch-can employment for a kid with no special talents or qualifications. Not well-built, Allen was weak-eyed, wearing glasses in photos from boyhood, which is perhaps why he did not go 'on the land', the most common option around our way then and for many years since.

When Britain declared war on Germany in 1939, Allen had just turned sixteen. Conscription applied immediately but only to those aged between eighteen and forty-one. Farming was a reserved occupation, leading my future Uncle Charlie to be denied his wish to join up by his father – he had to settle for the Observer Corps rather than the RAF – and the younger Uncle Tom, with more hair to brylcreem, to miss National Service in its last post-war year of existence on the application of *his* father. Allen enlisted in 1941, whether directly from the grocer boy's job (to me the image of forty-something David Jason and his bike in *Open All Hours* is irrepressible) or some other. Perhaps because of his limited vision or what he had learned of the grocery art trade and business, he went into the Royal Army Service Corps (RASC), responsible for provisioning the service with everything except guns and ammo. His main job in the forces was lorry driving. He spoke to his younger brother of coming under shellfire at least once, which was 'not very nice'.

Joyce Elizabeth was the oldest of four children, born on 28 September 1927 to George Edward Hills and his wife Dinah (so everyone called her, though her baptismal name was Elizabeth). Like Allen's, Joyce's family was unimpeachably working-class, equally that of a village, one right on the border between Cambridgeshire and Norfolk. Outwell is less than half an hour by car to the south of Sutton Bridge, with Wisbech, 'Capital of the Fens', roughly halfway between the two. Following the River Nene from the Bridge to Foul Anchor, you will pass on your right in the otherwise featureless landscape an impressive stand of seventeen trees, a landmark known as Nineteen Trees until the gales of 1987.

Grandad George was born and lived all his life in Outwell, as did three of his four siblings (the adventurer, Uncle Will, went working on the railways out of March, a good ten miles away). Born on 5 December 1903, George was too young for active service in the First World War, too old for the Second except as an Outwell Home Guarder. No stranger to land work, he spent forty-five years driving buses, first for the private business of a Mr Robb, then – or which became – the red double-deckers of Eastern Counties. Intensely shy outside his family, he liked being shut off in the cabin, towards the end of his career declining to move to single-deckers where the driver also issued tickets.

George's button-nosed bride, Dinah Goldsmith, grew up in Norwich, a sickly child who survived, unlike some of a dozen siblings. Her mother Elizabeth had moved to Outwell from her hometown of Norwich in 1918, when she was widowed by the war that four years earlier had claimed one of her sons, named Robert like his father. Dinah's courtship by George included him cycling to Norwich, more than forty miles, for the girl slightly older than him, born on midsummer's day 1902.

Nana and Grandad wed around September 1926, with Joyce arriving a respectable twelve months later. She was followed over the next decade by Doreen (1929), Edward (Ted, 1932) and Shirley (1937). The fact that none of the children went to Wisbech Grammar or High School was no more a reflection on their intelligence than in Allen's case. Joyce's cousin Pam's recollection that the two scholarship successes from Outwell each year – one boy, one girl – were always councillors' children may not have been strictly correct. Mum told me she herself passed two of the three examinations for the eleven-plus as it was known. She was in isolation for the third with measles, along with another cousin, Eileen, with whom in infancy she had also shared a pram and whooping cough.

Leaving school aged fourteen, Joyce entered the labour market around the same time as Allen signed up. Like his, her first job was at a grocer's, 'having to write out little tickets, George Mason's was the shop, beside Woolies'.

Woolworths was on the marketplace in Wisbech, where she also had a brief spell at Smedley's canning factory with her best friend Marjorie Sutton, before returning to Outwell. There she worked on the land of Uncle George Brown, husband of Grandad George's oldest sister Ivy (or Ive sometimes). There was additionally casual work to be had on Grandad's own land, particularly during the strawberry or fruiting season.

I long thought Joyce left home in her teens after some falling-out with her father, but she set me right that he ceased talking to her *because* she left home. Her falling-out was with an Irishman called Jim, to whom I think she was actually engaged, rings and all. He was a great favourite with Shirley because he let her have his sweets ration, and with Uncle George and Aunt Ive because he was a churchgoer, albeit a Catholic one. There was also an American, who against all odds returned from the States with the promise completed of a house ready to take her there. I believe George disapproved and somehow put the kybosh on it.

Was Jim or Joe (let's call him) the one, or one of many, who sent Joyce Valentine cards? She was always careful to clarify that, while Dad never marked the day in their years together, she had not missed out entirely on these sentimental tokens.

'Where did you meet this Jim, then?'

'Oh, up Wisbech, there was a whole colony of Irish at Lynn in them days. We kept writing for a couple of years after I moved away, nearly up till I met your dad. I just made sure he wasn't there or I didn't see him when I went home.'

'What was he, a navvy or something?'

'No, a bit like your dad really, he had a job something to do with drainage, excavating. We tried to get a job in the NAAFI, Marjie and me, but we were too young.'

The celebrations for Second World War Victory in Europe on 8 May 1945, known as VE Day, saw Joyce aged seventeen cycling over thirty miles to see Jim in Hunstanton on his twenty-seventh birthday. Strictly forbidden to do so by her dad, she swore up and down to George when she saw him back at Wisbech that evening she had not gone. She reckoned without his bus driver and landsman's knowledge of the route. 'What's all them rhododendrons in your front wheel then?'

While Joyce would have had to elope to Gretna Green to get married without her father's permission, his authority did not extend to keeping her at home as a single girl. Marjorie accompanied her to a series of live-in jobs, including a post-war convalescent home for soldiers in Baldock. There was a place near Dunstable, a miners' hostel out Nottingham way. The chronology is uncertain, so I may be wrong to think of these as Bevan Boys, men who without going to the lengths of becoming conscientious objectors preferred digging coal to trenches as their contribution to the war effort. Mum talked of them watching, motionless, tired perhaps but with an altogether modern sense of gentlemanly behaviour, as the young women employed to cook and clean for them strained to lift heavy urns of tea or tubs of washing water.

During Joyce's heady flight to independence her father would at first not speak to her when she came home for weekends or holidays. He would, however, write to her at the various addresses (the hostels and later hotels where she worked provided accommodation as part of the deal), enclosing say a cooked chicken leg to ensure she did not starve. She was eventually brought back to earth and Outwell by a serious illness.

Young Joyce

Joyce was laid up for a year with a malady she could never name to professionals enquiring of her medical history. This was not from reticence or forgetfulness. As she explained it, 'they didn't tell you nothing in them days.' She would have been about nineteen. If the doctors had wanted to be more specific to her father, I can only imagine George delegating that dealing with strangers to Nan Dinah (as he would to me, as a teenager, going in the ambulance with Nan and her broken arm).

Mum spent a good deal of time in hospital for tests; rheumatic fever are words I throw down without really knowing what they signify. She speculated that she had perhaps strained or ruptured something internally on one of those heavy lifts, scorning any help if grudgingly proffered by the conscripted colliers. Nan Dinah had spent periods of her own childhood laid up. I think we'll have to leave it that Mum was 'poorly' – very poorly even.

I don't believe the illness was life-threatening – while she was presumably medicated, there was no operation. Still, it was a severe blow for someone so active and ready to attack life. Perhaps boredom and a need to test her willpower were partly why she was carried to the strawberry fields at fruiting and picked lying down, dragging herself along the rows. I guess that George would have approved such a willingness to work at the harvesting of his crops, and that his approval would have meant a good deal to her.

Allen did not rise above private in the army. I heard he was involved in the Normandy landings, not on D-Day itself but on D plus a small number. The only confirmed 'sighting' of him after that is in a photo with a pal taken at Wommersom (in Belgium), on 18 August 1945 according to the writing on its back. His mum would send him cigarettes and other treats during his service, but Allen rarely wrote home. He later followed the almost universal convention of not talking about his war, for all that it would affect him deeply. How could it not, when it still cast a long shadow over us, the children of that generation?

Demobbed Allen, like many who had learned in the forces, never had to take a driving test. It would be years before he could aspire to a car, but he drove lorries before graduating to draglines, in the latter like his father before and brother after him. This is not to suggest any degree of nepotism, though Grandad Bailey did make at least one phone call to help Brian get into the job aged about twenty.

Apart from his driving skills Allen had acquired an ability to play the cornet and an abiding affection for brass bands, so much a part of the post-war landscape until they became a victim of rock and roll. It was at a dance or similar social event that he first dated Joyce Hills, recovered from her illness and working as a chambermaid at the Duke's Head Hotel on the market square of King's Lynn. She was on duty when they were introduced, entrusted with the whole set of hotel keys on a great ring at her waist, so that his initial impression – he confided safely later – was of a gaoler. Their date was a double one, the other female Marjie if I had to bet.

All of George and Dinah's children exhibited a strong degree of independence, or perhaps wilfulness. Their second daughter Doreen was eighteen in November 1947 when she walked up the aisle to the aircraft-spotting Charlie Rowell. I long imagined the early part of Mum and Dad's courtship conducted with him in uniform, but Allen was home from the war by 1946 at the latest. His sister Jean remembered his arrival on leave or discharge, seeing him through the window of their house in Railway Lane before he came round the corner to its back door. She ran out to meet her adored 'Algeebub', to be carried back inside by him. Keen to see his little brother, born in September 1944, Allen went upstairs to find Brian at their mother's breast.

Mum and Dad met in March 1949, marrying within the year on 15 October. On their wedding certificate Allen's 'Rank or Profession' appears as 'Lorry Driver'. There is nothing but a dash in the corresponding space for Joyce.

Chapter Three

Striking Out

St Clement's was no doubt for centuries the spiritual as well as the geographic centre of Outwell. Now it shares a vicar and services with Upwell, the two villages a single settlement called Wella back in the doomsdays when John was mislaying his jewels in those parts.

Nowadays far from a social hub, its door usually heavily locked, St Clement's must have been livelier in the forties and fifties when George took his three daughters successively, if not exactly in age order, down its aisle. Only Aunt Ivy from either of my parents' families was a regular churchgoer, but they did things in the time-honoured way. There they are in Joyce's wedding photograph, the principal group, fifteen of them. It is black-and-white, yet looking at it I never feel cheated of a riot of colour. The who's who on the back in Mum's neat handwriting specifies that the bridesmaids' dresses were 'blue with wine ribbons'. The local press report cited below for her own wardrobe adds to the blue dresses matching headdresses and bouquets of blue flowers.

Joyce wore a 'gown of white marocain with a full-length veil held in place by a headdress of heather, and carried a bouquet of red carnations and trailing fern'. Those bridesmaids were the youngest Hills sister Shirley and their cousin Betty, one of Uncle Fred and Aunt Peg's children, along with Allen's two sisters Margaret and Jean. As befitted an already married woman, Aunt Doreen was matron of honour. The two mothers wear hats, dark skirts and jackets.

The men are all buttoned up and buttonholed, white shirts under shades of black jackets and ties. Joyce's brother Ted, an usher for the occasion, stands tall at one edge of the frame behind their mother, beside Uncle Charlie, bald from an early age and in those days with no option but to stay that way. Grandad George is also bald, under the church door, Grandad Bailey square and solid at the other end of the photo. The best man was Eric Scott, a friend of Allen's from the Bridge, probably pre-army days. I never saw or heard anything of him during my boyhood.

The baby of the group, aged five and in short trousers, is Allen's brother Brian. Still now as I look at the picture, I feel he is somehow there representing me. It would be nearly forty years until his own wedding. Ted had a good twenty to go before a ceremony at Downham Market Registry Office broke the St Clement's thread binding George and Dinah's kids' nuptials.

That thread was almost snapped by Joyce, who said once a serious fall-out with Nan Dinah in the build-up left her prepared to make her wedding a registry office do. Her parents got wind of it only through the banns. George stepped in and insisted not only on giving his daughter away but paying for everything. He did her proud, from the look of the cake. Around a hundred people were reported at the reception in the Swan, just across the river. Uncle Sid got conspicuously drunk on strawberry wine either then or at the wedding a generation earlier of his brother George.

Joyce and Allen were looking for a place of their own, on the council housing lists in both Sutton Bridge and Outwell, as they began married life in Railway Lane. Joyce continued to work at the Duke's Head, travelling daily to King's Lynn by bus. Allen would cycle to work on the lorries then his bright red dragline (one of my earliest toys was a metal replica), not a company vehicle you could swing for personal use.

How long before my birth on 1 November 1955 (All Saints' Day, as I always add) they moved to Princes Street I don't know. It came on offer at the same time as a tied cottage in Outwell, with Allen's job as well as the relative merits of the two properties influencing their decision.

Although in his whole life Allen would never draw a weekly wage of more than twenty pounds, I imagine him and Joyce in the childless years of their marriage and into the first few with me as comfortable enough financially: this in the context of an upbringing for both by no means luxurious, if only – and it was not only – from war and post-war shortages. It was a big plus that neither was subject to the seasonality of land work, though Joyce would always do that to supplement their income.

During their courtship and early marriage, they would go to the pictures with some regularity, later taking me as an infant to sleep and bawl through Westerns, war films and biblical epics alike. Allen kept up his cornet playing for a time, with Joyce going along to watch. There were outings to pubs and dances, but a meal out would have been an extreme rarity unless you count fish and chips eaten on the way home.

Wedding cake

Socialising was mainly home-based, whether at their own, those of married neighbours or family. An exception was that Allen and Uncle Charlie (born in the same year) used to go to Fenland Park to watch Wisbech Town. I remember the odd football match not just there but to see King's Lynn and Peterborough, the only league team of the three. Charlie and his older son Barrie would keep up the habit longer than Dad, for whom, like his cornet, it did not survive long into my childhood.

'I want you to close your eyes and come outside with me, David. Come on.'

'What for?'

'We've got a big surprise for you. You'll see.'

'How will I see if I've got my eyes closed?'

Outside in Princes Street was a beige Ford, one of the big boxy models, new to us and perhaps factory new. I was encouraged to get into its back seats (I think it had two doors only) and promised a ride in it very soon. I distinctly remember wondering why I was supposed to be pleased, what this big new toy of theirs really had to do with me. I hope I made the right noises. Now I see it as a significant aspirational moment for them, their first car. (Dad had previously owned motorcycles, with and without a sidecar; Mum could not be persuaded to lean with the bike when it appeared to be taking her towards the road surface, so was less of a danger in her own cabin.)

Perhaps the Ford served not only to take us on visits to family in other villages but more adventurous outings. I have the photos, if not the living memories, to prove that with Mum and Dad I went to London and Cambridge: me outside the gates of Buckingham Palace; on a camel at the zoo; Dad trying to stop me scuttling away from him on Parker's Piece. I remember once talking with Mum of a more extended trip to London: 'And one day can we just go round the shops and do nothing but spend?' the greedy boy begged.

The car and the trips allow me to hope Mum and Dad did enjoy a brief spell of affluence, however muted. Lack of money would be a major concern for the greater part of their life together.

Well before I started school in September 1960 (at the beginning of the term in which my fifth birthday fell), I am told I was a fluent reader. It took no conscious effort. Nana Goldsmith was given the credit for reading to me constantly in my infancy. I have a vague recollection of a benevolent white-haired presence, one not too benevolent to greet my biting phase by biting me right back, sportingly taking her teeth out first to make the fight fairer.

Before moving in with George and Dinah, my great-grandmother had perhaps kept house for Uncle Fred, the only other of her children to fetch up in Outwell. His wife, Aunt Peg, was an Upwell girl. Their bridesmaid daughter Betty's older siblings were Eileen and Bobby, with David the youngest of the four.

Nana Goldsmith shared my birthday. She was bedridden for some weeks as we approached eighty-two and four respectively, dying on 16 October 1959. I would go into her bedroom early every morning. Overnight when she died, Grandad rigged a bolt or other mechanism on its door to prevent me entering and finding her still. According to the local press notice 'affectionately known to everyone as "Gran"' (but always Nan or Nana to me), she left only three surviving children – Ollie in Norwich, Fred and Nana Dinah – seventeen grandchildren and twenty-five great-grandchildren.

I am supposed to have astonished my parents by reading out the instructions on the cardboard boxing of the Baby-Glo that warmed my bed of a winter's night. This was a carcass of, I'm guessing now, metal ribbing enclosed in plastic, which would lurk in the bed like some barrel-chested dwarf reading under the covers by the soft pink 'glo' of its central heating bulb. It worked off the electric, which must have been a constant source of trepidation for Mum. My small bedroom had a storage area with enough space between it and the ceiling to stow the heater, which as spring came changed places there with the tortoise waking from hibernation.

My bed may have been warm but it was not a refuge. As I was left to sleep each night, I remember being frightened at the prospect of what dreams would come. I was careful to lie always on my back, on the alert so to speak, which I later read may not have been the best strategy. The play of light and shadow from Princes Street could have stimulated the imagination far more, closed eyes no barrier, than an unrelieved view of pillow would have.

The scary dream I remember specifically was of a witch grabbing at my legs to drag me off the bottom of the bed. I woke with my feet furiously tangled in the sheets to provide an easy rationalisation. Things were not so bad that I was regularly surfacing in terror with cold sweats or soaked pyjamas (I learned the useful trick of waking myself from dreams when they turned too nasty). Although I don't think I ever mentioned it to anyone, the fear of falling asleep is a vivid memory of my early childhood.

My family were not physically demonstrative, either to me or among themselves. This reflects the conventions of the time. I was indulged plenty, rarely hit, for all that smacking was an accepted part of the adult arsenal of coping strategies back then.

I only recall two smacks from any adult in the days when corporal punishment, even from people outside the family, was an allowable check on children's bad behaviour. The first was on entering the back door of Princes Street one evening. I kicked my shoes or wellingtons off behind me. One of them struck Dad on the shin, and he administered one of the 'clips around the ear' that have passed into legend as the beat bobby's universal, unfailing remedy for juvenile delinquency. (The concept of beat bobbies and the phrase 'juvenile delinquency' have themselves passed not into legend but the dustbin of history.) In the present case it was not any pain from the boot's impact that drew the smack, more my carelessness or conceivably that I laughed and sinned against the respect owed to parents.

If I asked anyone in my family to guess the other smacker, I'm confident none would point the finger at Uncle Tom, married to Joyce's youngest sister Shirley. That gentlest of men had carried me around Yarmouth on his shoulders throughout a hot summer afternoon so as not to wake me, when all the time I was only faking sleep. I tested his limits to destruction on Grandad's strawberries one year. He was trying to pick, I was trying to stop him; after more than enough warnings he grabbed me and slapped my backside. I remember my shock that he would do this, Uncle Tom who was always ready to play. It taught me work is a serious matter.

Although I never felt under any direct personal threat, I was conscious and nervous of growing tensions between Mum and Dad. Wanting not to hear, helpless not to listen, I followed my instinct whenever possible to remove myself from their shouting matches. Striving for pathos, I wrote as an adolescent or young adult some paragraphs on this.

They were at it again. The child was neither a part of nor party to their rows, but he was there. He always seemed to be there. They were shouting now. Perhaps later there would be blows. His mother would lose then even if she had won the shouting match. After the blows would come tears, then hugs and reassurances for him. And he, pretending to be reassured, would not be.

'I'm just going to get a drink of water,' he mumbled. Neither of them replied so he rose from the settee and walked through the hall into the kitchen. There he took his high-backed, black and white

plimsolls, his baseball boots, from under the chair and hastily tugged them on, listening in dread of discovery to the noise from the living room. He turned on the tap and left it running as he went out the back door, closing it behind him as quietly as he could.

Cutting across the untended garden so as not to be visible from the living-room window, the boy was soon beyond earshot from the house. It was still raining, though not hard. He did not like rainy days because then he was not allowed to play outside.

He walked to the end of his street, then turned right into the rec' road. The rec' was deserted. He walked across it, keeping to the paths, past the site where the British Legion was building a new club. Coming towards him were two slightly older boys, brothers, his second cousins. He was cheered. Their mother allowed them to play out in the rain.

'Where you going then?'

'Home,' replied the younger.

He knew if there was any trace of an appeal in his voice he was lost. 'Why don't you stay out a bit longer?'

'We've been out all afternoon. Where were you?'

'I expect his old woman's just let him out, now the rain's nearly stopped,' said the older brother in a factual tone.

'Anyway we're off in for tea.'

'All right, see you later.' The boy walked on until they were out of sight before turning back towards home. If Roy and Stevie were going in, there was no one else out.

He let himself in by the back door as quietly as he had left. He pulled off his baseball boots. He filled himself a glass of water and turned off the tap. They were still at it.

The real me close to the surface of this was shocked that my friends would refer to a mother, any mother, as 'the old woman'.

I did not know what lay behind the rows (Mum's invariable word for them), which were explained to me as a normal part of married life. She would always seek me out to provide reassurance when normal service was resumed, except that the rows themselves became part of my normality. From my bed at night, I would hear at least the pattern, if not the actual words, of her recriminations, his voice deeper and less frequent, thuds and bumps eventually and her crying. It always ended with that, whether he hit her or not. My helplessness to prevent the tears was what distressed me most.

I suspect Mum would have been a volatile partner for any man. If she had felt a need to bottle up her emotions while living with her parents-in-law, perhaps it was a relief to have her own house to shout in whenever she wanted. Problems were always kept behind the closed doors of our semi, hidden from the rest of the family. Without necessarily any open sharing of confidences, some of our neighbouring 'aunts' and 'uncles' saw and knew more.

It would have been a matter of pride to make any marriage work, especially with a child involved. I was possibly oversensitive to some of the normal give-and-take (blow and counterblow) of married life. Be that as it may, somewhere around the time I was learning to read, Dad was taken to Rauceby hospital near Sleaford. The clue to its speciality was in its former name of Kesteven County Asylum. Allen would be there on and off for a couple of years. He would never hold down a full-time job again.

Chapter Four

Battle Fatigoo

I would commute in my pram with Mum between Sutton Bridge and Outwell, the Bridge to Wisbech leg by train until that line closed. The Wisbech to Outwell tram was already only for freight, passengers served by the likes of Grandad George and his bus. Joyce must have found it easier to work for family with live-in crèche facilities than to keep fixed hours as at the Duke's Head or with any land boss outside the family. Although Nana Goldsmith 'spent much of her time nursing people locally and in areas as far away as Ely and Cambridge', her active travelling days likely ended after a serious illness aged seventy-five also reported in her obituary.

I remember going once to work with Dad, or at least a snatch of that day. I was playing around happily in the mud when he came out of the dragline cabin to see where I was. I subsequently built this moment up to a dramatic rescue, a last-minute escape from being buried under tons of wet Fenland soil. If this was a story I'd heard, or embellishment of one, it was not known to Mum.

Clearly a flat landscape of strawberries or potatoes was a safer place for a child than one of excavators and sudden huge earth movements, for all the allure of the latter. It was patently the wife's responsibility to care for children even if both she and her husband were working. Patently in the fifties and early sixties, at any rate.

Grandad George had what seemed a vast expanse of land at the back of his Wisbech Road bungalow, split in half by a grassy earthway just wide enough for a vehicle. At the end of this, which gave on to Robb's Lane, was a small shed. Outbuildings opposite the house included a garage, between what we called the hovel and a couple of pigsties. In the narrow hovel could be found

Dragline drivers

any manner of thing Grandad might need about the house or land. He always seemed to know which of the ramshackle banks of shelves and trays housed a nail or screw (pre-loved, often enough) of a particular size. The axe in the middle of the floor held a fascination for me but was always buried securely in a chopping block, from which at that age I could not free it.

Grandad was working the land for some years before he was able to put his own home on it (the family moved from the Cottons in the early fifties). He may have been gifted the plot, or helped to acquire it, by a lady I knew only as Aunt Ducky. Her given name was Clara, from a house along the Downham Road boasting greenhouses with grapes and asparagus. Grandad's father kept his horse Prince in a shed nearby. Ducky's mother Alexandra was said to be the first woman from Outwell cremated, because she had cancer (then thought to be contagious).

When she moved across the river to a cottage past the Sluice, Aunt Ducky lived with two aunts of her own, known as Cook and Teacher. When Joyce fell ill as a teenager in Nottingham, it was Ducky who drove Grandad to fetch her, proving unable to turn her car round for the trip home. The eventual builder of George's home may have contrived a split between him, formerly Ducky's man-of-all-work, and his benefactor. Earlier and more positively, the same man gave Ted his first job, as a carpenter's mate.

George's nephew David Goldsmith, an architect, helped him with the planning permissions needed because the plot was beyond the generally accepted bounds of the village (marked by the Radio Garage at Gill's Bridge) and therefore green belt. The bungalow was a prefab, the classification of which David was also instrumental in converting to that of a permanent dwelling. The name 'Maillebourne' picked out on the frosted glass at the top of its front door more likely came as part of that door than being George's choice. We learned eventually that it had something to do with the French for milestone.

Grandad's full-time job at Eastern Counties mainly saw him ply the 360 route from Wisbech to Welney. I don't recall him doing weekend special contract work such as Sunday-school seaside outings, as he had at one time. His smallholding was for spare time and holidays, probably at least two acres. A football pitch would have fitted comfortably in each half – not that the land was ever used for anything as frivolous as sport, only to produce income. Piecework labour would be drafted in as required, mainly at fruiting. This always meant strawberries, apart from a few raspberries nearer the house for home consumption. At the front was a small lawn, with flowers in a round bed at its centre.

Casual labour was usually family, which was plentiful for Grandad in Outwell. Doreen had escaped to marry her own farmer, working *his* father's land in Parson Drove, on the other side of Wisbech. The Rowells had livestock as well as crops, as did the Thorpes in Tydd St Mary, not far from Sutton Bridge. Tom senior was still active in running the farm, to which Shirley's husband Tom, perhaps unlike Uncle Charlie, had a vocation. Married in 1959, her main occupation would become land work, but in my early childhood Aunt Shirley was an assistant in a dress shop called Francis on Wisbech marketplace. If her own dresses were shorter than Mum's, she was ten years younger, and we were now in the sixties. It was a treat from Shirley to eat chips and beans upstairs at Purdys, all maroon leatherette banquettes, while she and Mum had coffees.

Ted was reputedly the fastest strawberry picker of them all, when he could be bothered to do it. On leaving the army in 1965, after twelve years with the 13th/18th Royal Hussars – which saw combat duty in Malaya (now Malaysia) – he worked away as a prison warder, before returning to Maillebourne as a lorry driver with Hannam & Davy and then Walpole Fruit Packers. It seems reasonable to me, now as then, that he would not have wanted to pull family land work during his free time, Grandad's concept of which only began when it was dark outside.

George's two sisters also lived in Outwell, in properties either side of the Sluice. Aunt Ive has already been mentioned as the wife of George Brown. As he died aged fifty-seven in 1959, I have no memory of Uncle George, whose spinster sister Beattie lived in one of the bungalows across the river before the turn-off to Churchfield Road. George and Ivy were childless; she apparently accepted it as his right to leave all his lands but the bungalow in which they lived to the Brown side of the family. He was a smallholder of some standing in the village, with the list of mourners running to two columns in the local press and 'a lorry-load of beautiful floral tributes'.

Aunt Gert, whose mail would sometimes be mixed up with that of Grandad George (another G. Hills less than a mile down the same road towards Wisbech), would throughout my boyhood generally spend her nights at Ivy's. The two were often also together during the day, whether working or at home.

Gert had raised two daughters. Aunt Pam married and moved away from East Anglia to southern England with Ian, a building surveyor. Their three children of my generation were Elizabeth, Bill and Alison.

Gert's younger girl, Ena (from Georgina) wed an American serviceman, possibly from the Mildenhall airbase. They were living with four daughters in Florida, where Aunt Gert would later come to spend the winter months of each year with them.

Uncle Sid was often at one of his sisters' houses. He worked on the land full-time for a Mr Brown unrelated to his deceased brother-in-law. Sid's wife Edna was reclusive, always spoken of as 'a bit funny'. Their daughters Sheila and Colleen had also married Americans and headed to the States.

If Sid was shorter and leaner than George, he shared his liking for flat caps and the fleshy Hills nose inherited by Joyce and Ted. Uncle Will at March was an almost invisible figure in my boyhood. He and wife Lydia lost a son Billy aged fourteen to a perforated appendix. Their daughter Sylvia, in Joyce's terminology of the day 'crippled by St Vitus' dance', was married with three children. I would occasionally see Paul (John was older, Sharon younger), at Aunt Ivy's during school holidays.

Grandad's most constant source of (unpaid) labour was his wife, Dinah. I never knew the slim and elegant lady in that 1949 wedding picture. Nana was always a stockier, rounded figure to me, no hard edges either physically or metaphorically. Their tone towards each other was of good-humoured banter, except during card games when Grandad would grow genuinely furious at her perceived (I grant he had a point) incompetence. She was unrepentant. She loved to play and didn't mind losing the few pennies involved. She was far more devoted to bingo than her husband was, though George would sometimes go with her.

In other circumstances I can imagine Dinah as a gambler, like several of the men on the Goldsmith side of the family. I saw her brother Fred rarely, but whenever I did he would give me ten shillings or later fifty pence, no mean sum then. Dinah shared this open-handedness, of which I would be a major beneficiary through the years.

I strolled my backyard kingdom, acknowledged and greeted as 'the gaffer', wearing braces just like Grandad did. I don't remember him playing games with me, until I was old enough to manage ones like draughts or dominoes. He is alleged to have boasted of me as an infant prodigy to a friend, on the strength of some 'bonnie baby' ribbon I won from my pram in Sutton Bridge. It was enough to hang around with him, being made to feel I was contributing to this endless world of work.

Of Sutton Bridge Infants School, I have little memory other than its location (in Wharf Street, I later confirmed). We would walk up to the main road – without having to cross it – past tonsured Lennie Laytus' general store, where you could get anything from gobstoppers to a haircut, towards the village's main bridge then down a couple more side roads. In a hall just before turning right to school I saw water turned to wine. The goal was no doubt religious instruction or reinforcement. Curious the mindset that would see this fostered by reducing the miracle at Cana to a parlour trick.

The headmistress shared my surname without being related to Grandad Bailey. Mum had provided a note to say that I did not like salad (the child is father to the man) and should not be made to eat it.

'Your mum's far too faddy,' Mrs Bailey grumbled as she swept the offending item – a shred of lettuce, a slice of tomato? – onto the plate of fat Brian, sitting beside me on the bench at dinnertime. That was the only time I remember the matter coming up; perhaps the head was standing in for someone more attuned to spoilt bastard's special dietary requirements. When I relayed her comment, maybe not so innocently, to Mum, she was all for going to the school to have it out with her namesake. It did not happen. I ate no item of salad before reaching the age of majority.

That school was probably for five- to seven-year-olds. Mrs Beaney is the first teacher I recall, an elderly lady with big yellow front teeth and hair in a bun. I learned to tell left from right, for some time afterwards having to project myself back into that assembly hall of small children to be absolutely confident which was which.

Miss Spooner, my second teacher, was much younger, with black hair and glasses. She would dole out sugar lumps to children who had done something praiseworthy. I transmuted her to an Outwell teacher as yet unmet in what I probably thought of in my youth as a prose poem. I changed the schoolboys' names too. I have not altered anything in reproducing it here, judging the touching childhood vignette beyond improvement.

'Now, since Donald Sparrow is away today, I wonder if someone would like to take a note home to his mummy for me. Peter, you live on the same side of the road as Donald, don't you?'

'Yes miss.'

'Well perhaps you would be a good boy and do that for me.'

'Yes miss.'

Donald lived about a hundred yards along Princes Street from Peter's own house. Peter was desperate to go to the toilet when he reached home, but he was mindful of the responsibility with which the pretty young teacher had favoured him. He wanted to deliver the note before going in.

By the time he reached Donald (or bird-brain's) house the pressure on the back of his pants was severe. He wanted to stick his fingers up his bum as he stood at the Sparrows' front door, but what would bird-brain's mum think of that? And why was she taking so long to answer the door? Peter started going through his multiplication tables.

Seven sixes – at last – 'Miss Kerridge asked me if I'd bring you this note because bir… Donald's away from school and I live on the same side of the street so I said I would…'

'Thank you very much Peter. Do you want to come in and see Donald? He's in bed but I'm sure he'd love to see you.'

But the handing over of the note had been accompanied by a far more calamitous release. Peter muttered incoherently something about his tea, turned and moved off as fast as he dared, or indeed could while keeping his legs perfectly rigid.

Donald was a sickly child. Later that month Miss Kerridge needed another note taken to Mrs Sparrow.

'Peter, I believe you took me a note before to Donald Sparrow's mummy. Would you take another one for me when you go home this afternoon?'

'No miss.'

'But you do live on the same side of the street as Donald, don't you?' Miss Kerridge was a nice young lady. She wouldn't ask one of her children to cross a road as a favour to her.

'Yes miss.'

'Well why won't you take the note then?' Miss Kerridge was puzzled rather than annoyed. Her children, especially the little boys, were usually more than keen to do her such small services.

'Don't want to, miss.'

So Peter had no excuse other than a spoilt child's sullen obduracy. Miss Kerridge herself was still a teenager. 'Well then, Peter Wilkins, I shall never ask you to do anything for me again.' She would shame the child into compliance.

There are however degrees of shame beyond the reckoning or knowledge of adults, even pretty young schoolteachers. Peter remained silent.

Walking to school aged five, being entrusted with notes for other kids' parents, these are relics of a time when children were viewed as small adults, not princes and princesses to be indulged and obeyed by their parents. It was strictly against my orders that, she admitted years later, Mum had followed me and my friends to school at a discreet distance on at least my first day and perhaps a few after that. I can't see me leaving infant school nowadays at Christmas, laden with balloons and party trinkets, to get into a car with a man never seen near the place before. Quite right too, but quite right then also. The driver was Uncle Ted, on home leave from the army.

In my early schooldays I remember going to a neighbour's house each morning, the shipping forecast wavering from the radio on their kitchen windowsill with its remote names, Dogger, Finisterre, and its incomprehensible numbers. I suppose Mum would drop me to go off to work, leaving me to walk to school with whichever of my mates lived there. Although a similar pattern would be repeated in Outwell later, when I would go next door to the

Chapmans', I was never a so-called latchkey kid. There was always someone in the house when I came home in the afternoon.

Looking over for the first time in many years some black-and-white photos of a birthday party for me at Princes Street, I was shocked not only to see Jane there, but to hear Mum talk quite casually about my first grand passion as my 'girlfriend'. My only retained memory, apart from that of the strength of my feelings, had been of walking alone, a long way in the opposite direction from school, to sit on the pavement across the road from her house. Jane did not appear.

Missing that opportunity, I doubt if my love was ever stated. Jane had freckles and was the subject – 'object' perhaps is the better word – of my first recalled erotic dream. I don't think space hoppers had been invented then, but it was as if we were sitting on one together, she on my lap, bouncing along Princes Street. It felt great.

In those birthday snaps also sat Uncle Tom and Aunt Shirley, with 'cousins' from his side of the family. His sister Joy had three children with Uncle Len: Jackie, a year or so older than me, inherited her mother's height; David was my age, while Lorraine would come along a few months before Shirley and Tom's only child, my actual cousin Mandy, when I was eight.

For every happy birthday memory there is one of Mum crying soundlessly into her tea at the kitchen table, tears plopping into the Yorkshire pudding and gravy (which we then ate in the Lincolnshire/Yorkshire manner, as a separate dish before the meat and potatoes). There was Christmas morning between Mum and Dad in a bed covered with gifts and ripped wrapping paper; then there was standing at the television, turning it on, off, on, off according to the conflicting instructions issuing from them in turn (in such rapid succession that the blessed thing, in those prehistoric days, never had a chance to warm up enough for a picture to appear). For every smile from them both when I came in to tea chattering about a war story I had read as 'Battle Fatigoo', there were grim moments before Mum once again broke the silence, determined to have the last word. For every tale of a cowboy called Smoky Joe Dad told me, there was a tipping point of his temper lost against Mum.

The exact timeline of those years is lost, which rankles for the inveterate diarist I would become. As Dad's stay in hospital lengthened, while they sought the cause of what ailed him, Mum would be with me in Outwell during the week, returning to Sutton Bridge at weekends. Although they would have been paying rent, I suppose it was important to keep the house in Princes Street against Dad's eventual return.

While Dad was away at Sleaford, Mum and I came to an accommodation of life without him, easier for me than her no doubt. Fathers were more remote then from the daily doings of their children. To me his absence was welcome. Loss of Smoky Joe stories was a small price for not having to fear for Mum. By the time Allen came out of hospital, at first for weekends only, the balance of my life had shifted definitively from Sutton Bridge to Outwell, where I had been going to school.

Chapter Five

Sergeant Mash

Army boys
Allen is bottom right with soldier's hand on shoulder

Of Beaupré Community Primary School (I have an idea it was '*County* Primary' in my day), we were told its name meant 'beautiful meadow' in French. I heard it pronounced in the whole range from boo pree to bow (to rhyme with arrow) pray. In my sixties boyhood the ruins of Beaupré Hall still stood, back from Wisbech Road between Maillebourne and the village. There was by then not much to see in it. The legendary bloodstains on one interior wall, if we were identifying them correctly, looked no worse than a patch of damp; the mythical network of underground tunnels was never found. The whole thing was demolished at some point as I was growing up, word was to stop youngsters getting injured playing in or around it, leaving the bottom of the new Beaupré Avenue estate of bungalows as flat as the rest of the countryside.

The school was a conventional state primary, one storey with a sizeable playground extending to the bike sheds and a playing field we were allowed to tread if the ground was not too wet – through most of the year it seemed to be out of bounds to us. The headmaster Mr Booley was irreverently known by his forename, Stan. His wife, who took the top class, the one that sat the eleven-plus, was generally viewed as more fearsome, no Christian name familiarity for 'Old Ma Booley'.

The infant class at Outwell was taken by Miss Bailey, related to the irascible head at Sutton Bridge. She had been at the school since it opened in 1939. Of Miss Kerry's class, the second year and the one I joined, my only memory is of her lovely face and legs as I sat almost face-on to her desk. Young, blonde, beautiful, no wonder she left so quickly to become Mrs Something and pass out of my orbit for ever.

The soft, frustrating folds of Miss Kerry's skirts were followed by the sharply creased trousers of Mr Harry Wiseman. I don't remember the details of his classes, only that they were the real start of an education, moving away from sticking pictures into books or communal story times to the right or wrong world of sums, history, English.

Small – even to us children – and bald, Mr Wiseman ran his class on strict lines, only occasionally undermined by something faintly comical in the excessiveness of his rages. He was far from deskbound. My mate Hank (Anthony Hancock) remembered a painful clash of heads as Harry was chivvying him into getting some books out of a cupboard. I wish I could claim I was the one to christen the teacher 'Airbrakes', from his wailing exhalation when someone would give him a wrong answer.

'Right, now we've been through the tables in order all together, I'm going to see who's been speaking up but not keeping up. Adrian Smith, what's four times six?'

'Er... twenty-four, sir.'

'Very good. Now you Jeffrey, what's five times six?'

Silence.

'Come on boy. Let's hear it.'

'Er... twenty-four? Sir?'

'Twenty-four? Sssssssssssssss,' then a closing louder 'sssss. How can five times six be twenty-four if your friend has just told us that's four times six? Angela, what is the answer?'

'Thirty, sir.'

'Correct. And what's seven times six?'

'Forty-two, sir.'

'Yes. You see. I knew she'd know it.'

Harry had his favourites among those he saw as the brighter kids. I was one of those, a pattern that would persist throughout my schooldays without leading me to be written off as a swot, creep, apple-polisher or arse-licker. Perhaps my behaviour, both with my peers and the teaching community, was abrasive enough, consciously so, to ensure that.

Hank said he thought the very first day I arrived at Beaupré that we would get on. He was dead right. With my split residence, I remember him as the only friend from Outwell ever to come to Sutton Bridge. We played in the big park where the Bridge football team had its pavilion home – wasn't there a library on the left on the way into its grounds? Steve O'Reilly did make the reverse journey from the Bridge, perhaps only once.

From weekends in Sutton Bridge I would return each Sunday evening to Outwell. Apart from his weekend releases there was possibly a time when Mum and Dad lived together again during the week at Princes Street. Equally I remember them staying together in Maillebourne, if only because I had a bed in the same room.

The exchange point was King's Lynn. Nana and Grandad would take Aunts Ivy and Gert there to play bingo of a Sunday evening, and me off my parents' hands afterwards. Beforehand, I don't know if we did anything there. I was taken to the cinema for such films as *Exodus*, that one probably before I started school. At the Bridge I went to the flicks on Saturday mornings with friends. Mum took me, uniquely boarding a bus in Railway Lane, to see *Zulu*. My abiding memories of it were the Zulu women's bare breasts and the climactic ridgetop gathering of all the Zulu men.

Grandad's job at Eastern Counties was not a nine-to-fiver. Sometimes he worked evenings and Saturdays, yet it is he I remember usually preparing my schoolday breakfasts, often poached egg on toast. They had a proper poaching pan with individual cups for each egg cracked onto a dab of butter or marge. The trick was to ensure you had at least a tiny sliver of egg with every mouthful of toast from the two rounds. Once I took this to its extreme, getting through four or five rounds as he continued toasting them. If Nana cooked, the yolks would sometimes be hard. I flatly denied having said this when Dad tried to grass me up on it to her. One of the most memorable snacks of my life Nan knocked up for me was two thick slices of fried potato, each big enough comfortably to hold its own acceptably runny fried egg.

Once in later years Grandad conducted an experiment. I had read the same thing he had in the newspaper, of points at the top and bottom of any egg that will not break under tons of pressure. Sadly, the ones we had were not equal to the fourteen stone applied through his slippered foot. Dinah intervened to end the sport after his third attempt, left with nothing but the makings of an omelette. He was equally profligate when I sold him on the delights of pickled eggs. He prepared a huge jarful, probably two dozen, of which he grumpily passed on to me twenty-three when he discovered he did not like their taste after all.

Nan Dinah was equally impatient with him when he once held out some evidence of a minor domestic misdemeanour to her in the living room. She looked at it for a moment or two then said, 'Shut up, you daft bugger.' He protested, partly for the benefit of his audience (which may have included others than me), that he had not opened his mouth. I guess he looked at her in the wrong tone of voice.

I was not prone to disrespect George, thinking it innocent enough to apply to him once a joke I had read in my comics. 'Did you know Grandad should be in the FBI?'

'Why's that?'

'Because he's fat, bald and ignorant.' The only quibble was with the third adjective, which Mum told me it was, well, ignorant to call someone.

My first school report, from Harry Wiseman in July 1964, noted I was a keen reader. There was no lack of material at home. Along with Grandad's morning newspaper, most days there would be a comic for me: *Valiant* on Monday, *The Dandy* Tuesday, my favourite *The Beano* on Thursday and *The Topper* on Fridays. There would be time at least to glance at these by the Rayburn in the kitchen, Grandad polishing our shoes before we went off to our buses.

It was over half a mile from Grandad's house to Wenn's Bridge, so called for Charlie Wenn the butcher's shop. His walls were choked with a profusion of big waxy leaves changing to purple every autumn (we were made to fetch samples to class one year for some reason). The bridge separated Wisbech Road from Downham Road, leading to St Clement's at the heart of the village on the right and Beaupré past the Co-op to the left. The fare was tuppence ha'penny each way. Every day Grandad would give me a fresh silver sixpence, with the two ha'pennies in change mine to keep. He would convert them back to silver for me when the weight of coppers threatened to rip a hole in my jacket pocket. My outgoings were few or none, with Nana always ready to treat me to the latest bubble-gum card collections. I had cigarette cards too, discards from family smokers.

The variety of my collections was impressive, judging by their remnants refound many years later: the whole set of 'Flags of the World', more than fifty bulletins of (American) 'Civil War News', cigarette cards from series of 'Wildlife in Danger', 'Asian Wildlife', 'African Wildlife', 'Butterflies of the World', 'British Butterflies', 'Tropical Birds' and others. There were famous footballers, trains, cars, boats and planes. From film and television there were 'James Bond' (Connery vintage), 'Batman' (Adam West) and 'The Man from U.N.C.L.E'. The latter two would form a larger image if all their backs were laid together in the right sequence.

You will realise, in these years when The Beatles were on one of the sets of cards Nana collected for me (it went to a second series as they grew bigger and bigger, photographs, each card 'signed' by one of the four Scousers), I am talking old money. The tanner, or sixpenny piece, which as a coin did survive a while after decimalisation in 1971, would now be 2.5p, albeit infinitely richer in purchasing power. For one thing, sixpence would buy a soldier from Woolworths.

Uncle Brian played with lead soldiers as a child. Although their production was not banned (because of the alloy's toxicity) until the mid-sixties, they had already been almost superseded by plastic ones in the fifties. I don't know a time when I did not have a collection of these, the main recruiting office Woolies on Wisbech marketplace. The sheer range available was evidence of their popularity as boys' toys. We played at soldiers, and we played with soldiers: Steve O'Reilly and me, me and Hank, me alone, especially me alone, building a world of increasing detail, if no great intellectual complexity. As a child unable to control the outside world, it was good to have an alternative one where I could literally call the shots. I don't think my parents or grandparents understood why I would hurl half-bricks down on the armies I had so meticulously assembled. It's easy with the hindsight of psychological blah blah to say I was acting out anger I had to repress in other areas. Not for nothing though, boys do like to smash things.

After school I would catch my bus back to Maillebourne, from the shelter past Wenn's Bridge facing the Red Lion and backing on to the river, the Well Creek which marked the boundary between Norfolk and the Isle of Ely, part of Cambridgeshire. One day I chose to walk on from the stop rather than wait for the bus. I was fleeing some kind of confrontation. Three hundred yards along the grassed-over tram lines, which in turn once ran over a choked river course, the big double-decker pulled up, between stops, something unheard of. Grandad was driving. Since he was enclosed in his cabin there was no conversation as I boarded, nor do I recall any later. I suppose I still paid my tuppence ha'penny that day.

I would get a cooked dinner at school, learning years later that I was entitled to free meals because of my parents' financial situation, only saved from any stigma of having these by Grandad's insistence on paying. That was a romanticised version, I was told later yet. Mum and Dad did apply but were found ineligible, while the village doctor was granted them for his children solely because he had four. Mum was scandalised at this.

Whatever the exact version, I was retrospectively glad to have been in the mainstream of paying children. I know I would have found it hard to bear being outside that group, though it would likely have been a problem of my own making. I have no memory of which individuals received the state benefit, nor how it might have been possible to tell. The doctor's twin boys (who went to school in Upwell) would not have been seen as disadvantaged, free scran or not.

Grandad was acknowledged to have paid for my dinners and shoes, the latter initially because he insisted I could not go to school in plimsolls, whether other kids did or not. I imagine he and Nana met all my expenses while I lived with them, and perhaps beyond. He also gave me half a crown (a single coin, two shillings and sixpence, 12.5p) every Monday for a savings plan administered by Beaupré.

'Mr Wiseman said there's not a lot saving in our class this year.'

'I doubt there's many taking in more than half a crown,' Grandad observed after a moment of silence, not addressing me directly. Horrified that he might think I was being ungrateful, I was at haste to clarify the teacher's comment.

'No, I don't think anyone does. All he meant was there's not as many of us who save anything at all.' This, nothing but the truth, seemed to satisfy him.

I don't remember the dinners at Beaupré, free or otherwise, nor whether my salad-dodging continued to be formally countenanced. I was becoming chubby, to say the least, with tea at Grandad's another cooked meal. He would knife a sergeant's three chevrons into my mashed potatoes for our amusement. I used to ask him when I could have striped trousers like him, not a pinstripe you will have guessed but a broad yellow band down the outside legs of his bus uniform. I never had such a hankering for the peaked cap, which at home would be swapped for a flat one. He had no vanity or shame about his substantial baldness, as outside his own front door he would always wear a hat *except* when 'dressed up' – back to Mum's wedding photo.

We would have tea by five at the latest, unless on occasion we waited for Grandad to come home from work. Nana did most of the cooking. His flourish with the mash was his main invention and intervention, except during busy times on the land when he would prepare something at midday. This might be just potatoes with cold meat, something he could manage between weighing and carrying up the strawberries from the rows, where it made sense to keep the pickers (including Nana) at their task as long as possible. Dinner was the midday meal but not necessarily as substantial as tea, the evening one. Lunch was something you had between starting work on the land in the morning – after breakfast or not, as the case may be – and the midday break for dinner.

Apart from bringing up her four children, Nana Dinah worked for many years at Hannam & Davy, one of the village's main employers. Any Davy had long since disappeared and the company was usually known as Hannam's. Richard Hannam, who had a big house set back from Rectory Road, ran a Rolls Royce as well as the fruit and vegetable processing factory for which Mum in her turn would put in a shift of over a quarter of a century. While George was uncomfortable outside his own close family – never known to speak directly to anyone not at least ten years married into it – Dinah liked company. She would continue going to bingo three or four times a week, capable of managing multiple cards in each game, long after he stopped altogether. One of Mum's press cuttings is a photo of me with thirty other small children at a party organised by the Outwell Women's Conservative Association, Nana standing smiling behind me as I look down at the tablecloth. In due course she would take an active part in the Over-Sixties' Club's social events and outings, as Grandad never did.

While George was exceptionally generous, financially and otherwise, to his family, he was otherwise as close with his money as befitted someone who had to work for every penny of it. Dinah was indiscriminately generous, always ready to give away personal belongings to the merest acquaintances who might express a liking for them. Her husband and eldest daughter might well at times have viewed such generosity as a fault; to others it was a loveable Goldsmith trait, shared by her brother Freddie as already mentioned. His and Dinah's equivalent of my daily ha'penny bus-fare change had been a weekly farthing: a quarter of an old penny, so the tenth of a current one, except again, instead of being something miles below any conceivable purchasing power it served them – shared, mind – as pocket money for doing their parents' shopping.

Nana was suspected, by Mum at least, of subsidising her only son's lifestyle. Nana Goldsmith's former bedroom, which Uncle Ted had occupied during home leaves, became his own when he began to work at Hannam's, whose depot was up the road from Maillebourne, across the bridge on the way into Outwell. A driving job at that time was not entirely sedentary, sometimes involving heavy lifting in loading and unloading the vehicle. I assume Nan Dinah took money for his keep; perhaps sometimes she did not accept it all, or 'loaned' him some of it back. Mum commented indignantly once that Nana had given Ted a good steak for tea, sitting George down to a fried egg when he came home from work the same day, so generosity was in kind if not necessarily in cash.

How then did two spoilt bastards like Ted and me get along under the same roof? The truth is, he was a peripheral figure within the household, working long and irregular hours. While he showed as strong a work ethic as either of my grandads, he would often go to Wisbech pubs of an evening, suppering (the final meal of the Outwell day) on scampi and chips when fish shops had only just brought in that exotic alternative to cod or plaice. When he deigned to notice me, it was usually with a rough benevolence. He would rub his unshaven chin against my face until I squealed, practise wrestling holds on me till I submitted – I never had a hope of holding out against the Boston crab – but also play me at draughts often enough for me to learn to give him a good game. If I sometimes appealed to Nan and he dismissed me as a baby for not being able to fight like a man, we were ready enough to resume combat the next time our paths crossed.

'Give it back to him, Ted,' Nana would say – I never in my life heard her raise her voice – as he held a soldier just out of my reach.

'Why should I?'

'Because he's mine. You know he is. I was only showing him to you.'

'Come and get him then. You know what I said.'

'But it's not right, it's not fair.'

'Tell your nan what I said then, see if you've learned your lesson.'

'You're not my teacher.'

'All right, I'll take Captain Morgan here with me to work then.'

'It's not Captain Morgan, he's Henry Morgan.' A jump well short of his six feet height plus extended arm.

'What have you told him, Ted? Give him the soldier back or you'll be late for work.'

'Only if he admits it's right. What did I say, boy?'

'Possession is nine points of the law.'

'There you go. Don't look so sulky. And might is right. Have Henry back and remember what we've taught you between us.'

I did.

Chapter Six

Saucerer's Apprentice

Land girls
Joyce is partly obscured second from right

If my contact with Uncle Ted was limited, I hardly recall him talking at all with his father. Only once did I see outright tension between them. It was a teatime when for some reason we were sitting down at the card table, red plastic top over metal legs. Nana was bringing in stuff, Ted came to sit and involuntarily jogged the table, spilling or nearly spilling some tea. George said nothing, but tutted, which led his son to spring up and head to his room, to pick up a jacket and go out, despite Nana's bewildered efforts to make him stay. He may have muttered 'for Christ's sake' (or 'Jesus wept' – he'd taught me that was the shortest verse in the Bible) as he rose from the teetering table, but there was no confrontation with George.

I never saw Grandad drink anything stronger than shandy. There were then at least five pubs in Outwell. His brother Sid would go to the Swan, beside Charlie Wenn's. Uncle Fred was a more frequent visitor to the Rising Sun, down Cemetery Road. I remember once being sent to fetch a pitcher of beer (or perhaps it was just cigarettes) from the first one to close its doors in my time, the Bridge Inn not a hundred yards from Grandad's by Gill's Bridge. Then there were the Crown and the Red Lion. I never knew him go into them or any other pub.

I do not mean to suggest George was a puritan killjoy, not by any means. Wrestling, with Kent Walton as commentator, was a must-see on Saturday afternoons from four to five, before he would summon all his concentration – tongue peeping out the corner of his mouth was the giveaway – for the football scores. Reading glasses on, he would carefully mark them off against his pools coupon. I would also be listening closely, eyes averted from the screen. It was easy to guess the visitors' score, momentarily before the announcer read it, from the intonation he gave to that of the home team.

At one time, not only Ted but George would wrestle on the floor with me. I remember Grandad rolling there, clutching his head in both hands. Small I may have been, but when I jumped right on that head it must have hurt. I was not punished, since the crowd had been egging me on: 'Jump on his head,' were Uncle Tom's exact words.

That sore head may have marked the end of our rough-housing, which was never a feature of my relationship with Dad – not that I was deprived, with Uncles Ted and Tom to pick up the baton. Of all the male influences in my formative years, it was Grandad I most sought to emulate, to whom I listened most carefully. Apart from wanting to wear braces with my trousers, which would ideally have a big yellow stripe, I asked for a haircut like his with nothing on top – 'you can't have hair *and* brains, boy' was one of his stock sayings.

Other instances of being like Grandad were not as welcome to Mum. She might have been expected to raise an eyebrow at sorcery, but saucering was harmless enough. If the cup of tea was too hot to be drunk comfortably in the conventional way, the top inch or so went down a treat once it had been poured into the saucer. Mum did not allow this. She further took me to task for shovelling food into my mouth from the bowl of the fork, rather than its outside. By then I was not living at Grandad's, who was condemned *in absentia* for setting me the example. A week or so later I was able to report that I had unobtrusively checked George's cutlery management. If not impeccably genteel, it was innocent of the common horror she suspected. Dad confirmed, as the three of us sat at our own tea table, that he had made the same observation. If I was uncouth, it was of my own devising, or a fault shared with my schoolmates.

Mum saw her parents occupying her own and Dad's place in my upbringing, however temporary and necessary an expedient it was. Life was extremely tough for her physically, emotionally and financially. I was shielded from it all. At Grandad's kitchen table I happily signed some kind of savings book, understanding and not minding at all that whatever money was in it would be transferred to Mum. 'And when things get better you shall have every penny of it back, plus an extra five pounds,' I registered her saying, without knowing why she was being so emotional about it. I had no conception of her life away from me. If she kept me by her while working at Grandad's during the day, as soon as Nana came home from cutting carrots at Hannam's, Mum would go there to put in an evening shift.

Nobody we knew had a phone, so when we were apart during the week we would exchange letters. I deciphered one promising me a BIG SURPRISE at the weekend. I had found in a comic a rudimentary alpha-numeric code, which Mum was sporting enough to go along with in our correspondence, until something else caught my interest.

The shuttling between Sutton Bridge and Outwell became a permanent, and final, change of home for our dog. Nick was a black Labrador acquired in more optimistic times, a pet and companion for me (though I have a vague idea he used to go to work with Dad). He was with us from my earliest days, witness the story of my standing in the bath arcing a stream of piss accidentally straight into his yawning mouth, which I assume I wouldn't have been doing much beyond infancy. My memories of him begin at Grandad's, and there most vividly peering miserably out from under the kitchen table. Maillebourne was on the Wisbech Road, where he had been run over, somehow dragging himself home with a broken back. The vet was fetched to put him down.

Grandad could never see the final surprise guest on Eamonn Andrews' *This Is Your Life* (the one from fifty years ago and fifty thousand miles away, 'You haven't seen him/her since…') without his lip trembling, without piping his eye. He sometimes seemed more moved than the celebrity guessing the wrong name. I know this sentimentality, or rather a purer and proper sentiment of loss, would have extended to poor Nick's demise. He was not, however, as soft-hearted with the succession of pigs, all called Gus, kept in the yard's sties. I was allowed to ride on the big animals' back; it was not a treat I requested twice. The piglets were at times kept in the oven overnight, a foreshadowing of their eventual fate, but in their first days only a measure to keep them alive. I saw one being drip-fed by the fireside from a baby's bottle, to the same end.

Boy with braces and dog

Endearing though the little ones may have been, the adult Gussies were less so, while the boar Guses who appeared occasionally could be frightening. For Grandad they were a commercial proposition, expected to benefit the household economy, though he never took the cost-benefit analysis to the lengths of doing his own slaughtering. At some stage, just as Uncle Tom gave up cattle for arable farming, he stopped keeping pigs. I later suggested the sties could be converted to nuclear fall-out shelters. Grandad must have been too busy to carry out the work, since he had agreed the idea was a good one.

Nick was not immediately replaced. The dog or dogs that Ted brought home didn't come close. I have in mind Toby, a yappy black-and-white Jack Russell, which rode in his lorry till it too fell victim to Wisbech Road. Another could not be house-trained so that Nan Dinah eventually had enough of it. Equally abandoned by Ted was a yellow Mini, over the years becoming embedded into the landscape where the driveway petered out into the beginnings of the strawberry rows. I can't imagine the quickly doorless vehicle offered much in the way of shade, for all that Ted would at first pretend to enjoy sitting at leisure in it while others worked around him.

If Ted showed no interest in land work, George – Daub (my spelling) was his nickname on the buses, without anyone ever able to tell me why – might have expected more from his two sons-in-law who were working farmers. That, and being married to Hills sisters, were perhaps the only two things Charlie and Tom had in common.

We have already met Uncle Charlie at Joyce and Allen's wedding. To me he was a benevolent yet somewhat remote figure, always dapper in jacket and tie when they came to visit. Baldness, glasses and false teeth, none of these characteristics made him appear any younger. He also had a full weight of children, who naturally felt more warmth from him than the polite, detached affection he always showed me.

Joyce stood godmother to Charlie and Doreen's firstborn, Teresa in 1949. Two years later when her brother Barrie arrived, she would stay with my parents-to-be at Sutton Bridge, as Barrie would when after a similar interval Graham made three. Teresa would reappear at the Bridge, outside my memory but of an age reportedly to cut a swathe through the local boys, sneaking out through the window to meet admirers. I do remember her at the Rowells' house in Newlands Road, Parson Drove, screaming at The Beatles on the television, pointing out to us all which was which.

Barrie, my boyhood hero, was said to be the image of Grandad George as a young man. He spent much more time in Outwell – with his own spells at Beaupré – than Graham, who had Charlie's fair features and what one guessed to have once been his sandy hair. Graham was allegedly more favoured by the Rowell family, none of whom I ever met. No such preferential treatment was shown by the Hills side in their most frequently told anecdote of his boyhood: 'And we got so fed up, you dinged him round the head on one side and me on the other at the same time,' Joyce and Shirley would take turns telling of an occasion when he was sitting between them in a car.

Vivienne was born in 1960, the only one of them my junior. Like Mum, Aunt Dawn (as I called Doreen) seemed to have energy and to spare. She was always kind to me, singling me out for special notice at family gatherings as both nephew and godson.

Aunt Shirley, George and Dinah's youngest child, may have been thought of as his favourite by Mum for that reason (Ted would have been odds-on against all the girls if any of the Goldsmith men had made a book on Dinah's preference). As she became a teenager there was more disposable income in the family, with older siblings out in the world and George and Dinah working as hard as ever. There may have been an element of envy of youth, too. The difference in age between eldest and youngest sisters would have yawned the wider from the change in the world they entered as adults. Beginning a marriage before the long slog of the fifties was a big stretch from swinging into one on the cusp of the sixties.

Uncle Tom's relationship with his father was much closer and more relaxed than what we heard of Uncle Charlie's with his. I also saw Tom far more around Grandad George, despite Charlie's longer tenure as son-in-law. Only twenty when he married Shirley, who was two years older, Tom's good nature and obliging attitude showed an impressive maturity, as well as making him universally popular. Over six feet tall with a full head of blonde hair and an open face that remained boyish, he may have been another cause for some to envy Shirley. The only fault Mum found with him, rehearsed many times to Dad who never got to give his own view, was that Tom was too easy-going, dominated by her sister, in a word henpecked.

Shirley and Tom began their married life in a tiny house in Hix's Lane, Tydd St Mary. I spent at least one night there, seemingly having a great time until I suddenly said, 'I think I'll go home now.' This was long past bedtime, and I was peaceably enough persuaded to stay. After a couple of years Old Tom got a good offer (£450!) for their cottage and sold it from under them. The young couple moved just up the road to live with Tom's parents in Henson House, where he had grown up.

Tom drove a Land Rover, a new kind of vehicle to me, canvas flaps at the sides of the truck bed (I would usually be squeezed in somewhere up front, never to suffer the same assault as Graham). He would bring Shirley back to her own former home in Outwell every weekend. If my grandparents respected the rule of the Sunday roast dinner, eaten any time between noon and three, tea was the social event there.

The only hot thing on the table would be the teapot, left by the fireside once everyone's cup (finer china than the weekaday, so no saucering) was filled. I recall no salads, but perhaps I just blanked them out. Beetroot featured every week, also ignored by me. Ham, pork pies, haslet, perhaps a tin of salmon decanted brine and all into a dish, were the staples, a plate of white bread – I didn't know there was any other colour – and butter, the latter melted to spreadability by the fireside it would vacate for the teapot. I wasn't much of a one for sweets, usually sticking to the juice from canned peaches mixed with evaporated milk ('apporated' to me as a toddler). I'm sure there was a wider selection than that, maybe a trifle. Seldom was anyone but immediate family there. Dinah would certainly have pressed anyone happening by to join us, but who could that be on a Sunday afternoon? I never knew George to spend social time with anyone outside the family.

The fact that Maillebourne was almost at the limit of Outwell, that short bus ride from the centre of the village, limited my own social life once school was done. Trevor Longmuir lived down Robb's Lane near the midpoint of George's land. If there were hopes that he and I would pal up, it didn't happen. The main thing I remember Trevor for was an accident, a clumsy approach to the vaulting horse in the gym leading him to fall and break his arm. Never one to miss a teaching opportunity, Mrs Booley told us later it was nothing to worry about and was called a 'green stick fracture'. That innocuous term didn't stop it hurting Trevor, we had all seen.

Although I also went once or twice to another classmate's house further down Robb's Lane, beyond the dyke that ended home territory for me, I could not swing a pass to a neighbourhood event when one slightly older girl had reportedly promised to take all her clothes off. Most evenings would be spent at my own games, soldiers mainly, or in front of the television. If Grandad was working late, Nan would always let me sit up with her watching whatever (limited) choice of programmes there was, until we heard his footsteps crunching down the gravelled driveway.

Other nights Nan would be at bingo, so Grandad and I would sit watching comedy wherever possible. Once he'd finished outside work for the day his hat would come off, the white of his bonce a startling contrast in summer to tanned neck. He would never be without a cigarette in his mouth during the day, yet in the evening never thought of smoking. This was not an heroic anticipation of keeping indoors smoke-free, which would have appeared a ludicrous affectation to anyone back then. All men smoked. Women were free to choose, as long as they didn't do it in the street (Mum and Nan Dinah did not smoke, Doreen and Shirley did).

I think, without being too fanciful, in shedding his flat cap and fag George was simply removing his land uniform, just as he would remove his bus-driver's when coming off shift. There was no longer any need of a protective carapace against the world, unless and until he had to face it again – walking a dog last thing, for example, when it was a reflex to pull the cap from its nail and light up. He could relax, cry at *This Is Your Life*, laugh at the *Beverley Hillbillies* or Benny Hill. Wednesday was a golden night, when we would contentedly instal ourselves from seven to nine for four half-hour programmes, including *Coronation Street* at seven thirty and possibly with the Hillbillies as its highlight.

The only threat to this safe and happy Outwell life was that, away in Lincolnshire, my dad might be getting better.

Chapter Seven

Moonlight Flit

Courting couple 1949

'Children weren't allowed on the wards then. Uncle Tom had to hold you up at the window to see your dad.'

'What was he doing there? Did he used to take you to the hospital?'

'No, normally I'd go on the bus. Just sometimes he'd turn up and take us all in the Land Rover.'

'You used to get a bus to Sleaford?'

'No, this was to King's Lynn. Your Dad was never at Sleaford.'

'But I thought that was where he went when...'

'The mental hospital was at Rauceby, not Sleaford.'

So Allen was first taken to the general hospital at King's Lynn for physical investigation before moving to the former asylum – or was it vice versa? The doctors at one or both facilities had at last concluded that home was a better place for Dad. Under their care he had needed for a spell to be shaved by the ever-helpful Tom, enough removed from his former self for his young sister-in-law Shirley to find him a bit scary. I heard he was given electric shock treatment at some point; also asked by a doctor to write down how he got on with his dad, something that kept him up all night. I would like to have read that (those father issues again). Mum never showed any indication of having done so or interest in what it might have contained – perhaps it counted as privileged medical information and was never offered to her. Allen was also kept occupied physically, producing a varnished coffee table Joyce found presentable enough to make a fixture in our living room, and a blue tray that also survived for many years.

No doubt I was too young to be given details of Dad's illness. As I grew older, it was so much the accepted way of things that I never felt the need to ask. Mum was hugely indignant to have learned of, if not herself overheard, her mother-in-law at Allen's bedside laying the blame for it squarely at his wife's door. It generally went, if named at all, under the catch-all heading of 'nerves'. The main physical symptom seemed to be an excessive need to go to the toilet, Barrie offering to bet me how many times my dad would leave the table during one of the leisurely teas at Parson Drove (Aunt Dawn's table was famous, particularly in the article of desserts). Trailing around Wisbech with Mum one Saturday, I was no further enlightened by a brief conversation she had with a woman in the street.

'And how is Allen nowadays?' followed comments on how long since they had last met and the like. I never did find out who the woman was.

'Oh, he's all right, thanks.'

'Funnily enough I was just thinking of him the other day. A friend of mine is bad with colitis and I remembered that was what Allen had, wasn't it?'

Possibly so. He took various tablets. My interest never extended to knowing what they were, beyond paracetamol, which is hardly informative. The theory of 'nerves' was supported by an origin story I heard only years later. Mum's cousin Eileen and her husband Hugh had come visiting one Sunday. All seemed well, a convivial afternoon, but the next day Allen would not go to work, nor any day thereafter. It was on a Friday when Mum brought home her own wage packet, as he no longer did, that he threw an unopened tin of beans or something at her, the first sign of violence. She took to inviting a workmate in for a cuppa with her on paydays, not an ideal or comprehensive solution.

My sense is not of Dad coming home from hospital a different man. Perhaps all my memories of him are from times when he was suffering to some extent, or perhaps there were already rows when everyone was in the pink. If there was a spell when he left hospital only at weekends, maybe there was also a time of out-patient treatment. Did he go back to his dragline? There must have been some indication, or at least hope, of a former life being resumed, since they took me back to start at the bigger primary school at Sutton Bridge.

I lasted one day.

'You came home and said you weren't going back there, you weren't even allowed to do joined-up writing.'

I was unusually stubborn, wilful or – all right – spoilt, if I was allowed to decide my primary school fate that swiftly and unilaterally. My memory of the new school at the Bridge, across the main road on the same side as the playing field, church and picture-house, is of confusing numbers of children running between classes and of meeting up again with my 'cousin' Micky. Not a big portfolio of snapshots, though it was a surprise to learn my stay there had been quite so short.

My formal school records, religiously preserved by Mum, begin when I was admitted by the Isle of Ely Education Committee to 'The Beaupré Primary School, Outwell' on 16 September 1963. I was thus nominally under the care of the Sutton Bridge ladies Bailey, Beaney and Spooner for up to three school years, though for the latter part of that period I would have been in willing thrall to Miss Kerry while living at Grandad's in Outwell.

Mum and Dad had talked before his illness about emigrating to Australia. In the event, they got no further than 15 Isle Bridge Road, Outwell, moving in March 1964. 'You did a moonlight flit because you couldn't pay the rent,' I was told by a girl at Beaupré living down my new road soon after our arrival. It has the sound of something overheard from adults. It was the only such comment I heard, and what did I care anyway, since it came from a girl?

Before the move I was taken to visit the semi-detached three-bedroom council house, the last set back from the road on the left before two in a similar block faced it at ninety degrees, the three sharing a garden path. Number 15 had the big gardens front and back of all the other houses from the main road down. Their potential for conversion into cash-earning strawberry fields was plain. A runny-nosed girl I recognised from a year below me at Beaupré came to the door behind her mother. I have the impression of other kids, but nothing else from that first sight beyond a feeling that neither house nor garden were as neat and tidy as ours at Princes Street.

It seems we were on an inside track for our new home. The man in charge of allocations from the council was someone on whose land Mum briefly and Nan Dinah longer and more importantly had worked. I'm told I asked him if the house had two toilets, and on confirmation said it would do then, a rare instance of me looking out for Dad.

While I have no recollection of the move itself, I doubt this is because I was smuggled in a blanket as Mum and Dad pushed a handcart through deserted midnight streets. I was probably at school. The sole break from normal routine was to spend a night or two at Aunt Ivy's, the only time I ever went upstairs in her house.

As well as a parish councillor and Conservative Party worker, Uncle George Brown had been a church sidesman and warden. His widow Ivy continued regularly attending St Clement's in preference to St Andrew's Methodist Church, always known as the chapel, almost next door to her at the top of Robbs Chase and with a much bigger congregation. Bright blue-eyed behind tortoiseshell spectacles, with a lot of freckles on her face, Aunt Ivy was in a constant, often bickering dialogue with her younger sister Gert, always seeming the calmer of the two. Maybe setting the clock on her mantlepiece half an hour later than the correct time ensured she rarely needed to hurry. If for any reason I couldn't stay at Grandad's, Aunt Ivy was a reliable substitute. She would always give me beans on toast for tea. Afterwards we might play whist, dealing the whole pack out between us. Once I was railing at my terrible hand. Not to be outdone, she insisted on showing me some of her own cards to illustrate equal bad luck. (I knew it was unnecessary, that we could deduce what each other had from the start. It just felt better to express and share our misfortunes.)

There were occasions round that time when I slept at Grandad's with Mum and Dad in a double bed beside me. I knew that Aunt Shirley was 'expecting'. I had pedantically clarified with Mum that this was the preferred term to use when talking of women, 'pregnant' being appropriate for Gussies. One of Joyce and Allen's conversations in bed, which I would hear a bit lopsidedly – either his voice was too low for me to register, or he simply didn't reply most of the time – related to this.

'Do you think David will be jealous?'

'Of what?'

'Of the new baby.'

'Why should he be?'

'You know how Shirley and Tom spoil him. He won't get the same attention when they've got one of their own.'

'I don't think they'll treat him any different.'

If I wasn't supposed to be asleep, I could have reassured Mum more confidently than Dad tried. The idea of being jealous had not occurred to me. I am sure Joyce's concern was genuine, while masking a dig at her sister, as if I were just a stop-gap plaything for the young couple, apt to be discarded when they were lucky enough to have a child of their own.

I had ample reason to be grateful to Shirley and Tom, although at the time I took everything as my due, the normal course of things. Perhaps having to be grateful on my behalf rankled with Mum. One example of their kindness was summer holidays. They would for some years go away with George and Dinah. I went too, with each couple paying everything for me on alternate days.

Stories from before my time were trotted out as common family currency: Grandad needing the toilet on a public green space, improvising by lying on his belly to urinate into a wormhole; Tom finding himself in a toilet without the wherewithal, having to use ten shilling or pound notes to wipe his arse; a policeman stopping George for some traffic infraction, seeing the stripe of his busman's trousers and waving him on with an 'I expected you to know better, sir.' Shirley would usually introduce them, 'Do you remember that time…?', concluding 'well we never laughed so much, ha ha ha.' (She would say the words, it is not my lazy reproduction of a laugh.)

My own memories are of trips to Devon and Cornwall, Yarmouth and Blackpool. Nana and Grandad shared with Shirley and Tom ownership of two caravans at Hunstanton and another at Heacham. Those were our default destinations on the Norfolk coast. The vans were rented through the summer to family and acquaintances, as well as occupied by the owners, occasionally other than when opening them up for the season or battening down for the bleak east-coast winter.

Great Yarmouth remains my favourite seaside town. Its main attraction was not the sandy beach, where I suppose we did spend some time – paddling at most in the sea itself – but the brightly lit front ending in a funfair that dwarfed those I saw on tour at Wisbech (and just once in Outwell). The figure-of-eight was top of the bill. There was a moment of genuine fear as you came over the top for the longest and steepest drop, a trick of perspective making it seem that the whole train would smash into the wooden scaffolding beside and over the track. It cost half a crown, with a cut rate if you stayed on for a second go. We always did. Shirley and Tom were the ones for the rides rather than Nana and Grandad.

At some point in the day, often on our way back to the van early evening, we would buy in the street bags of the piping hot doughnuts, rings of wonderfully moist fleshy interiors and crisp brown coatings, dipped and nuzzled liberally in white sugar. These were regular delights, but there was little on offer we did not sample. This included the horse-and-cart trips along the front (nothing special), and once a helicopter ride, of which I would be leerier now than then. During the day we ate mainly on the hoof, though at least once we sat down as a group inside a fish and chip shop. Thinking to be helpful, I picked up a sixpence from the table as we were leaving.

'Here Grandad, you left this behind.'

'No, put it back, Jim.' (That never was my name to anyone but him.) 'It's a present for the waitress.'

'What for?'

'So she'll remember us, then next time she'll treat us a bit better than anyone else.'

'What, like give us more chips?'

The investment struck me as a poor one. The huge throughput of customers and serving staff made it unlikely we would be recognised, should we ever return to the cafe. Still, it was an example of doing the right thing, the tanner tip neither ungenerous nor ostentatious.

I know it never rains on these remembered childhood holidays, yet if it had there were plenty of indoor activities to keep us amused. Nan would need her fix of bingo, in which everyone else could join, me looking greedily at the various prizes suitable for children (Nan was typically not fussed with winning anything for herself) before playing slot machines or shoot-em-ups around the arcade. There was a branch of Madame Tussaud's at Yarmouth and the day's biggest television names appeared live in summer season at the main resorts. We would always go to a couple of these shows. The best, by some distance, was Ken Dodd. I didn't want him to leave the stage, and for a while it seemed he wouldn't. Like the helicopter ride, Doddy may have featured in my personal history at either Yarmouth or Blackpool – conceivably both, since he put on a show in almost every sizeable theatre the length and breadth of Great Britain.

A trip to the south-west, Devon and Cornwall, was an ambitious novelty in that we would be touring from place to place, looking for bed-and-breakfast accommodation as we went. It seems nothing had been booked in advance, because all five of us spent one night wrapped up in the car. On another – or perhaps the same one – we were looking at some kind of boat for sleeping quarters, or would have been if Nan had not flatly refused to set foot on the wooden walkway towards it, water lapping gently underneath. On arriving at each port of call the first task would be to patrol the streets, searching for windows in which the jackpot combination of 'B and B' with 'Vacancies tonight' appeared.

The freedom of the open road may have palled against the stress of constant foraging for a place to lay our heads. Any shortness of temper was limited to Grandad against Nana, who would take it in her stride, paying him no heed. He did give Shirley a furious bollocking at the bottom of a hill somewhere in Devon. She and I had been running down it, hand in hand, when I lost my footing and was scraped along a few feet as she struggled to keep me upright. No harm was done beyond taking the skin off my right elbow, treated with some cream from a nearby chemist and soon ripening to a slippery bright purple splotch.

It was on that holiday I temporarily lost my taste for sausages. The hosts at one of our staging posts warned their portions might be too generous for me. Grandad and I knew better. I cleared up the three fat monsters, to what I thought were gasps of wonderment at my man-sized appetite. Except for Nana and Grandad beaming with pride, they were more likely grimaces of horror at the chubby kid's bulging cheeks. While I kept the meal down – only a breakfast, of which the sausages were only a part – I ate my fill to the point where it was years before I would face another one.

My cousin Mandy, born to Shirley and Tom in May 1964, would long be the youngest member of my generation in the family. It was natural that their style of holiday should change once they had a baby. At the other end of the age range, perhaps the days of going away with parents had also run their course. They spent various annual holidays in Mandy's childhood at Bournemouth. George and Dinah continued to take out a touring caravan, once as far as Scotland with a day trip by ferry to Ireland thrown in for good measure.

I felt no sense of loss, much less deprivation, at the end of holidays with George and Dinah and Tom and Shirley. I suspect I didn't notice it as an end at the time, the year between summer holidays marking a huge difference in perspective, development and other circumstances for any child.

There may in any case have been an intermediate stage. It might have felt odd for Nana and Grandad to be thrown into each other's exclusive company away from Maillebourne for a week or two. They had no friends in common (no friends, in Grandad's case). They perhaps missed having me live with them full-time, although I often stayed at weekends or during school holidays. Whatever the case, I trust my memory that a holiday with them in Blackpool was just the three of us, though I may be conflating or confusing it with a trip to see the illuminations in autumn, one George had made many times driving an excursion bus. For us it was a start in the early hours, to arrive only in the evening darkness of the same day.

I was given the chance to see Blackpool play at home to Manchester City, most likely on Saturday, 24 September 1966. I took an alternative offer, which may have relieved Grandad, who had no interest in football beyond the pools coupon. We definitely saw the lights, the tower, if not Doddy on that occasion then maybe Mike Yarwood or Ted Rogers. Blackpool is second only to Yarmouth in my seaside hit parade.

There was one break for just Nan Dinah and me, staying in their caravan at Hunstanton. Mum and Dad took us, left us for the night, got halfway home then returned at Mum's insistence because one of the gas filament lights in the van had been flickering and she feared we would be blown up. We could not understand the fuss. It was a good time, starting at the bingo as soon as it opened in the morning and accumulating between us plenty of prize vouchers (Nan gave me all hers as a matter of course), since there was a bare minimum of players at that hour.

It was on another seaside holiday, when it was not always possible to be outside and there was no television indoors, that I found the trick to leave consistently the single peg in the centre of the solitaire board (the card game of that name, also a reliable pastime, we always called patience or clock patience). I heard Nan Dinah say, when told that I had mastered solitaire, 'What don't he master?' Although I suppose she and Grandad were as pleased and proud of any achievement of mine as most grandparents, it was rare for either of them to comment in that way.

Mum specifically recalled March as the month of our move to Outwell, so there would have been the rest of Harry Wiseman's year to negotiate before any summer holidays. My parents had been careful to let him know that if I appeared to be chewing gum in school it was only the braces I was wearing to straighten out my top front teeth. I caught the eye for a different reason of some visiting dignitary or schools inspector, who reportedly asked Mum and Dad which university they were thinking of for me. I never wondered how they happened to meet this personage. I don't recall any parent-teacher events or open days until secondary school. I was not told of the incident at the time and, if I had been, doubt it would have meant much to me. I was already integrated into the classroom side of Beaupré. Now that I was living in the village, I would have to decide which gang I joined.

Chapter Eight

The Run and the Chase

'It was on Tuesday evening,
On Wednesday yesterday night,
Ten thousand miles away I saw
A house, just out of sight.
The back was at the front.
The front was at the back.
It stood alone between two more
And it was whitewashed black.'

These were the lines I first remembered, to which also came, as I wrote:

'The flowers were singing sweetly,
The birds were in full bloom,
I went down to the cellar,
To sweep the upstairs room.'

and

'The moon lay thick upon the ground
The snow shone in the sky.'

I don't claim these lines to be definitive, nor Grandad's recital as my own work (or his). He was helping in the practical task of settling us in at 15 Isle Bridge Road. Mum was proud to say that we redecorated every single room. This went further than just wallpapering, at least in the case of the third, single bedroom, which for some reason we designated 'the office'. In a filling of concrete beneath its floorboards must still be my initials, carved before it set, at Grandad's suggestion.

The front door was rarely used except by the postman and paperboy. Jehovah's Witnesses might have betrayed their ignorance of the neighbourhood by knocking on it. Dad earned a shrill rant from Mum for accepting, with her at work, one of their tracts for me to read. I backed him up, saying it did look interesting. I doubt she was concerned that we might be converted. More likely she feared money had been spent on the booklet; more likely yet, she resented strangers being allowed into our home in her absence.

Turning off Isle Bridge Road down the shared garden path, first on the right lived Mr and Mrs Betts, with their similarly aged lodger Sid Cole, then Freddie Churchyard and his wife. Their son Michael was a year or two older than me.

A ninety-degree left turn brought you to our house. One impertinent paperboy, years later when the front garden had become lawn rather than strawberries, took to cutting the corner. Mum dragged down a thick concrete gatepost that had become as redundant and loose over the years as our front gate itself, unhinged and converted to firewood. She laid the post as a heavy sleeper in the grass at an angle to have put the lad over his handlebars, had he failed to spot its installation and persisted in that route.

The chastened paperboy would have ridden along the pavement, dropping off our *Daily Express* then whatever the Chapmans took at the house attached to ours, front doors separated by just a few feet. The real way in to both houses was through a door at either side of the building, facing in our case a small rockery and the hedge that protected us from the disorder of Freddie's garden.

Before entering the house proper there were a coal-shed and toilet to your left, a wash-house to the right. Mum had a mangle to squeeze clothes dry. I was not strong enough to work its handle when a sheet was going through.

Downstairs was the small kitchen where we usually ate, with two rooms leading off on the right from the hallway. The first was where we and the television lived, with the same Rayburn coke (coal in smaller lumps, as far as I could tell) fire and cooker Grandad had at Maillebourne. The second room had an open fireplace, generally unused, as was the room itself. It was not 'kept for best' (though it would always be as spotlessly maintained as the rest of the place, Mum being house-proud almost to the point of OCD). I was free to play in it with friends, as in my teens I would be to listen to music. The three of us

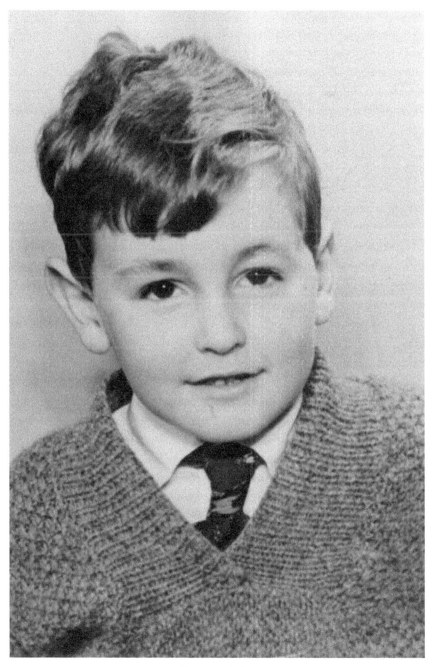

Boy aged six

occupied it as a family only once, when the television broke down. Sitting in front of the blank screen the first evening everyone soon became tetchy, a row looking the most probable outcome. On the second, someone had the happy idea of dragging the settee into the back room to sit in front of an open fire. The remarkable thing is, it worked. There was cheery conversation and Mum and Dad agreed it was just like the old days, we should do it more often. We never did – the telly never went dark again.

At the top of the stairs was the bathroom/toilet, with the two double bedrooms looking over the back garden. Mum and Dad had the one nearer the toilet. Both had open fireplaces. I don't recall mine ever being used. The other one sometimes was, when Dad was bedridden, a testament to Mum's caring side given the fag of hauling coal up the stairs.

With the downstairs rooms and the office available for me to play, I spent little time in my bedroom other than to sleep. I soon had a double bed, though I think at first it was two singles, from a memory of Barrie staying over, whispering to me in the dark from the other my first dirty jokes.

'There was this girl called Fuckerada. They had a boy staying in the house. Her dad wants something and starts coming up the stairs. "Fuckerada," he shouts. "Fuckerada." "I can't mate, I'm already fuckin' 'er as 'ard as I can," the boy shouts back.'

I'm not sure if Mum thought I was in danger of becoming a loner because of my ability to play alone for hours, or was simply trying to provide me with playmates in the absence of siblings. As well as my favourite cousin, she was always pleased for me to have friends round the house – the bonus being she knew where I was and would not have to worry about me out on the streets.

Mum once voiced a suspicion that some object or money might have 'walked' from our mantlepiece after one of my schoolmates had been round. This proved as groundless as Annie Walker's paranoia about the young Bet Lynch in a similar *Coronation Street* storyline. Luckily, it had never quite overturned common sense to the point of accusation. It was another example of a generalised fear that nobody outside the immediate family could ever *really* be trusted. Once adopted, this mindset is extremely tenacious of life.

Friendships were to some extent compartmentalised between school and home. Children's village legend spoke of a pitched battle on the solid river (so in the 'big freeze' winter of 1962-63) between gangs running onto the ice from their own bank, their own county. Outwell was not a big village. On the Isle of Ely side it straggled along the Creek, with Isle Bridge the biggest council estate

– and that no more than a single road. On the Norfolk side Churchfield Road, longer and curving around behind the school, with the volunteer-manned fire station at the far end before the village petered out into single dwellings and fields, was equally the biggest single address for my friends and schoolmates.

Hank lived in Churchfield, a couple of doors from Aunt Peg and Uncle Fred. Jim Wilson from the year below me at school and Stevie Metcalfe from three above were there too, as was Adrian Smith (always called Aidi – spelling mine as I've not seen anyone else write it of him), with whom I shared a desk in Harry's class. I don't mean we were huddled uncomfortably over a single inkwell; we had one each as the desks all through primary school were designed for double occupancy. One of Aidi's eyes was lazier than my left one, which I would say is only occasionally inattentive.

Playtimes at that age, before we discovered football, would all be spent in 'fighting'. The inverted commas are because this was rarely of the kind to do serious harm. We would sometimes be rebuked by a teacher – there was always at least one in the playground during our breaks – but generally they left us to it. Ian Coe, who lived on neither Churchfield nor Isle Bridge Road, led our eternal opponents, a gang whose other members I don't recall.

Stephen Allday was a smaller boy than most. With him on piggy-back we had a good unbeaten run at mounted combat, me charging around head down while he tried to dislodge the opposing riders by whatever use he could make of his arms.

Stephen's main sidekick was Steven Buzzard, a taller kid with fiercer freckles than Aidi and a red-haired crew cut. He gave me my first taste of real fighting, punching me in the mouth one day in the cloakrooms. It hurt. I was shocked, thinking this wasn't supposed to happen. His manner was matter-of-fact. He punched me again in the face, an accurate jab, not a kid's haymaker.

I dragged Buzzy all round that floor, crying myself from a mixture of pain, humiliation and rage while laying into him with fists and feet. He scarcely put up a fight. He was totally taken by surprise. Well he might be, since Christopher Buzzard had not seen me get hit by Steven, who had strolled away, job done. The two boys were not related.

Allegiances could shift quickly. At one time I found myself outside the gang altogether, reduced to wandering the playground alone between the girls' skipping ropes and the boys' rougher pursuits. This had nothing to do with the smack from Steven Buzzard (the reason for which is lost forever), since he made an approach to bring me back into the fold, waiting in ambush for Coe one day round the corner from the milk crates. I can say I had never defected to his side, while it is also true I do not remember Ian or any of his minions trying to recruit me.

Although I think Steven Buzzard left Beaupré before going through all its classes, generally there was little change in the composition of these. From Isle Bridge Road there were no other boys in my year, but two or three girls.

My next-door neighbours on the right were Steve and Ricky Chapman, both eventually to be known as 'Chuffer'. I would go to their house, a mirror image in design to our own under the same roof, every morning before heading to school, where I had no further contact with either of them. Steve was a year older than I, Ricky a year younger. We once all sweated at digging a hole in their back garden. I don't know what our intention was, if any. When adults appeared, we had already made sufficient progress for a lecture on the dangers of being buried alive if it should have collapsed.

Across the road an old friend of Uncle Ted's, Graham 'Grady' Smith and his wife were raising five children. The oldest Trevor, known as 'Plug', 'Henry' or once unkindly by a girl in the queue for the pictures at Wisbech as 'Rabbit-teeth', was exceptionally friendly and good-natured. He never made me feel his ten months' seniority, in a higher class at school until we coincided during my first year with Mrs Booley.

In the same year as Henry (the nickname that would stick, given him by the village fish-shop owner) was Michael 'Fiddle' (after his dad) Sutton. The three of us would hang around together, in Isle Bridge Road more than at school. Fiddle was the oldest boy in a big family, on my side of the road a few doors further up towards the village. It was his Aunt Marjorie who was Mum's boon companion in those teenage flights from Outwell. Across the road from us lived a friend from even further back, with her husband and two children. Iris Rumble, as a year older, had been entrusted with taking Joyce from next door at the Cottons to her first day at primary school.

Dad's only interaction with Fiddle in our house was a painful attempt to understand the younger generation.

'Why do you call him that?'

Fiddle had no answer.

'I mean you're friends, aren't you? You always seem to be playing together.'

'Yeah.'

'I just think it sounds horrible, using people's surnames when they're supposed to be your friends.'

This one-sided exchange suggests we were in my early days in Isle Bridge Road, before I had been given my street name. Adults were not dealt these back. We would dutifully ask them if Anthony or Trevor or Michael could come out to play. I ended up with the uninspired 'Bail', to lengthen which to 'Bailey' eventually became an invitation to fight.

Most of our time was spent away from grown-ups, including after dark in those days when the road had working streetlights. Fiddle and I developed a circuit of the village we would make when nothing better presented itself. With or without Henry, we took as granted permission to go down his garden path and scramble over the fence, into the Chase. This was a dirt road, wide enough and occasionally used by cars, leading from Aunt Ivy's house at the main road through to the Cottons.

Off the Chase, level with the Smiths' back yard, was the 'Recreation Ground' opened in 1904, the Rec' as everyone knew it. In my earliest memories this had swings and one of those roundabouts you work yourself by running and pushing one of the metal spokes, before jumping aboard off the footplate. It once hosted a proper fair, an offshoot of the Wisbech Mart, with rides and flashing lights if not perhaps the star attractions. There I'd executed a wrestling pinfall on Stevie Metcalfe, older but no bigger than me, for taking the mickey out of my clothes. 'Grandpa Braces' was the offending term he found and repeated.

When Fiddle and I were making our run, as we called it, the Rec' was overgrown and disused. We crossed it from the five-barred gate to a square, brick building in the corner. This survived because there was nothing to vandalise, just solid walls with one doorless entry and a flat concrete roof. Before my time there were reportedly battles to occupy this vantage point, using apples for grenades. We would later develop a form of football squash at the wall facing the field, kicking a ball against it so as to leave your opponent (or yourself if playing alone) no possibility of hitting the wall again from the spot to where it had rebounded. Sometimes there were signs of fires lit inside, or other human detritus, but the block held no attractions for us as a clubhouse. We assumed it had something to do with the war, perhaps an old air raid shelter. We were right on the war, but not the purpose; it had been an ammunition store.

A path was worn at the crossing of the dyke near the building, beside which we would hide in the undergrowth on the banks any objects of interest found on our travels. Perhaps we recreated the game I had played at the bottom of his garden with Martyn in Sutton Bridge, filling an old pop bottle with whatever we could think of to make the vilest potion: mud, weeds, worms, nettles and our own piss. If there were no treasures to admire, we would skirt a ploughed field along the line of the dyke, separated now from the Rec' by a thick hedge (if the dyke had water, it was barely more than a step across even for kids like us). A wooden fence was scalable at the right spot – a convenient foothold halfway up – to bring us into the back yard of the Methodist chapel.

That was the best of the run. It only remained for us to turn right out of the chapel yard along Isle Road, past Aunt Ivy's, Tuck's Bridge and the Crown, and back down Isle Bridge Road.

'Say it, Bailey.'

'What?'

'You know, like I just said it, like Plug did: "He's a… fooking bastard".' Each syllable of the last two words was enunciated slowly, given full weight, perhaps copying a quaint pronunciation of one of the fishermen who came from 'up north' to stay at the Crown – it always seemed to us a strange kind of holiday.

Caught between the promise I had given Mum from my improvised bathroom in Princes Street and the need to talk the same language as my mates, I suppose I did repeat the swear words after Fiddle. He must have spotted my reluctance or perceived weakness and forced me to confront it. Younger kids in any group are always having to prove themselves one way or another, which is not to absolve myself from blame in the raid on the pop factory.

Past the church to the left on our way to Beaupré, where old folks' flats would later be built, were premises owned or rented by Corona, in those days a major brand of fizzy drinks rather than a Mexican… well, not so much changes. In a village like Outwell it can hardly have been a major depot. Perhaps it was no more than an overnight lock-up where the delivery driver would leave his lorry with its crates of Cherryade, Orangeade or Dandelion and Burdock (my personal favourite). The bottles were something over a pint, glass, with money back on their return. If we saw them at all, canned drinks were far less common.

While a drink of pop was a treat, it was not an unimaginable luxury. As with petty theft of sweets where the shop owner was too decrepit or inattentive to catch you, which I had tried back in Sutton Bridge, the idea of boosting a bottle or two was more a test of nerve than born of deprivation.

It was just the two of us. We were edging along between a lorry and the wall of the depot – full dark, so it was winter – when we were challenged, not from outside but by a voice from deeper within the premises.

We ran. I can easily relive the moment I passed the full bottle Fiddle, ahead of me, had let drop as he belted along. It didn't smash, at worst someone would lose a bit more than usual to froth-over when it was eventually opened.

The driver, or whoever it was, did not bother to chase us up the street. There were no 'Wanted' signs posted on the sheet-metal door when we went to school the next day. If we were worried that we would be recognised and our parents told, we were clearly not so notorious in the pop-rustling world that those fears had any foundation.

Two boys will either fight or get along fine. When three are together, one will often become the butt of the other two. Henry generally took any ribbing in good part, but he was not a doormat. Once goaded a bit too far, he came back at Fiddle with a vicious insult that may not have been strictly relevant to his own teasing: 'Yeah, well your mother's…' Surprisingly, or not if you'd ever seen the red mist descend on our lanky, bespectacled friend, it didn't come to blows between the two of them.

If Fiddle was shocked into silence, there was a time when Henry left me too without an answer. I don't know how the conversation began; we were sitting in a minibus or van, so perhaps it was on a Boys' Brigade outing. I can't imagine he would have bragged about having more brothers and sisters than I did, but for some reason I was keen to emphasise that I was at no disadvantage as an only child. 'I bet I've got more aunts and uncles and cousins than you have,' I crowed, more than ready to bring all my great-aunts, every second cousin from Uncle Fred's family, Uncle Tom's nephews and nieces, into the count if necessary.

'I don't… oh, I get it. That's only cos you're adopted.'

Chapter Nine

Cibola and the Zunis

Westward Ho!

When Mum and I went alone to King's Lynn on a Saturday we came to call it a 'Great Day'. We would go by bus, crossing the 'Big Puddle' (aka the Great Ouse) on our way into the town. Among my regular treats, she reminded me years later – as she did of the Great Days themselves, shame on me – were a Swiss roll and a bottle of Lucozade.

She had found ways to indulge me since the earlier days commuting between Sutton Bridge and Outwell, from where the bus would drop us at Wisbech Horsefair. This big open space near the town centre was the most convenient spot for double-deckers to manoeuvre as they began and ended their journeys. We would walk to the railway stop for Sutton Bridge in Harecroft Road. It was there, beside Wisbech Grammar School's sports fields and the sign Grandad told me was once edited to proclaim the town 'Hospital of the Hens', I would greet a horse. He came to know us, to approach the fence every day for the sugar lumps I would feed him, as Miss Spooner did her pets. Our own dear Nick got no such reward, despite always appearing punctually at the Bridge to greet us on our return, after being left to his own devices all day in the streets there.

Our other regular stop – except on Wednesday, half-day closing – was at Woolworths, to buy me a sixpenny plastic soldier or two. A broad expanse of counter was occupied by them, all standing free to touch, behind no protective glass. Obviously they were not just for my benefit; those years of the sixties were in the golden age for collecting them.

There were soldiers, in the sense of men in uniform: British Tommies and German roundheads mainly, but also Russians, to be distinguished by their fur caps or Cossack hats. In the two-shilling Airfix boxes of about thirty figures not half an inch tall, there were Japanese soldiers and French First World War regiments (one of the few things I heard Dad say of their part in the Second was 'we liked the Germans better than the French as soldiers'). Although I would develop a good secondary collection of these, my main interest was the ones three to four inches tall, and in these I don't remember seeing any 'Japs' or 'Nips' as we called them. The former was viewed as descriptive only, not disrespectful. Nobody bothered with 'Japanese', though I did like the sound of 'Nipponese' when talking about the specially evil ones.

There was an ample choice of figures in no conventional uniform. When I came to classify my men as the people of Cibola, a while after those first visits to Woolies, I would identify four races: Army, Westerners, Knights and Pirates. These were also the international teams for my football and cricket matches.

Apart from war games, cowboys and Indians was another staple of my boyhood. Back in Railway Lane we had argued which would be worse: to be captured and tortured by the Japs, or the Mexicans. Stereotypes of the cinema or television were repeated in the plastic figures. Germans could be found with arms outstretched, having just taken a bullet, or with arms raised – 'Hände hoch!' right back at yer – in surrender, attitudes not seen in the British fighters. Mexicans always had the huge sombrero, on their head or down their back, with slicked hair and a moustache if the facial detail was fine enough to allow it. Indians ranged from chiefs with feathered headdresses trailing to the floor – one hand raised in a greeting you knew was 'How' – to loinclothed Mohicans with rifle and a bandolier of bullets.

I read a children's novel called *The Gauntlet* (by Ronald Welch), the adventures of a boy who finds himself transported back to the Middle Ages. In my mind we had in England castles and knights at the same time America had its cowboys and Indians. There was an ample supply of figures to feast at a round table or forge a crusade.

Anyone who did not fit into any of the other three races – and the odd renegade who did – was classified a Pirate. These ranged from actual pirates in the seafaring, wooden-legged, one-armed tradition, to kilted Highlanders, to Arab tribesmen, Cavaliers, Vikings, Zulus, Foreign Legionnaires, Conquistadors, Robin Hoods and their merrie men. I hardly need say the Pirates were the biggest charge to my imagination.

It was a lively, engaging but far from peaceful world I created, long before I called it Cibola populated by Zunis (names from half-digested reading on a North American Indian land and its tribe). The destruction of the soldiers began almost as soon as I started collecting them. Their folk memory was of a plague that had decimated the population long before I moved – it was a perilous migration for them – to Outwell. There, 15 Isle Bridge Road became the capital, Blood, while Maillebourne was and remained Casablanca.

It was not a solitary obsession. Although he did not have armies of his own, Steve O'Reilly joined me in games with mine in Sutton Bridge. Perhaps it was on leaving that I gave him the pick of any of my men, not to keep, oh dear no, but to name. So it is that Tommy O'Reilly is the leader of a clan – of turbaned Arabs, armed to the teeth and frequently bearded.

It may have been the first summer holidays after I arrived in Outwell that Steve came to stay. Walking the streets of the village we could pick up any number of lollipop sticks from the gutters and pavements. Although it was difficult to link these directly with the soldiers, they did provide the raw material for an air force. Take three and fan them out with your thumb and forefinger gripping the ends together, before weaving two more between and across them. At the base of the inverted triangle move the top stick to the bottom and you have a rudimentary bomber. The cargo, of marbles say, fits in theory between the slats but in practice fatally compromises the airworthiness of the craft. Requiring in production slightly more manual dexterity, justified by an enhanced boomerang effect, was the V-shaped four-stick fighter.

The flying machines were not exactly robust. As you skimmed them away from you, it was odds-on they would disintegrate on landing. Then again, they were easy to rebuild. The most spectacular flight ever ended on the side of Dad's head as he was talking to a neighbour. It was a total accident. It could not have hurt, though it clearly caught him completely by surprise. We managed to keep a straight face for the telling-off, me and Steve, then creased up as soon as we could escape from view. The mention of it alone was enough to reduce us to fits of laughter for days afterwards.

As Hank took Steve's place as my best mate, he also started playing with soldiers. His house became Zanzibar. To colonise it went an intrepid band of my best men, led by no less a figure than the great Tommy. They were gone an age, given up as lost for a large part of it, before they found their way back to Blood (Casablanca was Tommy's hometown, showing that he was with me before the city of Blood was discovered and populated).

Among my earliest games with the soldiers was wrestling. Kneeling on the floor with one in each hand, I would release them against each other with a degree of force. The more solid one had the chance of battering a submission, while pinfalls were self-evident if one should fall on top of the other in the right way.

Wrestling before long gave way to football. The first all-star team I formed from my soldiers in Casablanca, the Young Faithfuls, apart from the ubiquitous Tommy O'Reilly as defensive linchpin, had several players whose names I learned during the 1966 World Cup: Zito (from Brazil), Yashin in goal (Russia), Más and Onega (Argentina) and Luis Suarez (Spain). They played against pick-up teams until Morgan's Marauders were founded, skippered by Henry Morgan, a Scottish clansman, whose team's name owed something to the seminal war film *Merrill's Marauders* I saw at the pictures with Dad. Of the four brothers who completed the Casablancan Marauders' forward line led by Henry, only Rab Rory's name hinted at the Highlands: the others were Bene,

Albert and Asparuchov, after Eastern European strikers at their peak around that time.

Early games had soldiers with viable stands and ideally of similar height to act as goalposts (no crossbar). If this seems an unenviable role, it was better than that of the man whose head became the ball.

There was no shortage of balls. Grandad's land had enough corners where nothing was growing to provide fantastic battle terrain. A two-foot-high stack of branches that would eventually become firewood, for now was the Little Rock Candy Mountains where the Pirates lived rough. If brought to justice, an effective guillotine awaited in the sharp-edged base of Ted's rusting Mini where once a door had fitted. Most men died more messily. It was useful to have a squat body with no neck (the Arab Luis Suarez was a prime example) to withstand jagged half-bricks rained down by me in various skirmishes, battles or mano-a-mano confrontations.

The family was generally indulgent, if uncomprehending. I was mightily impressed when Uncle Ted, in a moment of attention to my activities on the living-room floor, made excellent guesses at which positions various soldiers would play. Uncle Tom patiently helped me glue The Hulk's legs back to his stand, propping him up by the post-Christmas fire to dry. Grandad was concerned that the flying bricks, which occasionally caught me a painful bouncing blow on the shin, might go through one of his greenhouse windows. I know he also resented the wastefulness of buying toys then deliberately destroying them. Mum made this point too, while valiantly struggling to be part of the world, accepting the chairmanship of Ajax when that team was created in Blood. Her role was largely honorific or clerical, copying out teamsheets and the like, my compulsion to annotate and record finding early expression.

I write of Cibola not to vaunt my powers of imagination or creativity. Many other boys (girls too, if you will, but far fewer I bet) all around the Empire will have constructed from similar material worlds far more coherent and elaborate. So be it. This was mine. My soldiers were as important players in my boyhood as most of my schoolmates and would continue to be so for years after that first treat at Woolies. Decades beyond schooldays they would provide the cast for *Seventeen*, my first published novel.

Chapter Ten

Extended Family

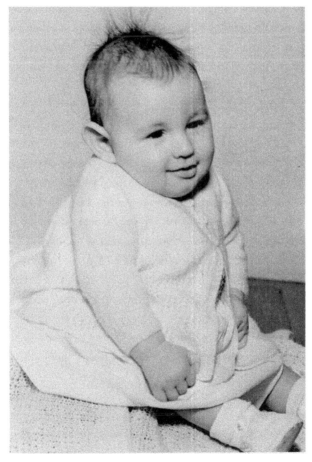

Baby in first months

When Henry said I was adopted, he was not telling me anything I didn't know (nor trying to; he was devoid of malice). Surprised that *he* knew, with other people on the bus I was disinclined to ask how. The moment passed without embarrassment, and the topic did not come up again between us.

I have always been grateful that Mum and Dad were honest about my origins from my earliest consciousness. Until 1976 the law stood that separation from birth parents was final, with no prospect of further contact, or of details to allow it being released. I had a birth certificate that made no reference to adoption, naming Joyce and Allen as my parents. If there was any debate between them, I imagine Dad as the stronger voice for full disclosure, but this is pure conjecture. I never asked.

The first time they saw me was on Christmas Eve of 1955, driving through a snowfall from Sutton Bridge to Lincoln. They took me home with them in January, two months old. My birth mother was unable to take care of me. She was working in service for a doctor and his family. My putative father was American, Mum further told me as a teenager. She relayed a suspicion of Nana Dinah that the doctor was the actual father.

Whether Mum and Dad's attitude was an enlightened one or accepted practice for the time, I think it has been proven correct, in general as well as in my own case. Because I knew I was adopted as soon as I knew anything, I never as a child felt it was an issue, much less any cause of trauma or regret. Mum and Dad stressed that they had chosen me, been delighted to choose me. Mum, my only source of information on this topic, said they had made it clear to the whole family that I was to be accepted unconditionally, or the break would be with her and Dad too. I can imagine the spiky comment, but not that anyone in the family on either side would have given them reason to make it. Not one of my full set of grandparents, aunts, uncles, or cousins has ever mentioned to me being adopted. More significantly, I don't recall any of them ever *not* mentioning it, tiptoeing around the subject or being overly solicitous of my feelings on it. Perhaps it seems not such a big deal, to love and accept a baby, adopted or otherwise. Still, I honour and thank them all, starting with Mum and Dad.

Because the 'news' of my adoption came at an age before that of reason or memory, my reaction to it is lost to me. I would in any case make a strong distinction between the impact of the news and the impact of the event. I have kept in these pages mainly to the perspective of childhood, without too much foreshadowing of future incidents or fates now set in time. From that perspective, it is true my adoption was no big deal. I am, however, convinced it was central to the child I was and the adult I became, in terms of defining my character. I haven't yet put in the hours of therapy – nor shall not neither – or self-analysis (which is ongoing) to decide whether for good or bad. Probably those words are not the right ones to start with.

Mandy as a child expressed surprise that someone so much bigger than Aunt Joyce as David could have come out of her body. Aunt Shirley passed on the comment, suggesting that although she had been told, my cousin had forgotten I was adopted. I never forgot. My self-consciousness, manifest in so many ways from compulsive diarising to shyness in company, I ascribe more to the isolation of an adopted than that of an only child.

Speculations on the forming of self belong to a different part of my personal narrative than this – one that may never be written, may be impossible for me to write. I know now that adopted children can tend to the extremes of rebellion or conformity, aggression or people-pleasing. One day at Beaupré we were held back in the corridor. Those of us nearest the closed classroom door could see the back and arms of Headmaster Booley through its glass. He was pressed hard against it, as a pupil thrashed and kicked at him, raging to get out. Maybe this had nothing to do with the lad being adopted, as Mum told me at some stage he was (it did not make friends of us). If early abandonment or separation from mother – not adoption itself, which may improve matters – was a factor in that savage outburst, then I was closer to the other end of the spectrum; at least as a child I was, at least on the surface, at least in my interaction with the adult world.

I should probably extend this pseudo-historical viewpoint another paragraph or two, in reviewing my arrival into the lives of Joyce and Allen. As a child, with the evidence of their devotion to me and my welfare unmissable, I was probably conceited enough to think they had got quite a good deal, especially as teachers regularly praised my academic progress, by which Mum and Dad set such store. I had no idea – little interest, if truth be told – of the process that brought them so providentially to Lincoln that snowy Christmas Eve.

I knew that Mum couldn't ever have children (slightly odd sentence to write). This was either a result of, or discovered at the time of, her long teenage illness. Just as the doctors did not deign to tell her what the sickness was, they did not give this news direct to her but to Nana Dinah. By the time I came to know Nan, she was the archetypal loving granny, the soul of kindness and gentleness. She had the toughness, though, to survive childhood in a family where more than one sibling did not, overcoming her own periods of significant ill health. Mum remembered Dinah, when a mother bringing up her family on a limited income, as more than capable of holding her own in garden-fence skirmishes with neighbours in similar straits. With a grim symmetry to the doctors' indirection, it was by way of Dinah that her prospective son-in-law found out that Joyce would not be able to bear him children, something Joyce had perhaps not been told herself.

I thought for years that Mum went into her marriage keeping this secret, her haggishness if you like, from Dad. In fact, he learned it within a few weeks of their starting to go out together. George was apparently annoyed with his wife for breaking the news. Joyce was I-could-never-forgive-her furious, saying the whole matter was none of her business.

While she did not know for sure, Joyce guessed similar oversharing from her mum to Irish Jim. As she was seeing him on to his bus back to Lynn one Sunday, she said as usual, 'See you next weekend.'

'It's over,' was his reply as the doors closed on him. By this account he wrote later seeking a reconciliation, but she was 'not getting caught out twice'.

Allen's reaction was different. When they next met after he had been briefed by her mother (or was it in a further refinement by his own parents, who had some independent social contact with George and Dinah at that time?), he asked Joyce if she had anything to tell him. She said no. When he told her what he was driving at, he knew from her reaction it was as much news to her as it had been to him. Telling him he could clear off if he wanted, tearful and furious she set off back to the Duke's Head. It was not only because he had her purse in his pocket for safekeeping that he followed her. He said he was going nowhere; they could always adopt and in any case miracles do happen. Three months later they were married.

Perhaps because her infertility was based on a report from her mother rather than direct word from a doctor, perhaps just in hope, Mum and Dad went through some months of tests once married. He went for the first, at any rate, not impressed to be sent into a room with 'mucky books'. Mum was more persistent, accompanied by Nana Bailey with a clean skirt and underwear for her, to King's Lynn every Tuesday. When she told her mother-in-law she really did not have to keep coming with her, she was told to hush, that was the only time she got a meal out paid for by Grandad Bailey.

We were sitting watching television one night in Isle Bridge Road when some godforsaken corner of the earth – Scotland? – was described as 'barren'.

'Just like me.' Mum lobbed the grenade calmly enough.

'Don't say that.' Dad smiled over at her, affectionate, protective.

'It's true.'

'It may be, but I don't like to hear you say it.' Did he add, 'It doesn't matter?' It doesn't matter. He conveyed that impression clearly enough, and Mum was mollified. She would not have expected anything more extravagant in language or gesture.

Childlessness in marriage was perhaps more often in those days a result of infertility on one side or the other than a conscious choice (some who did have children might have preferred not to, or not as many). Mum said that at one point a friend – not one of her closest in Princes Street – suggested fostering. Dad set his face firmly against that, on the basis that it would break her heart to have to return the child or children. It was adoption or nothing.

Whatever the availability of children for adoption – much greater then than it would become, certainly – the process was a stressful one. They got their choice of a boy with a clear medical certificate. They were not, however, pleased enough with my first posed picture to put it on general display. I am sitting (propped up) in Sutton Bridge, looking very like I did in my promo photo when they first met me aged two months. It was years before I saw myself, hidden away in an old album. They did not contract Crome Studio of Norwich again, but Lilian Ream Ltd (a well-known name in Wisbech) for the 'camera portrait' of me aged one that would long reign framed in Isle Bridge Road and is also reproduced in this volume. Judge for yourself.

I asked if I was really white in my early teens, when my curly hair and dark complexion led to me being called 'coon' once or twice. The word, in much more open usage in those days, was said jokingly, by only one friend, in a school where there were neither black children nor of any other category but white, none of mixed race as far as I could see; still, I felt the enquiry worth making. Evidently at the time of my adoption someone else felt the same way, or the question had been forestalled – that American father thing? – as Mum could be categorical in her answer.

That was perhaps the only question I did ask. I knew the subject was not congenial to Mum. While they had felt bound to take me to see Lincoln Cathedral as a child (a trip of which I remember nothing), she told me later she was nervous the whole time we were in the city. Dad was also uneasy enough to hurry us back to the car and the road home. Irrationally so, as there had never been any contact between them and my birth mother, who could hardly have recognised me either. On another occasion, Mum felt the need to share a terrible dream she had. My real mother (that's the phrase she used) had come to look for me and I'd wanted to go away with her. I could not find any appropriately reassuring words.

Running away from home did enter my head. Joyce recalled Steve O'Reilly's mum in Sutton Bridge coming round wondering where we had got to. We were up around the golf course near the bridge, having gathered some few provisions with the longer-term plan of living in dustbins. This piece of my history I'd forgotten, but I do remember agreeing to meet Hank under the Outwell church tower at one o'clock in the morning with the same purpose. He confessed first the next day that he hadn't been there. I resisted the temptation to lie that I had. It hadn't seemed quite urgent enough to get out of bed.

Although I may have initiated both abortive plans of escape, I think I was mainly adventuring. I had no fantasies of running to or rescue by my birth mother. The family that brought me up is irrevocably mine and, yes Mum, it is my real family. The plan to provide me with a little sister by the same adoption route was scotched by Dad's illness.

Chapter Eleven

The Tuck Shop

Boy racer

It is a commonplace that childhood haunts revisited are smaller than in the mind's eye. This effect was startlingly evident, in accelerated form, in the case of Harry 'Airbrakes' Wiseman. From the safety of Miss Bailey's musty and Miss Kerry's fragrant petticoats in the first two years, he was an ogre, a giant lurking in the middle of the school whose eruptions could be heard everywhere in it. Once we were in his class, he was still formidable, but recognisably human, a martinet without being a real hard case. Free from his clutches, we found him immediately smaller, his rantings provoking more of a smile than fearful whispers.

Mrs Lawrence was known to Mum by her maiden name of Alvy Jones. While not in Miss Kerry's league, the young wife who taught the class between Harry and Mrs Booley was an attractive woman. It was a pleasure to pull milk monitor duties for her. Bringing the crates in from the yard to the classroom at morning break, one boy at each end, was the only pleasure associated with the free drinks that later earned Margaret Thatcher the title 'Milk Snatcher'. She could have withdrawn the benefit in 1964 without any protest from me. The bottles, a third of a pint in each, were too warm in summer, too cold in winter. I didn't dislike the taste, only the temperature. Everyone drank it, anyway. The same boys for a week would lug the empties back out to the playground.

We were progressing in maths, English and other subjects as we moved through the school. Harry had started us in the times tables but drills in them probably continued, the rote learning reinforced by Grandad. He would try to catch me out with, for instance, eight times eight. 'That's a proper one, Jim, cos you can't cheat on it.'

'How do you mean?'

'Well, say I ask you what's six eights. If you give me the right answer – that's it, forty-eight – it don't mean you know your eight times table. If you're clever you might just switch it round and go eight times six.'

'But I'd still get the right answer.'

'I know, but you might only know your six times table, not the eight.'

The limit of our ambition with tables was twelve twelves are 144, which number we were also taught was one gross. We were shown all the wrinkles, the curiosities as with the nine times table: 'If you take one off the number you're timesing, that gives your first number. Then the second number is always what it takes to add up to nine. You see? Seven nines, take one away gives six, and six plus three makes nine, so the answer is sixty-three. And it works all the way through that table.'

The only thing I remember learning for sure in Mrs Lawrence's class was the colours of the rainbow in order: red, orange, yellow, green, blue, indigo, violet. 'To help you, all you have to do is remember the word – well it's not a real word,' she conceded with a smile – 'ROYGBIV.' Alvy, Alvy, were you sleeping in teachers' training when they gave out the mnemonic about Richard battling in vain?

While cousin Mandy, eight years younger, would struggle to remember, let alone convert back to pre-decimal money, its twists and terms were ingrained in me at primary school: bobs, tanners and joeys (long before we learned that 'thrupenny bits' was rhyming slang) were literally our common coin. Similarly, a healthy temperature for me will always be ninety-eight point four, not some figure in the thirties.

Imperial weights from pounds to stones, quarters and hundredweights were all around us. 'A pint of pure water weighs a pound and a quarter,' as Grandad told me, tied these to liquid measures. When it came to distances, it was easy to get entangled in chains or scourged with rods between the yard and the mile. All easy enough to check up and reconstruct now, but to what end? We didn't really need to know them even then.

There was a daily assembly in the big (now little) hall. Apart from parish notes, it would be prayers and hymns. I fancy Harry would play the piano, unless Mrs Booley chose to accompany herself while leading the singing.

'Stop a moment, Mr Wiseman, will you please? Right, now, who was that grunting?' We were practising for some concert or other. 'It sounds horrible. We're going to start singing again, and I want you to listen to the person next to you and tell me if it's him.' Somehow we had already known it couldn't be any of the girls.

'Is it me?'

'No, is it me?' Jim Wilson asked me back, receiving equal reassurance of his tunefulness. Our headmistress was not prepared to accept that everyone's silence meant her ear could have been wrong. She began stalking the rows. I was soon pinpointed as the cause of the disharmony. Diagnosed instantly as tone deaf, I was urged from then on to move my lips to the words, without allowing any sound to escape them.

While I had enjoyed grunting along to the more stirring hymns, I cannot claim to have been too dashed by Mrs Booley's gagging order. This was before I had reached her class. At some later stage, with a dreadful smile, she talked about the two of us seeing if anything could be salvaged. Her 'just in a friendly way' was terrifying. Luckily, she never found the time to plink out a tune for me to drop all over the floor.

Better mute than singing, it was soon apparent I had no talent for drawing either. This was barely remarked, since I don't recall any of the teachers showing a special interest in the visual arts, as Mrs Booley did for music. Dad fancied himself a bit at producing a good likeness of objects, if not people. We never pretended there was anything to be compared between my own and my parents' characteristics or talents, and they were far happier to see me doing well at 'academic' subjects than artistic ones.

How hopeful were they then of my stage debut? I'm not talking of a silent tea-cloth-headed Joseph I may have been in an infants' nativity play, but of a leading, perhaps title role: Mr Bumble.

All I remember of the piece is that it involved me, in character, growing horribly confused between different babies. I had to shuffle dolls about from one pram to another. Mr Booley, coming in on one rehearsal, tried to demonstrate how it was done. 'Show a little more expression, boy,' he boomed. 'You've got to make the audience think these are real babies. Project yourself, here, make big gestures.'

I thought none the worse of Stan when I heard him talking in pre-production to a visitor watching us rehearse (I say 'us' without any idea who may have been Mrs Bumble or other characters – I suspect there was not a large cast): 'The trouble is, the children we can trust to learn the lines are not the ones who may have any acting talent.'

I'm sure Mum and Dad were in the audience on the big night (afternoon?), with nothing but good things to say about my performance. I believe I got all the words out in the right order and juggled the dolls correctly. Perhaps the sheer busyness of this kept me from any thought of stage fright. I was confident enough to take the stage again (or earlier), the older Chuffer messaged me (emojis deleted) of something I had forgotten:

> *The earliest memory I have of you is, wait for it,,,, Walking on stage at Beaupre school in a play, you were about 7/8yrs old, and played a French policeman, Your line was BAH!!,,,,I was in the audience, cos only the brainy kids got to act, (Mr Booleys favourites).*

Despite all this positive evidence, my career as an actor... well, let's consign it, like singing and painting, to a path not taken, and for equally good reason.

Stan did not have a class to teach. Walking the school corridors his head would be held high, keeping most of our doings well beneath his line of vision (unless it was a troubled kid hacking away at his shins). Perhaps he would have stepped in if a teacher was absent. I never recall any of them being away. He did appear in Mrs Lawrence's class one day, stationing himself at the back where hamsters were kept to be fed by the girls and tormented by the boys at playtimes.

'Right. Now who can tell me what this is?'

Everyone looked at Mrs Lawrence, who gave us the nod to turn and face the headmaster. Finally, someone ventured 'a weighing machine, miss?' We were well enough trained to address our teachers politely at all times, used to adding 'miss' to the end of each sentence. Mrs Lawrence herself was often called 'sir' in the first few days of each new intake from Harry's class, and long beyond that in certain cases.

Ignoring the nervous titters, and the furious blush of the girl who had called him 'miss', Stan extracted the positive from her answer: 'Yes, that's right. It's what we call a pair of scales, and these are the different weights that go with it. Have the children learned their weights yet, Mrs Lawrence?'

'Yes, Mr Booley.' She added kindly, 'They know there are sixteen ounces in a pound and fourteen pounds in a stone.'

'Good. I won't need to ask them that then, will I? Now, let's do an experiment. Who can help me? David Bailey, come over here.'

There was no culture in Beaupré of children standing in front of the class, for good or bad work. I was in the back row, near the window looking over the empty playground, with Stan's prominent suited belly in the foreground.

'Right David, I want you to tell us how much this book weighs.' It may have been some other object, just as there is an element of invention in the dialogue thus far. I only remember it verbatim from here on.

I stood there, holding the object as if I was trying to reach the answer by heft alone. Stan was not an aggressive man, but nor was he the most patient. 'What's the matter?'

'I don't know how to do it, sir.'

'What? Oh, you don't know how to use the scales. Well, never mind. That's what we're here for, isn't it, Mrs Lawrence? We've got to be able to teach you something.'

The bridge that separated Norfolk from Cambridgeshire at Outwell is a narrow one, whose sharp turns have embarrassed more than one lorry driver and many in cars too. As children it was the height of our ambition one day to join the youths who perched on its railings, feet on the raised kerbstone that could never justifiably be called a pavement. They had their own title, 'bridge-hangers', bestowed by Stan himself on those we should strive mightily to avoid becoming once we reached our teenage years.

The general stores on either side of the river were Buck's and Tuck's. The latter, by far the senior, gave its name to the bridge then and many years after the shop itself closed. It survived as a business long beyond what seemed feasible to a child looking at its owners, each seemingly closer than the next to the confines of extreme old age. We would never have addressed any of them directly – though they were probably not as deaf as we thought – but everyone knew their Christian names.

Mabel was the one most frequently in need of assistance from one of her brothers. Tiny, hunch-backed, goggle-eyed behind thick spectacles, she had perhaps never married. As well as her relatively rare appearances behind the counter – what could she reach on those shelves stacked fifteen feet high? – she supposedly kept house for the widowed Walter, and Bernie. These two were patently of the same blood, balding and stooped, noses to compete with Grandad's in size. Walter was the less spry, wearing a drab brown butcher's apron even after Olga Parker, mother of Paul a year below me at Beaupré, took over the bacon slicer in a snazzier blue-and-white-striped outfit. 'At least we won't be getting the dewdrops from Walter's snout on our ham anymore,' Robert 'Doey' Dolan remarked.

Bernie, sometimes almost dapper in a grey three-piece suit, was the only one of the siblings I could imagine in a broader human context outside the shop's heavy double doors. He was still a prominent village figure, the Tucks' face to the world. The family were significant landholders, noted benefactors of the chapel. None of this would have cut any ice with us, had we known it. Their defining characteristic was to be *old*.

Old yet never disrespected by us children, who saw our parents address them formally as their own elders. This might have been a legacy from days when the dynasty (a John had his name on the frontage, possibly the father of 'and Sons' Walter and Bernie) would run a slate for people in hard times or between markets. Another son Alfred, a Great War survivor with a ruined arm, had lived at the top of Isle Bridge Road before my time or beyond my ken. The remaining Tucks earned their respect by being nobody's fools. They were not at all fazed by decimalisation. Bernie's mental arithmetic and perhaps a grubby crib-sheet for Walter and Mabel were enough to run for their customers parallel pricing systems and conversions – always scrupulously accurate – as long as was necessary.

From a child's viewpoint, how to contemplate pinching a few sweets, when they nestled in big glass jars behind the counter, reachable with infinite care and often a stepladder only by one of the brothers? Infinite patience, too; they wouldn't mind how many different jars you picked from to get your quarter or half pound, nor would they have to use the scales except to show you a fair deal before they twisted momentarily shut the white paper bag. If Mabel was entrusted with this final step, Fiddle remembered her always popping one of our sweets into her own mouth before handing them over. You don't get rich by giving things away, as the old village saying went.

Stan was a permanent parish councillor; it was perhaps in that capacity he bought our whole class lollipops from Tuck's one day, after a surprise excursion from school. I remember his expansive arm-fling as he vaunted his munificence, but we deserved the treat for an afternoon's solid physical work on a hot day. The Rec' had been neglected and become a place where nobody went anymore, at least for the innocent pastimes it was meant to serve. Our brief was simple. Fanning out across the field, we had to pick up all the stones we could find. How many there were, what we did with them, who worked beside me, to what purpose, all gone. Without the lollipop, the day would be lost forever.

Any resurgence of the Rec' was short-lived. A bigger village project than one based on primary school labour was a new playing field, a new Nest for the Outwell Swifts. I went just once to an earlier home ground, somewhere by the Basin not far from Grandad's. One of the team's heroes of the day, a Hanslip (John or Derek, names have become confused with those of subsequent generations) was pointed out to me. Uncle Fred's older boy, Bobby Goldsmith, had played for them on the wing during the fifties.

Crossing the Sluice footbridge from the chapel to where Aunt Gert lived, turning left along the Wisbech Road, on your right is a flat space – aren't they all in East Anglia? – big enough for fifty cars or so. A waist-high one-rail metal barrier ensures vehicle access is only by the paved road on the Wisbech side.

Although the council bought the land in July 1966, the playing field was not formally opened until June 1969. While the Swifts may not have moved in till then, my memory has us kids playing there much earlier. We quickly wore a path to it from the village end of the barrier, easily vaultable but in any case with a gap big enough to walk through between it and the clapboard fence of the property next door. The son there (Greg Wilkins), a year or two younger than me, had never been so popular. He had a football. We would always call to fetch them out to play.

The playing field eventually had not only the Swifts' pitch, full-sized goals with round metal posts and stanchions plus wooden backboards, leaving only the nets to be strung up for matches. Crossways to it, the council thoughtfully put up smaller wooden goalposts for us kids. One from Upwell soon busted a crossbar by swinging from it. The goal was removed but never replaced, while Hillsie was not welcome for a while in our village.

We were too old to play on the swings and roundabout, not old enough to hang around them with girls. The commendable initiative of two hard-surface tennis courts would not interest me until later. Otherwise, within the field boundaries of dykes on three sides there were only the pavilion, where the teams would change and take their half-time cuppas, and a smaller wooden shed by the halfway line. With an earth floor and without seats of any kind, this offered some little shelter from the elements for the hardy Swifts fans.

That I have related my undistinguished footballing career in another piece of work (*Midfailed General – My B-rilliant Career*) will not spare you its beginnings here. The first FA Cup Final I watched was Liverpool v Leeds in 1965, breaking away at half-time to play football in Isle Bridge Road with Henry and Stevie, one of his younger brothers.

At school, while the girls were occupied at something indoors, there would be an afternoon game once a week for the boys in Mrs Booley and Mrs Lawrence's classes. At the younger end of the age range from eight to eleven, I counted my participation in this by the number of kicks I had, usually between zero and five. Stan was nominally in charge. Beyond seeing the sides picked up in the corridor outside his office, he took no interest. If he came out to watch at all, it was for only a few minutes. There was no coaching, and at that stage I was not watching football on television. Apart from street games I remember playing with Hank on a small patch of grass down Churchfield Road, taking alternate shots at each other's goals, and with Cousin Barrie, shooting at each other three-and-in. Football fever was some months away. The field was being built and we would come.

Chapter Twelve

Angel Cake

Boy with braces and monkey

At home, the move to Outwell brought about an improvement in relations between Mum and Dad. She may have felt more relaxed back in her own village. Apart from George and Dinah, she had Aunts Ivy and Gert. Uncle Sid, not a friend or support to her in the same way, would often be found in Aunt Gert's small kitchen, a benign if taciturn presence, usually speaking through teeth closed around his pipe. Mum now only had a bike ride to work, not the hassle of a train and bus commute with me in tow, which would only have become harder. She recalled a crowd turning out at the Bridge to mark the train's last passenger stop while we were still living there.

Many Outwell people, more women than men (and me in due course), put in a shift at Hannam & Davy. Work there varied according to the season and the job in hand between day and piece work, with permanent staff supplemented by casual workers when required. I am sure the wages were not extravagant, but Mum was well-suited to piece work, where the more productive you are the more you earn. A degree of flexibility in the hours was also helpful. The only drawback was the visibility of working for a company, subject to whatever employment regulations were then in force, whereas local farmers would pay cash in hand, without the burden (or benefit) of 'the stamp'.

One of my Beaupré compositions caused consternation in the family. Mum and Dad were always keenly interested in my classes, their 'what did you do at school today?' more than a form question, not to be satisfied with the eternal schoolboy answer 'nothing'. There was never homework at Beaupré, so I must have told them what I had written about our family circumstances. These included Mum working at Hannam's carrot-topping. They were genuinely fearful, perhaps that benefits from Dad's incapacity might be prejudiced if the extent of our family income were known. I was gravely warned, by Grandad as well as Mum, to keep our business to ourselves.

I don't imagine Grandad minded no longer having to supervise Barrie and me once he could come to stay with us in Isle Bridge Road. Indoors at Maillebourne there was a radiogram, which I never knew Nana or Grandad to use. Of the few records in it, I would beg Barrie to play Frankie Vaughan's 'Tower of Strength' time and time again. Grandad could escape this. When we invaded his land, he had more reason to be careful.

The boundary with his neighbour's orchards (from which we took the odd apple without any qualms) was a dyke nearer to the house, then Hall Dike, a continuation of Robb's Lane with dykes on both sides. From pigsties to the halfway shed, which held little of interest for us on the rare occasions it was not padlocked, was about 150 yards. At the shed the dyke broadened and deepened somewhat, to the point where it was worth throwing stones in. One day Barrie and I began a more ambitious project.

The land was freshly rotavated. There were plenty of fresh, sizeable clods for us to hurl into the dyke just below the shed. Although some landed on the banks, it did not take long before we were markedly impeding the flow of water.

In family legend, tragedy was only narrowly averted. Like the reaction to my school essay, Grandad's temper seemed disproportionate. Did he really believe we would block the dyke, backing up the water to flood all his land? He sounded as if he believed it. Sending us scurrying for cover with curses and threats of a thrashing, he was not quite concerned enough to scramble down in his wellies and overalls to bust our dam. The whole family heard about our criminal vandalism, nevertheless.

Barrie was fondly imagined as an ideal playmate for me, a suitable male role model, the older brother I never had. I agreed wholeheartedly. Mum's faith was sometimes tried.

Ladies of Spain I adore you,
Lift up your legs, let me explore you.

'David, where did you hear that?'

I told the truth in saying from Barrie, and that he had it from Uncle Charlie. Was I not allowed to sing even at home now?

In the first months of our tenancy, bringing that home up to Mum's standards, I was allowed to help in the congenial task of stripping off wallpaper, several layers thick in some places. The new rolls would be put on a table, slathered with paste then step-laddered onto the wall, with the utmost care to ensure the banal flowered patterns matched seamlessly. No doubt there were arguments – there would be with any married couple collaborating on such a task. Generally though, once Dad got started on a job he would attack it enthusiastically enough.

This enthusiasm did not extend beyond the house doors. The good-sized patches of land both front and back were immediately marked out for strawberries, the key cash crop for householders for miles around.

In their first year 'maidens' are straggly rows yielding little and soon picked. They thicken out for the next three years, after which standard practice was to rotate, with onions, potatoes or cereal crops, which on being ploughed under would refresh the land for the next lot of maidens. It was important to arrange things so that at least one of the front or back gardens had a mature strawberry crop. I don't recall either one ever lying completely fallow.

The plants need to be sprayed against disease. The earth between the rows is covered with straw, not for the eventual pickers' convenience but to avoid rain splashing up and ruining the growing fruit. A purist view is that the straw should be tucked under the plants themselves to stop the strawberries being corrupted by the earth. Uncle Tom's dad walked his fields with a stick to ruffle the leaves, to ensure his strawers kept to this practice, or later in the season that his pickers had not missed any fruit, in which case he would call them back.

It was a matter of course for Grandad to do our spraying – tank strapped on his back, nozzle in hand – and strawing whenever he did his own. Dad played no part in the process, nor ever in any land work.

Strawberry picking, the 'fruiting' that might last up to a biblical forty days between the highly prized first pick and the 'shacking' of the stragglers at the end, took place mainly in June. So integral to the villages was it that Upwell Secondary Modern closed for a fortnight in advance of the main summer holiday, accepting that most of its kids would be out picking anyway, either with their own families or as casual labour elsewhere.

There were never enough kids. Fruiting saw the influx of what seemed like a whole new population. Early signs of its arrival went up in some of the village pubs: NO VAN DWELLERS SERVED HERE. Others took a bit of additional aggravation for a dollop of additional revenue.

I was too young to know how great any additional aggravation was. Villagers were leery of those most politely known as 'vanners', otherwise as 'diddicoys' ('diddies' was Nan Dinah's variant) or 'gyppos'. Mum was always quick to point out that they weren't real gypsies just because they lived in caravans. I didn't hear the term 'pikies' until later years. They styled themselves as 'Romanies' or 'travellers'. Perhaps they stood out more because any new faces would in our small village. If they had come singly, they might have been more welcome. No doubt with their own habits of self-preservation, they were rarely seen alone.

It was accepted lore that if you fought one vanner you fought them all. Their puniest boys could take liberties with much older and bigger of us, safe in their knowledge that we thought that way. Their parents were usually strict in enforcing politeness and respect for elders in public. However many of a family of theirs were picking a given field, all the money went to the head man.

They were rumoured to come to us from the hop-fields of Kent, or perhaps head there from us after fruiting. We envied their children for not having to attend school. I became friendly with one exception to this. While most of the travellers had their camps dotted around the outskirts of the village, by night with the traditional open fires and unwelcoming dogs, John Raper stayed in Tom Russell's dad's field, where he would take back the same few families to work for him each summer.

I went to John's home at least once, because I remember his mother serving us angel cake in the back of their van. I went home full of (in both senses) this new sweet. I bet Mum dutifully bought some for us, and that it didn't taste quite as good.

Tom Russell was a year above me at Beaupré, and as such scarcely noticed me there other than casually bestowing on me the nickname Beetle Bailey. It didn't stick. Maybe only Tom was familiar with the cartoon character. I was not, despite being still on a heavy dose of comics. *Smash* came late to the party with some of the Marvel stable, notably The Incredible Hulk.

Outside school, at least for a season or two, Fiddle and I hung around a lot with Tom. I was the junior partner, with Fiddle always entrusted the errand, the fetching and carrying for Tom. There was an evil donkey in their field I was persuaded to mount one day. I say evil because of the outcome. Perhaps it was just a slap on the rump from Tom that startled the poor brute into a run, ending with me catapulted over its shoulders to the ground. Although I was physically unharmed, Aunt Shirley later made great sport of the way I hung on so desperately to a docile creature on Hunstanton beach, assuring the child leading it that, no thank you, I did not want to go any faster than a gentle walk.

On another occasion the three of us were recruited for a day's beating. Spread out beyond earshot of each other, we were expected to tramp over heavy, open ground to scare up birds for the guns. I thought it would never end. I saw nothing but mud, heard not a single shot.

We spent one Bonfire Night at Tom's. His profligacy with fireworks astonished me. He careered around the massive fire with a duffel bag overflowing with bangers, Roman Candles, Catherine Wheels, rockets, lighting them one after the other, scarcely waiting to see them burn. My attitude was the reverse. I lit my more modest stock sparingly, wanting to ensure I had one or two remaining till the very end. There was food in abundance, hot sausages in buns mainly. The adults were all cheerfully unconcerned at our doings. They felt no need to supervise us, although a spark in the shed from where Tom refilled his bag would probably have exploded the whole house. Now *there* was a spoilt boy, I reflected smugly.

At school we would be given each year a lesson on the history of the celebration: Remember, remember the Fifth of November... We knew roughly who Guy Fawkes was, preparing his effigy with straw and clothes discarded by dads to sit atop the heap and burn. The teachers may have warned us to be careful. If not, Mum would certainly have been on full alert, not wishing to entrust me with anything much more than a sparkler.

My birthday falling on 1 November meant I could expect at least one box of Brock's fireworks as a present. These appeared in every grocer's or sweetshop in the build-up to the big night, celebrated on the fifth, whichever day of the week that happened to be. The next morning, while bonfires still smouldered in many a back garden, the fireworks had vanished from the shops.

Burning household or garden waste was a common thing. Grandad had for some years no more profitable use for a small part of his land than to burn damaged pallets dumped there under contract from their yard by the creek. Apart from the cash received he fed the fire in his grate (at the expense of a new hearthrug for Nan every so often, since the wood crackled and spat). As fireworks night approached, the normal pile would be allowed to expand in readiness.

The two Chuffers and I shared a bonfire one year. We went all around the village, in competition with other kids begging material for it. We struck paydirt at the fish shop, whose owner (Frank Retchless) casually said we could take away everything in his back yard. There alone were the makings of a worthwhile blaze, cardboard boxes of every size as well as paper and wood. Failing to elicit a promise to reserve it for us if others came calling, we had to rush back home for the big flat barrow used for loading trays of strawberries. Somehow we manhandled this back across Tuck's Bridge then home again, struggling to keep our booty from sliding off in all directions.

The guy had an important function before he went up in smoke, one that justified pimping and primping him as much as our limited wardrobe and zero budget allowed. The more lifelike he was, the argument went, the more we could realistically expect in contributions, though the formula was always 'penny for the guy, please', whether delivered door to door or from a prime pitch outside Buck's, as Guido lolled slackly in a wheelbarrow or propped against a wall.

Looking up Isle Bridge Road we could see three or four other fires. We had built ours stick by scrap. We had stuffed and touted the guy. We were eating our mums' food, watching our dads launch the rockets from milk bottles, getting close enough to the fire to feel its heat flush our faces, to inhale the smoke from its gradual collapse (nowadays even our indoor fuel must be smokeless). The land, like the houses, may have belonged to the council, but it was ours on Bonfire Night.

Chapter Thirteen

Family Matters

I don't think I became ashamed of Dad until I left Beaupré. As in those adolescent years you may dread questions exposing your lack of experience with girls, I was constantly worrying that I might have to reply 'nothing' if asked what my father did for a living. It may be my morbid imagination suggesting that question was posed more often then, by well-meaning adults seeking some conversational foothold as well as in all sorts of official and unofficial contexts. It was as if our fathers' occupations defined us. I came to feel that was associating me with failure.

Dad's illness was a settled thing by the time we moved to Outwell. Perhaps there was concern that a new doctor might take a different view on his entitlement to benefits, ability to work. The only time I knew Dad to visit Dr Rushmer was with me, to see if I should have the mole (or 'beauty spot' as I was not yet shy of calling it) beside my left eye removed.

'No, I'd suggest we don't need to worry about it. As you get older it will look smaller on your face. When you have wrinkle lines around it, like your dad or me, that will be soon enough to think about taking it off, if you still want to.'

The initiative for that visit had not been mine, so I was not too fussed one way or the other. Once later, when playing football in Isle Bridge Road, I took a knock to the mole. I asked Mum, as she tried in our bathroom to stem it, 'I won't bleed to death, will I?'

'I don't know,' she snapped, continuing to dab away. The old superstition clearly kept a hold on us both.

We never had a doctor in the house. When Dad sank into one of his 'do's', a few days in which he stayed in bed, it was understood we had to wait it out. There was no cure, no shortcut either.

Part of the problem may have been depression. Dad was gregarious enough to miss the work world of male camaraderie, apart from the wound to his pride in no longer being the breadwinner (though of course there were other men, in Outwell as elsewhere, who were in the same position). Except during one of his housebound spells, Dad was sociable and seemed well enough liked around the village. He was not a regular at any of its pubs, though not averse to a drink – witness the bottle of Mackeson Uncle Norman had so kindly treated him to along with a weekly packet of cigarettes when he first became ill back in the Bridge. He continued to smoke the unfiltered Park Drive in packets of ten.

The days may have seemed long without any occupation, with Mum at work and me at school. If he could be said to have a routine, it was to rise just before noon, when Mum would come home from work to serve him – invariably – grilled bacon with some bread and butter. Not a big eater, he probably weighed less than eleven stone.

Television would not begin until late afternoon (with a possible exception for Test cricket). Dad had a small collection of hardback novels from the Bridge and earlier. *Treasure Island* was inscribed to him at Railway Lane as a Christmas 1934 gift 'from Grandmother', the single-sheet start of a retelling folded into its front cover in his own tidy cursive: 'Jim Hawkins, (the hero of this story), has climbed aboard the ship "Hispaniola", and has pulled down the Jolly Roger...' There were Monsarrat's *Cruel Sea* and Shute's *Town Like Alice*, while Remarque's *All Quiet on the Western Front* was inscribed to Allen as a Christmas 1958 gift from Joyce. Her own name (Joyce Bailey, so already married) was in her own hand in a *Lord Hornblower* I might have expected to belong to Dad. *The Saga of Billy the Kid* (by Walter Noble Burns) was one he lent a friend and neighbour. Perhaps there was traffic in the reverse direction, from Derrick or others, as occasionally Dad would devour something new, to the exclusion of all else for a few hours. A library van sometimes parked outside Tuck's. Mum, who liked detective fiction, introduced me to its Wisbech mothership. Dad patronised neither. He would read the *Daily Express* we had delivered, switching brands on Sunday to *The People*.

Our main meal was tea, the three of us eating it at the kitchen table. The habit ingrained in early childhood was by now only a gabble of grace: 'ForwhatweareabouttoreceivemaytheLordmakeustrulygratefulAmen'.   Less durable was 'please may I get down?' after bolting my food and giving whatever account of my day was required. Sometimes Dad would mention that in his father's house none of the children were allowed to speak at table.

Years later at a golf school for weekend warriors I stumped the pro, who was trying to improve my short game.

'I tell you what, have you ever swept a floor with a broom?'

'No.'

'You've never in your life swept a floor.'

'No.'

Although we both finished the course close to despair, I was not being deliberately obtuse. As a boy I was never asked to do any household chores, at home or anywhere else within the family. If anything, I was discouraged from them, with Mum almost hustling Dad and me out of the kitchen so she could do the washing-up. She would only join us in the living room when everything was squared away to her satisfaction, all in its time-honoured place.

Whatever could be classed in any way as 'housework', from making the beds to cleaning, washing, shopping, cooking – all was done by Mum. Although she worked full-time outside the home and did all the gardening, she regarded this as the natural way of things. Allen and I were not expected to make so much as a cup of tea. We did not demur.

Mum did not run the household in a spirit of martyrdom. In some ways, as she had always worked, she was continuing the pattern of their early married life, when Allen worked too. This clear division of duties between man and woman – on whose side anything to do with children also fell – was more the norm than peculiar to my mum and dad. To do anything less would have made Joyce feel she was failing in some way as a wife or mother, shirking what was fairly expected of her.

I hope there is no element of special pleading, no weasel words here to justify criminal laziness on my part. I was spoilt, of course. Guilty. Sometimes you just have to get over it.

As regards Dad, there was something nobler in Mum's attitude. She told of a time early in their marriage when she had entered a pub to give him some message. He felt belittled in front of his friends, that his wife was coming to drag him home, and 'called me everything' (once they were out of the pub, one assumes). She vowed she would never do that again. It was important for her to preserve a pride in her husband. She knew also how important it was for him to keep pride in himself.

Within our early years at Isle Bridge Road, the living-room Rayburn was replaced by an open fire. Whether this was at our own instigation and expense or part of a general modernisation programme by the council, I twitted Mum long after that she would miss the Rayburn. It was great for keeping hot drinks warm on its top. Its oven beside the fire always received the first batch of chips at Saturday tea, to keep warm while my fish fingers and their wet fish were being prepared in the kitchen. They tasted all the better for a few minutes in there.

Through winter the Rayburn would be banked down at night. This process, which involved juggling pans of glowing ash, meant it could be stirred to life again in the morning with a poker and some fresh coke. The open fire, when we were allowed to use it (first we had to admire its newness for a few days), was a different proposition. Much more dangerous, for a start. The fireguard had the landlord's share of the heat it threw out over the years. It also needed relighting every morning, and there we came to a labour demarcation issue.

It was accepted that Mum would light the fire, so the room would not be too cold for Dad to venture downstairs. While it was not one of her prime skills, she would nestle the kindling in strips of newspaper to start a flame strong enough to ignite the first lumps of coals. Dad's job was to chop the kindling. He was not always on the ball.

As I was getting ready for school, the kindling controversy was a regular one. If there was not a supply of the thin sticks ready in the wash-house, then Mum would have to produce some, throwing her morning schedule out. I used to dread her mutterings escalating into an outright reproach to the man upstairs, leading to a row and all it entailed. Normally there was no time for that, and by evening the matter was out of mind. I don't know what finally eroded the bone of contention. Most likely Grandad was so gorged with spare wood from the pallet yard he could provide kindling for us too. An option seemingly never considered by Mum was not to make up the fire.

Door-to-door salesmen were not common in Outwell. I only remember one calling at our house. He was Indian or Pakistani, selling I don't know what. Surprisingly, Mum shrank from the back door, calling her husband, who gave him a far rougher reception than he had once a Jehovah's Witness.

'Go on, bugger off out of here, we don't want anything,' Allen shouted from his armchair by the television. I was struck by the sheer *nastiness* in his tone, the unusual aggression. It was not a racial thing, unless he had heard something in the poor fellow's voice, since he never saw him. It was another example of him being the man of the house and being egged on to play that part by Mum. She was always scrupulous to invoke him as the maximum authority in matters relating to my behaviour (even if she could hardly use the traditional 'wait till your father gets home'), or expenditure on any item of significance. If they happened to be out together, he would always have the money in his pocket to buy the round. Propriety was all-important.

Motoring was a significant area of family life where Dad's role was clearly defined and never threatened. We somehow always had a car. I don't think anything came between the Ford and a black Morris Minor, which was eventually followed by an automatic Cortina. The first was the only one we possibly had from new.

Mum never learned to drive. She explained this to me more than once as a deliberate strategy, fearing that if she did so Dad would cede those duties to her and never have any occasion to go out. In short, he would become still more dependent.

While my aunts Doreen and Shirley could drive, I never saw either of them do so with her husband as a passenger. Mum appeared content with the shotgun seat, occasionally passing him a cigarette. She would light this and take the first drag. It was the only smoking I ever saw her do, though she confessed to having finished one or two in her single days. From the back seat I was allowed to sing out loud all the songs we learned at school, over and over, a true mark of their love for me.

We did not generally travel far afield. Mum and Dad entertained the concept of 'going out for a ride', getting into the car for the sake of driving, with no firm destination in mind. I never saw the point of that. I was much happier to go to Aunt Dawn's or Shirl's. This was done without pre-arrangement – we never had a phone and I doubt they did at that time – but they were always there, and we were always made welcome. An important benefit for me was that the risk of a row was minimised by such conviviality. If they were in enough accord to go out as a family, things were normally going to be all right.

Naturally we also visited Sutton Bridge. Nana and Grandad Bailey never seemed to change. I was disappointed that only one lead soldier of Uncle Brian's legendary collection could be found. Uncle Jack gave me an exceptionally generous birthday present one year (I have in mind a fiver, but that can't be right for the place and time). I was bored unless we happened to coincide with a visit by cousins Sue and Stephen. I had little more to do when we called on

Uncle Norman and Aunt Maud – they were the only ones from Princes Street who kept in regular contact, coming over to Outwell too – once the time had passed when I could call round to see if Steve O'Reilly was coming out to play.

By the unwritten rules of obliquity, it was rare for George to speak to Allen. The only time I ever heard him criticise Dad for anything was on a matter of driving. I had bragged of his daring in taking both hands off the wheel on one occasion as we went downhill. It was only a momentary treat to mock-frighten his son, but 'he should have known better' was the reproof from the man who used to drive with me on his lap, 'steering'.

I had been left one night with Nan Dinah, when Mum's face appeared around the living-room door of the bungalow soon after she and Dad had set off towards Lynn. 'We've had an accident,' she announced.

Her face was pale, but she gave us the story clearly enough. They were heading towards the Smeeth, not far past the Venni house I translated to myself, when an oncoming vehicle had cut the corner and hit them. 'You might ask how your dad is!' she snapped at me, when I tried to find out how badly the car was damaged.

'You already said he was all right,' I answered truthfully. Her first concern had been to reassure us that neither of them was injured. I don't know how she got back to Maillebourne. Dad was still at the scene of the accident; the police had arrived. There was likely to have been minimal traffic on that country road, with barely enough space between dykes on either side for two cars to pass each other at the best of times.

I think the case went to court, the other driver – also unharmed, I guess it was not a high-speed collision – was found wholly to blame so Mum and Dad got off without any major trauma, physical or financial. It was a shame their outing ended that way, for they rarely went anywhere without me. Grandad worked every other Saturday night. On those he was at home I would go to spend the night with them (Nan out at bingo), so money rather than lack of a sitter would have been the major inhibiting factor. I remember Dad once suggesting they should go to the pictures to see a film I was old enough to realise might have sex scenes in it. Mum didn't like the sound of it, and they didn't go.

They never walked together to any of the village pubs (still four then). One Christmas Eve, after the three of us had been to a carol concert or similar event at Beaupré, we could hear a noisy crowd behind the drawn curtains of the Crown, the one at the top of our road, by Tuck's Bridge. Dad went in alone.

With Mum's blessing, but still there was a tension in the house as the two of us watched Sid James leer and letch his way through *Carry on Christmas*. Dad was thankfully not too late in, and holiday peace was preserved. Not so in the year of the great family schism.

Chapter Fourteen

Christmas Carry-on

Aged four at King's Lynn

I have a feeling the custom developed in the Hills family of gathering for Christmas in the house of whoever had George and Dinah's youngest grandchild. My earliest memory of the day itself is diving into the back of the settee in Princes Street and kicking out my legs behind me, waiting for their green Morris, all curves as the Ford was all angles, to pull up in the road outside. Our decorations included a blue card in the shape of a stocking. Glued onto it were festive pictures cut from magazines, including a haloed Virgin Mary. I brought it home in my first school year, and it hung every festive season after from Mum's living-room ceiling.

If we did make a Christmas at Sutton Bridge for others in the family, it was possibly with their financial support. When we moved to Outwell, Maillebourne became the logical centre of festivities, though on Christmas morning I always woke in my own bed.

In those days children were sat happily on shop Santas' knees for a photo before receiving their gift. I think it was a mince pie and milk we used to leave out for the real Father Christmas, who never failed to consume them. Like many children (not my cousin Mandy, who found him a frightening figure), I tried to stay awake until he came; like most, without success or disappointment.

Not waking at some unearthly hour in excitement at the prospect of my gifts, I slept soundly enough. When I did open my eyes, it was to presents in pillowcases at the foot of the bed. I knew I could go straight to Mum and Dad's room, getting between them in the double bed to open everything. If they had any gifts themselves, I neither knew nor cared. I was shamefully late to realise that the festival (and the fun) involved giving as well as receiving. Aunt Shirley told me one year of Mum being upset: coming into money somehow earlier in December, I had spent it on myself instead of thinking of a gift for her. Mum herself had said nothing to me.

Apart from the convenient fireworks I remember little, few of my birthday and Christmas presents in those earliest years. There was a fort with real battlements and a drawbridge, men-at-arms to fight against merrie men. Soldiers were a staple, right through to Aunts Ivy and Gert coming with teenage me into Prams and Toys, off Wisbech marketplace. Saying they had another nephew with tastes near identical to mine – curiously, we had never met – they asked my advice in selecting each half a dozen of the latest Viking range (in a new material, superficially harder to the touch than that of my earlier armies but far more fragile under the weight of a brick).

118

I never had much interest in cars. There was a Land Rover-style vehicle that worked – for the briefest time – by remote control. I prized a two-storey garage, where cars could be winched up in a lift, to descend far more rapidly on a metal slide. I had a second-hand Scalextric at some point, not a Christmas gift, but any enthusiasm for it was short-lived. I found both track and cars too unreliable.

A train set was more favoured, growing to cover enough square feet of track nailed onto chipboard to make it a bit of a production to get out to play. Once I had tired of adjusting the points, I came to enjoy derailing the various wagons behind the speeding locomotive with a rocket launcher. Not destructive enough for soldier warfare, the silver-painted missile released by a manual spring mechanism provoked a satisfactory pile-up.

Whether Christmassy or not, many of the toys that occupied me for hours were football related. First there was a table with red and blue players, operated from beneath by magnets on the end of sticks. The control, the magnetic force, was stronger with some players than others. Less elaborate was a one-fold board game, where a dice moved the counter/ball. It fitted handily under the settee in Nan Dinah's living room. I wore the facing off that board, especially in the main traffic areas around the centre circle, where the midfielders scrapped to find a winger who could then cross to the centre-forward. He was the only player who could score, with a six (five earned a penalty, allowing another throw and an easier conversion).

The final stage was Subbuteo, which held a spell over different generations as *the* football game for boys, and lonely men. Here again my first two teams, the ones that came with the starter set, were red and blue, United and… well, Everton above any other Blues. Eventually I would have more than a dozen, among the ever more recherché strips picking up ones like Bradford Park Avenue, a team in which I otherwise had not the slightest interest.

I followed Barrie in my enthusiasm for Subbuteo. Flick the round-based players to kick the ball, flick two more in support then hit the ball again, the rules were swiftly enough explained to me. My technique soon became unorthodox if not illegal. It was so much easier to keep control by nudging the men around with your crooked forefinger rather than its nail. Most of my games I was playing both teams (as with the magnetised and dice games), so nobody lost out. My biggest legacy from Barrie was a splendid chipboard trunk, with individual slots for teams as well as various internal compartments. We haggled over it in the hall at the foot of their stairs. Money changed hands for me to take it home, with the blessing of both sets of parents. He'd built it himself. He made another, but acknowledged it was a poor thing, all cheap-looking cardboard partitions, by comparison to his first labour of love.

Barrie took his father's interest in aeroplanes to the extent of also joining the Royal Observer Corps. Like him, I had some of the Airfix models of Spitfires, Hurricanes and the like, though never hanging from my bedroom ceiling as they did in the Rowell home. I was cack-handed at gluing the tiny pieces together, never mind all the historically accurate paintwork. Dad helped me with some of them. There was one big white monster, perhaps a Flying Fortress. An aircraft carrier too, of which the lifeboats were one of many finicky details. In the Airfix world, as already suggested, I preferred the two-bob regiments of tiny soldiers to be twisted off their plastic stems.

There would always be books, loosely split between annuals to be inhaled before the new year and more 'educational' fare, in some cases still waiting for me to get round to it. The annuals were from the same comics I read each week, not rehashing material already published but with new stories and looking forward to the next year. My 1967 *Valiant* album was thus a gift from Uncle Ted at Christmas 1966. They might also be spin-offs from favourite television shows such as *The Beverley Hillbillies* or *The Outer Limits*, with a popular price nine and sixpence (47.5p) when the weekly *Valiant* comic was sevenpence (nearly 3p).

The Ladybird books about anyone from Richard III to Florence Nightingale, pocket-sized with a full-page illustration opposite each one of text, were easier to swallow than more expensive tomes on history and geography, all with our dear England at the centre of the universe. In a sense these could also be viewed as an extension of my weekly fodder, since Mum and Dad subscribed on my behalf to the *Joy of Knowledge* magazine. With this came periodically indices and offers of hard binders, the idea being it would build into an encyclopaedia. I *had* a set of encyclopaedias, eight volumes in alphabetical tranches such as AAR-COR, on a free-standing wooden shelflet with space to fit flat beneath them the accompanying Atlas of the World (I would later see an identical set at Fangs' house). Things like these showed Mum and Dad's commitment to giving me every chance to 'do well at school'. I am more sensible now of the financial sacrifice involved in a household where every penny had to count, yet grateful that they spent as much on frivolities for me, on *proper* toys.

At some stage on those Christmas mornings, we would make the short drive to Grandad's, taking a representative cross-section of my booty. Santa would always have called there too with something for me. Mandy and I benefited as Barrie with all those siblings could not, assuming an equal expenditure on each family of children rather than by individual. Our presents from Nan Dinah were numerous and extravagant enough, but it was Grandad George's prerogative to produce his as the grand finale, the showstopper.

I suspect the remote-controlled Land Rover was one gift unaccountably delivered by Santa at Grandad's for him to bring me at Sutton Bridge. I had a Raleigh bike from an early age, which it cost me time to learn to ride with confidence after first being pushed free to wobble down Robb's Lane. Following Mum up Isle Bridge Road between two parked lorries, I had to dismount, fearing the narrowness of the passage. Soon enough, I could accompany her on the main road by the river from Sutton Bridge to Aunt Shirley's in Tydd St Mary. On another occasion, we biked two or three miles from Outwell to the further limits of Upwell (which its locals would sometimes claim to be England's longest village). Uncle Johnny and Aunt Ethel had moved from the Bridge to a big house set in its own grounds. The thing that impressed me most was the offer of a packet of crisps, coming as it did from a whole boxful they pulled out from somewhere. The fact we cycled suggests that Dad was indisposed or undisposed to go.

We have all seen how the costliest presents are rarely those from which kids extract the most mileage. This was true of my go-kart. It came as a real surprise one Christmas morning. If they were in fashion, I don't remember 'haunting' for one. The Christmas-empty Robb's Lane again saw my first efforts, almost flat on my back only inches from the rough road surface as I worked its pedals and hung on to the racing (read 'tiny') steering wheel. That is the one time I remember driving the thing.

The only gift I noticed from Grandad George to Mandy is one where imagination failed him, improvisation coming to the rescue. It was a cuddly toy, a fluffy polar bear: a relatively cheap thing, except that sellotaped around its waist was a skirt of pound notes, causing much anxiety that it be kept well away from the fire.

One of my early tasks on Christmas Day was to read the rules of my new Waddingtons board game, before pressing adults into playing it with me. Already at the Bridge with Aunt Maud's boys I had shown off my knowledge of Monopoly, now very much *vieux jeu*. The figures that came with Battle of the Little Big Horn were too small and delicate to be conscripted into my own forces, though I would sometimes draft Indians in the other direction to make the odds against Custer even scarier. My respect for Cousin Graham soared when he beat me at this game, a feat the family until then regarded as impossible. He spotted, when it was his turn to have the Seventh Cavalry, that with a determined push to the corner of the board you could always carry the flag to victory before losing all your men. I was more wary after that of inviting him to play Risk, Mine a Million, Totopoly, Spy Ring or Buccaneer. Distracted uncles – Tom was always a good sport – were far easier prey, though again I would eventually spend more hours at each game by myself than with any other person.

On entering Maillebourne you walked from the kitchen through the living room (with a walk-in pantry off it) to the bedroom once occupied by Nana Goldsmith and later Uncle Ted, looking out onto the front lawn and Wisbech Road. There was another door off the living room, across a central space with a three-piece in it, rarely used except to access the bathroom and the other two bedrooms. Christmas was a time when this other room came into play, as well it might with a conservative fourteen of us in George and Dinah's house: Doreen and Charlie with Teresa, Barrie, Graham and Vivienne (which I never heard her called – Viv or Vivi was the baby of the family until Mandy came along); Shirley and Tom; Mum, Dad and me; Uncle Ted sometimes, if only for meals.

The trouble on Boxing Day 1963, when Shirley was four months pregnant with Mandy, began in a bedroom, or perhaps the kitchen. Recollections may vary. It was a spat between sisters. Someone wasn't doing their proper share of bed-making or washing-up. Suddenly the bungalow was loud with shouting and recriminations, battle lines drawn between Joyce and Shirley on the one hand and Doreen on the other. Teresa, feisty as ever, came to her mum's support by flying out at Shirley about the number of new clothes she had. No doubt, in the way of such things, much else was said that was not strictly related to who tucked in a few more sheets than the others.

While Nan Dinah tried to keep the peace as the action flowed through the house, the menfolk strove to ignore it. Someone had to maintain a semblance of small talk amid the tears and accusations, since Aunt Betty and her husband Brian had called in to offer season's greetings. Betty, Uncle Fred's younger daughter, bridesmaid to Mum, closest in age and friendship to Shirley, wisely kept out of the women's battle, struggling to hear what was being said through the shrieks of her cousins. Meanwhile Vivi, not quite four years old, like a *Titanic* bandsman forlornly played a toy guitar which had worked a respectful silence over all the adults only hours before.

Vivi's christening 1960
Joyce holding niece Vivienne, with David and Allen

Joyce, Dawn and Shirl vied with each other to storm out of the house first, hampered by their husbands' disinclination to break up a cosy fireside chat. The night before, Charlie and Tom had emerged from Ted's bedroom dressed in full pantomime dame outfits, including – heaven knows from where – wigs as well as lipstick. I found the sight of them mildly disturbing. Grandad silently communicated disapproval, and they didn't stay long in drag (for what it's worth, Uncle Charlie seemed more comfortable than Uncle Tom in a dress and heels).

The show would never be repeated. Doreen and Charlie took their kids home that Boxing Day (via Fenland Park, where Charlie and Barrie took the unexpected opportunity to watch Wisbech play), the last Christmas George and Dinah would see all their daughters gathered under one roof. For some years the only link between the sisters – two on one side, one on the other – was Uncle Ted, who saw no reason to fall out with anyone and had no wife to make him take sides. He may have had the further claim to neutrality of not being present for the row, as he was still in the army.

Chapter Fifteen

1966 and All That

Boy with cat at Princes St

After finishing 'Top Boy' in Mr Wiseman and Mrs Lawrence's classes, I entered Mrs Booley's on 7 September 1965. I wrote of a degree of nervousness in an early draft of these memories, before rereading a diary entry from when I had recently finished secondary school, which showed me more craven yet: '... I went into her class and on the first day I was quite literally trembling in my seat I was terrified of her...'

'Old Ma Booley' was a character twice as feared as 'Airbrakes'. Some of the pupils were in their second year with her, including Henry, one of whose meltdowns left us all goggling. The teacher was going on and on at him about something or other when he suddenly found his tongue.

'Oh, shut up you stupid cow.'

'*What* did you say to me, Trevor Smith?'

'You heard, you fucking old bag.'

He was in tears as he ranted, this was no cool bravado. He flung a plimsoll at her, which landed well wide of the blackboard. He never left his desk, while Mrs Booley had the sense to remain seated behind her own. Presumably she came out with some vaguely face-saving form of words before resuming the lesson, but she did not push Henry any further. There was no punishment, no repercussions.

If Henry had given us a thrilling illustration that the teachers ruled only by our consent, none of us dared pick up his plimsoll and run with it. There were no further acts of insubordination, let alone his outright mutiny.

It is hard to pinpoint what allows some teachers to maintain discipline without apparent effort, while for others it is a constant struggle. Mrs Booley had no need to threaten the intervention of her husband the headmaster. I don't think she resorted to corporal punishment of her own, which in those days would have been accepted by children and parents alike. She was not physically intimidating, plump with white hair and pearls in a friendly nana rather than wicked grandmother style. She had a bit of a humped back, and was old, yet we recognised degrees of separation in those features between her and Mabel Tuck.

Mrs Booley was possibly something of a bully, at least verbally. If so, I shared this characteristic with her, without any justification of 'cruel to be kind' or helping the children to learn by drilling them hard.

The first innocent victim of my spite was a kitten, a pet following rabbits (briefly, of no interest to me so too much trouble for Mum to look after) and tortoises (no interest required; Grandad George also had one) in my early years at Princes St. I am pictured outside number 42 with a black cat which may be the one, whose name I do not remember nor how it was presented to me. Perhaps dear old Nick had already gone for his long sleep, and it was an offer of compensation for my loss. My memory of it is at Maillebourne, where I would take it into the spare bedroom and slam it down against the pillows, in what I thought of as 'wrestling'. I went no further, but that was much too far. The creature would try to escape me, and I came to reproach myself that it had eventually fled the house altogether. Perhaps that was the case, perhaps it was run over and I was not told. The only adult comment I recall was from Nana Bailey: 'You loved it too much, didn't you, pet?' In public it may have seemed that way. I always wanted to have it on my lap or in my arms, wanted it to love me. Less charitably to myself, perhaps I just wanted to control it, be its master, not realising that cats are the animals least amenable to coercion of any kind. I am glad I didn't go further down the path of mistreating the poor thing, still ashamed of the steps I did take.

The turnover of pupils at Beaupré was limited enough for any incomer to stand out. Having been one myself, integrating relatively smoothly with the friendship and support of such as Hank, I might have been sensitive and helpful to someone in that situation. I was not, or not in any straightforward way.

A namesake of mine joined Beaupré in Mrs Lawrence's or possibly Harry's class. In truth I don't remember him in a school context, part of that selective blindness to juniors I had seen from the other end of the telescope with Fiddle and Tom.

David soon came to be part of our playing-field crowd, almost immediately stripped of his name. We tried out a variety including 'Pongo', but it was 'Stink' that became universal. I am sometimes credited as the one who came up with it; that may be so. He continued to hang around with us, anyway. It was not about physical abuse so much as having someone under our control. I say 'our' because Hank, if not others, was complicit.

'Who's your best mate, Stinkie?'

'You are, Bail.'

'Hank, he's just said I'm his best mate.'

'What? Come here, you little twat.'

And so we would bat him between us, applying whatever was required in the way of headlocks or arm-twisting to wring the admission of best-matedom from him.

Stink's house was on the way to the playing field. There was no contradiction in asking his mum if David wanted to come out to play. We all had home and street names. He also had a football.

Despite the element of bullying, which never escalated to real beating-up (that would have been totally outside the code against a smaller kid), Stink and I spent hours playing Subbuteo or board games at my house or his. In Buccaneer his vessels were expected to sail the seas as satellite craft to mine, not competitors in piracy; I liked to be the winner. Still, we became and stayed good mates.

'I'm not allowed to do it anymore, but it seems to work out that way,' was Mrs Booley's reference to her streaming method in the top class. The more academic pupils would be sat in pairs in the window file of desks, opposite her own, with second, third and fourth files to their left up to the solid wall adorned with artwork and the star chart.

If anyone farted – an offence almost as heinous as 'grunting', the teacher's nose clearly as sensitive as her ears – she would start her patrol to identify the supplier (we were all deniers) between the fourth and third files. This saved me from discovery more than once, the smell having dissipated somewhat by the time she reached the window seats. There was never any tell-tale accompanying sound. To trumpet a trump in her class would have been as suicidal as submitting Grandad's ditty for a composition:

A fart is a useful thing.
It warms the bed, it airs the bed,
It keeps the system clean.
There are eight kinds of fart:
The egg fart, the cabbage fart,
The wailer and the clinker;
The windy-buff, the brandy-buff,
The roarer and the stinker.

Line three is not canonical, and the wailer is expelled by me now rather than remembered (snorer or snorter better perhaps?), but that's the unfragrant essence of it. So, long-windedly (excuse me), I come to my seat at the same desk as John Goman.

If John was of Polish extraction, there was no trace of the exotic foreigner in him, Peter, or their younger siblings. They lived towards the bottom of Langhorns Lane, off the Downham Road leaving Outwell, before you reach the aqueduct; at the turn-off where the Crown caff (as opposed to the Crown pub) and a petrol station stood. This remove from the village centre may account for us not having met until we became deskmates – that and the year he had on me in school, as I did on Peter.

John's handwriting was recommended to us all as a model to follow. He won the class prize for it, despite labouring as I did under the handicap of being a leftie. It was easy to smudge the page as your paw followed, not led the pen across it. My own technique became to curl over my hand three or four lines above the one I was writing, as if anxious to prevent anyone copying from me. Nothing helped if you got an unlucky blob when dipping nib into inkwell. I came to write neatly enough, just not at all quickly.

In holidays or at weekends I would bike down to John's house, from where we would venture further afield with a bottle of squash or pop for company. It really was afield, there being no town or other village within our range or ambition as cyclists.

While not an outstanding footballer, John would make the school team at right-back in this his final year. He may have helped my breakthrough, in the sense of not defending against me.

There was enough excitement around a four-village schools tournament in summer term 1966 for Stan to decide he needed coaching support. So we came to know Mr Linford, owner of orchards beside Maillebourne. His son Martin was now in his first year at grammar school. Having skippered Beaupré the year before, he appeared once or twice with his dad at after-school training sessions.

There was no need for physical fitness training – forwards could run, defenders didn't have to. The main change from the games nominally run by Stan was Mr Linford's interest and enthusiasm. He would set what he saw as his first-choice defence in one team against the forwards in the other, with what went on in the other half of the pitch a matter of minor concern. It was there, however, as a makeweight forward against a makeshift defence, I scored my first hat-trick.

Without false modesty, I never had an inkling I could score at all, let alone three goals. I suppose the defenders on breaking down an attack would punt the ball forward – the full backs were categorically forbidden ever to cross the halfway line – so John may have provided me one of the through balls. The most important handshake of my life was Mr Linford's after my third goal. He could not have been more surprised than I was, but it was a close call.

I was the last player to be slotted into the team, which already held several of my mates: Aidi Smith (my deskmate in Alvy's as well as Harry's class) was

John's oppo at left-back, Henry and Hank the wing-halves flanking Tom Russell; Jim Wilson, a year younger and tiny, had no trouble claiming a place on the wing. Fiddle moved to inside-left from centre-forward, where he had played the previous year.

I could not have been prouder to wear the number 9 shirt, in principle at least as there were no actual numbers on our shirts any more than there were nets in our nets. Mr Linford commented in a pre-match pep-talk that we had a number of 'prolific' goal-scorers. That word, much used in football, was new to me. I checked and compared it to 'proficient' – I would take either.

A play-by-play account of the three matches would be a bit much even in this load-every-rift-with-bore narrative. We beat Welney 4–2, lost to Christchurch by the same score (but it didn't matter because I got a GOAL), then had our nearest neighbours and bitterest rivals Upwell to face. If the format was the same as the old Home International Championships, this was definitely England v Scotland – and my place was under threat.

The team's recognised twelfth man was Robert Laws, from the same year as me. He was close to playing in our first match, when Stan intervened in team selection to ban Jim. We had arrived at school one evening before any adult. The doors were all locked, but Jim was small enough to be boosted in through a cloakroom window, re-emerging with the precious football. Stan was not pleased at the unlawful entry. I wish I could say we pleaded a collective guilt (I'm Jim, no I'm Jimmy, my name is Wilson) to move our headmaster to pity. It was more likely to have been a word from our coach, or indeed Stan – far from an unkind person – deciding himself he had been too severe. In any event, Jim played, scored, and Lawsie had to wait for his debut.

He knew it would come, because Mr Linford had said so from the start. Having missed the first two games, or at least not played – like half the school and a good number of parents (including Dad), he was there watching – Lawsie looked now to have bagged his spot in the most important match of all to us kids. I was under no illusions that it would be at anyone's expense but mine.

God bless you, Mr and Mrs Upson.

Although these football matches meant everything to us, adults continued with their own steamrollering agendas. We were deprived of goalkeeper Derek Upson before our third fixture. The poor boy had to go on a family holiday.

Hank was versatile enough to go in goal without noticeably weakening the defence. Lawsie, an out-and-out forward, could not replace him at left-half (a midfield role should any non-football person still be with me). Mr Linford was not sure I could either. He did speak to me individually, shrewdly giving me the confidence to have a good run at the new position. Sadly, he did not see our 3–2 win play itself out. Falling awkwardly while refereeing, he fractured an arm, no little thing for a farmer with summer and fruiting approaching. His contribution was recognised by a 'small gift' presented by our captain Brian 'Brin' Chapman at the school's prize day.

It was a great time to fall in love with football. In that summer of 1966 England would win the World Cup at Wembley. I watched the tournament on telly from the start through to the final. I saw England's two hours of greatest glory on Saturday, 30 July at Maillebourne with Dad, Uncle Ted – who threw a cushion at the screen when Weber equalised for West Germany in the ninetieth minute – and Uncle Bob. A son of Nan Dinah's sister Leah, by then deceased, he and his wife Grace would come to Outwell from Norwich to help at fruiting. It was presumably something to do with that business, or a double shift on the buses, that kept Grandad away from the screen. He did not have the football bug, but I was confirmed for life with it.

And we still had another whole year to play for Beaupré.

Chapter Sixteen

MTGG

George Hills he was a bus driver,
Of credit and renown,
A bungalow and lands, had he,
Not far from Wisbech town.

Now one fine day his grand-son said
"Why do n't you grow things here,
But I shall want a part of it,
For mine was the idea."

"But I already grow things here,
As you yourself know well,"
'Ah, yes, but there's a difference,
For now they'll be to sell."

"By this means I do perceive,
I'll make a profit fair,"
"Ah, yes, Ah, yes 'tis true indeed
But don't forget my share."

"For even you must needs admit
That were it not for me,
This chance, which is so rightly yours,
Would never have come to be.

So George his grandson's advice took
And the very next spring,
He planted veg'es on his land,
And the till began to ding.

With flashy cars, and big cigars,
George a tycoon became,
But half the profits were always payed,
For use of grandson's brain.

Apart from confirming a lamentably long-standing weakness for doggerel, a slighter one at spelling and an unappealing mercenary nature, these schoolboy lines saved for posterity by Mum record a significant shift in Grandad's lifestyle. We sold no more than cabbage plants in the first year, the only one he split the profits equally with me.

So I was told. My own recollection must then be of subsequent years when I did manual rather than brain work. Picking out lobelias, petunias, 'messies' (mesembryanthemums if you must) and other bedding plants, I envied my friend Charles Robinson his day's pay. I could understand that to be given the sale price for the trays I prepared was a much better deal financially. It wasn't immediate cash in hand, is all.

Unless Eastern Counties offered him a deal to go earlier, George retired from the buses when he turned sixty-five and became eligible for the state pension in December 1968. He had always been a worker, including a Sunday paper round to the Smeeth, not as a twelve-year-old boy but a married man with children. He would bring them back a sweet or two from this extra job, which he eventually passed on to his younger brother Sid. Grandad could turn his hand to most things inside and outside the home, including running up on a sewing machine knickers for his older daughters as girls. My idea for a source of additional income must have appealed to him. He began to implement it before his retirement.

If it was not already in place, a low brick wall was built behind a narrow paved slipway, allowing customers to pull off the main road to park and buy. Part of the flowered border around the lawn was sacrificed to a counter area, a trestle table with an awning to protect produce against rain and shine.

Grandad may have offered strawberries for sale at the roadside, or on a pick-your-own basis, before my suggestion to broaden his scope of operations.

133

Fruiting remained the bonanza, with Mum, Nana and whoever else could be enlisted picking in punnets till late afternoon to keep the steady (almost overwhelming sometimes at weekends) stream of customers supplied. Vegetables and bedding plants kept the operation ticking over all year round, especially when George took out a cash-and-carry card, to add ice cream, soft drinks, confectionery and cigarettes to his stock list. He soon put up two or three greenhouses on the front part of the garden, for tomatoes as well as flowers. He installed two big freezers in the sudden conservatory leading to the bungalow's back door. These did double duty, allowing economies on the family's meat consumption. Instead of raising his own pigs, George could now benefit from the initiatives of other local small businessmen, who would sell mutton, lamb, beef and pork by the butchered and jointed, sausage-and-baconed animal or part animal.

One aspect of the venture would have been a trial for the man who refused to work single-decker buses to avoid any interaction with passengers. He had a phone installed earlier than most in our family, yet always answered it with a degree of trepidation, shouting UPWELL and the four-digit number that would become my forever PIN. In short, he was not a natural salesman.

Many of his customers were locals. Others, by dint of passing the same way year after year on their holidays, became almost friends. George would serve at the counter if he had to – there could be no question of letting a potential sale go by – but preferred others to do so, most often Nan Dinah or Dad.

Each had a weakness.

Mum and Dad would move into the bungalow for a week or two each summer when Nana and Grandad went on holiday. Apart from looking after the shop, this was to take care of our second Nick. Grandad may have acquired the lolloping black Labrador as additional security; he quickly became daftly devoted to it. If there were signs of any salmon being left in the dish at Sunday tea, I had to be quick to claim my own second helping before it went under the table to the dog. Neutered early, Nick grew fat. He was trained early too, by harsh words and harder knocks, not to stray beyond the driveway out onto the main road. Although there were no such animals in the vicinity of Maillebourne, Grandad somehow taught him to yap furiously at the word 'cats'. Nor was it only a theoretical, vocal hatred. Once down Isle Bridge Road he pursued a cat belonging to our neighbour Freddie Churchyard under the killing wheels of a car.

I happened to be at Grandad's when Freddie came round some days later. There was no question of moral or physical menace in the visit. Freddie, a bus-driving colleague of George who would hold the bus for me at the top of Isle Bridge Road if I was late (as long as I made a show of running for it), was a skinny fellow. Grandad had been known when younger – Uncle Ted told me this with obvious pride – to show his strength by lifting a four-stone metal weight in each hand to clap them together above his head. Now, as Freddie hoped perhaps for an apology, perhaps no more than an acknowledgement that the other man's pet had effectively killed his, George could only produce a silent facial contortion. It looked awfully like a smile but was probably closer to the crumpling of tears. He said nothing and Freddie eventually left.

Apart from house/shop/dog-sitting, Mum was working full-time at Hannam's. Nan would go to Wisbech bingo twice a week with neighbours of ours from Isle Bridge Road, Bessie and Suey (not a same-sex couple – Suey was what everyone called Cyril). They would drive her, sometimes having to wait a few minutes while she washed her knees at the kitchen sink after coming off the land. Bessie, closer in age to Joyce than Dinah, was a workmate of both at Hannam's. When Mum took her the usual weekly order of eggs, she was surprised to learn that Nan let her have them at something like half the shop price.

'She robbed your grandad left, right and centre. I said to your dad, "I'm going to tell him when they come back." I did an' all. I don't know if he said anything to your nan, or if she stopped, but I had to say because otherwise it would look as if it was us were leaving him short.'

What I steadfastly prefer to consider Nan's generosity – I benefited so often it would be rude not to – may not have been the soundest business practice. I suspect Grandad's prices were not pitched high in the first place, not from any generosity of his own but a fear of being lumbered with perishable produce.

Without bending the rules in any way, Dad was just as welcoming to customers as Dinah. Indeed, he probably had a larger fund of small talk and banter. For a while he worked with his father-in-law practically full-time. As well as serving at the shop, he would go out in our car to purchase stock and generally volunteer at anything in which he could be helpful. This was good in the sense of keeping him active, engaged in society, with a reason to get up in the morning. Unfortunately, it could not last.

135

Dad's illness, while genuine, could look very like malingering, especially to people unaccustomed to sickness in any but physical and visible form. I suppose it began with one of his periodic bed-spells. Given his own reserve and self-sufficiency, I doubt Grandad would ever have directly asked him to help out. It may not have occurred to him that any payment might be appropriate, beyond Park Drive at cost. Once Dad had failed to sustain his initial level of commitment, shown a measure of unreliability if you like, they never worked as closely or regularly together again. There was no confrontation, just a gradual dwindling of contact on anything but the (still frequent) social, family level.

Another temporary, unpaid shopkeeper, if only for a couple of weeks each summer, was Uncle Bob. Mum's cousin Robert King was perhaps a little older than Dad. He did wartime service with the Royal Marines (later giving me his medals and battledress tunic). There was a story that he had been disappointed in one fiancée's fidelity during his absence, before meeting and marrying Aunt Grace.

Not tall, Bob was broad-shouldered and solidly built under his ferociously short haircut – 'Nobody ever put me on the floor in a fight.' He worked with Carter Construction on major sites including Anglia Square, Carrow Road and the Mecca Ballroom. A perk he received on the last-named job became a treasure to me: a world of amusement in a blue box about six inches by six, brilliantly packed with a deck of cards, a set of dominoes, a pegboard and five gaming dice. Grace worked part-time, cleaning at the Woodcock pub on the Catton Estate where they lived.

If Bob was carrying a few more pounds than in his fighting days, his wife was equally well upholstered. Childless – I never heard whether by accident or design – she had a broader Norwich accent than Bob. Unlike him, she did speak at sufficient volume to make herself understood without difficulty. She wore glasses of the kind made famous later by Dame Edna Everage, and more make-up than was quite usual among the Hills women. I was astonished when she told me this included the beauty spot on her cheek, which I had thought not only in the same position but as natural as mine.

Bob, surprisingly for such a dour character, enjoyed serving at the shop as well as carrying up, traying, and weighing the chips of strawberries picked by the women. Aunt Grace was no great shakes at that job, even if Bob did help her, as Nan Dinah once told me: 'Here you are, boy, you take this chip of mine for yourself. He'll only weigh it up for *her*, if not.'

I accepted – Grandad had to pay everyone except his wife – not knowing whether it was true, or just another way to pass me a gift. Bob always showed the greatest respect for 'Uncle George and Aunt Dinah', so the comment struck me. It never became an issue among the adults, perhaps went unnoticed by Grandad (though I doubt it) as he was not keeping a running total of Dinah's picking for payment at day's end.

Bob never drove, so they came to Outwell by bus. I went with him to Wisbech one Saturday, waiting outside the bookies while he placed his bets. In this passion he was a Goldsmith, as perhaps in his younger taste for fighting. He would put on a smart blazer and polo-necked pullover to go out for a drink with Grace (port and lemon), Joyce and Allen. I was occasionally with them, sitting in the car outside with crisps and pop as was the only option for kids back then. I thus missed the time when Grace turned, not mortally offended, to smack Dad's face for twanging her suspenders as they walked. A van-dweller, never brought to book, was allegedly the real culprit.

Bob was good friends with Uncle Ted, whose army service in Malaya left him with malaria, which would revisit him from time to time for years. Less troublesome, more permanent legacies were tattoos on his forearm and in the webbing of his thumb (a blue bird, probably not an Outwell Swift). From what I heard, his career as a prison warder ran into the sand when he could not pass certain exams required to progress, or perhaps to remain. It was reportedly English that let him down. He was as quick with numbers as Grandad, whose physical strength he also inherited.

While Uncle Ted worked for Hannam & Davy I was sometimes allowed to go out on his lorry with him. I was jealous of Barrie, who got to set off in the evening and be out all night. The best I was allowed was a start at three in the morning, to be fair still a big treat. I remember looking at the clock on the bedroom wall at Nana's before going to sleep, then waking at the exact time agreed, before she came in the room to get me up (I hope she didn't have to do so routinely for her son).

I had little interest in where we were heading – central London was one destination, so perhaps Covent Garden. The thrill was in being up at that hour, as he unlocked the big shed at Hannam's to free the wagon on which we would go barrelling through the night.

It was not all motorway driving, far from it. I was startled at his daring the first time he jumped a wee-hours rural red traffic light (he had stopped to check nothing was coming). I was young enough not to want to be awake alone in the cab in the dark, so refused to guarantee waking him if he stopped at a lay-by to sleep. I disguised my fear, quite irrational – he would be only an arm's length away – as stroppiness, or perhaps said I wouldn't be able to stay awake myself. It was only for half an hour, he argued, then gave in with ill grace. He continued driving while insisting that I would be allowed no peace to close my own eyes. Sure enough, when I tested him by laying my head down on the middle seat, he reached out to ruffle my hair and wake me from a sleep I was only shamming. He was grinning, though; he was usually happy enough to have company, showing me how lorry drivers wore their wristwatch face inwards so they could see the time while driving, setting me riddles or tests.

'How do you say 'hungry horse' in four letters?'

'Don't know.'

'Come on, think about it, we've got hours in here yet.'

'I give up.'

Military escort
Allen, Nan Dinah and Ted

'Yeah, that's right, just like your football team.' (I'm sure he only pretended to support Leeds, just to give himself a platform from which to deride the only one United.)

'Go on, tell us.'

'How do you expect to get to grammar school if you can't answer simple questions like that?'

'I never said I'm going to the Grammar. Anyway, I bet they won't have questions like that in the eleven-plus.'

'You'd better hope they don't, all right.'

He would always tease me almost to the point of losing interest before giving out the answers, which is perhaps why I remember them still. He caught me out on the long name of the King of the Jews, and how to spell it ('I T'), then taught me the follow-up if someone had spotted the trick, which was to rattle through the real spelling so fast as to defy repetition: eneebeeyouseeaichaydee-enneedoublezedayar.

While he was happy to accompany wife and aunt to bingo – a form of gambling, after all – Bob would not miss a chance to go out on the lorries himself with Ted. They would also sit for what seemed like hours playing cards in Nan's living room. I prided myself on being quick to pick things up, especially games, just by watching, but the speed of play and calculation made this one impenetrable to me. Their bantering commentary was no help: fifteen two, the rest won't do; fifteen four, the rest won't score; Morgan's orchard here, apples and pairs; that's a nineteen (but then not moving the pegs on the board at all, let alone nineteen spaces); not to mention the talk of heels and knob. I did eventually learn to play, as I did that it was 'nob' rather than the fruitier homonym I had heard.

The best times were when I somehow got to be on Uncle Ted's side. His opinion of my intelligence underwent a drastic reversal when showing me off to his friends, like Terry who used to drink in the Wisbech Five Bells. It was in a different, long since demolished waterfront bar that he was invited to test my spelling one afternoon. Ted had phrased the invitation in such a way that it was not clear whether I was prodigy or moron. I still admire the opener Terry pitched at me to find out: ELASTIC. Another time, exceptionally, there were people at Grandad's one evening. Ted showed them my telepathic skills.

'I'll send the boy into the kitchen, you choose a card from the three I'll deal to you, and I bet he'll come back and pick the right one every time.'

I was duly banished for a minute or two. On my return Ted, cigarette in mouth and pack of cards in hand, invited me to pick the same one as his friend from the three on the floor. I did so every time, face up or face down, plonking my socked big toe onto the correct card or, the clincher, refusing to do so when they tried to get cute and pick none of the three.

I don't know why Ted left Hannam's to take another driving job with Walpole Fruit Packers. Perhaps the work was more local, though he had no wife or children to make long distances a problem. This was before the regulation of tachographs, so perhaps he felt he was being over-extended. Whatever the reason, it did not seem a big change.

Grandad sold his strawberries to Hannam's. He bought produce from his son's new employers, until the day they had Ted arrested. He faced a possible spell on the other side of prison bars from the one he had worked.

Chapter Seventeen

Handwriting Lessons

'They said they saw Dad standing on the Horsefair, near the shelter, in his uniform, and the tears were just rolling down his face.'

Without challenging it directly, Mum clearly had trouble believing Shirley's dramatic account. Me too. A dab at the eye during *This Is Your Life* was one thing, but *rolling* tears from a personal sadness and *in public* – no, that didn't sound like George at all.

His sisters always seemed to treat Ted with an amused tolerance, as if he had never quite grown up. When he came home from Wisbech as a teenager with a bloody nose, they called him 'My Hero' as if the fight had been a playground spat between five-year-olds. He generally knew better than to bring girlfriends into the family orbit, to avoid them hearing that and similar tales. Now that he had apparently done something a bit beyond naughty, he may have been slightly relieved to be away from his sisters' displeasure, while waiting on Her Majesty's.

I could not fail to be aware of the heightened atmosphere, without being privy to the agonised discussions that went on. Or perhaps did not go on. I could write an imagined scene between George and Ted. What I can't imagine is that anything like a 'scene' ever took place.

Walpole Fruit Packers must have been aware of more than customary loss of produce for some time. When the police moved, Ted was not the only one implicated. Mum's biggest fear was that Dad would be too, as a relative who had often been on the premises, buying for Grandad. Whether or not he bawled like a baby on the Horsefair, George suffered at having to destroy perfectly saleable fruit and veg, as he and Dinah were doing until the small hours in the initial panic. Hardly the drama of *Goodfellas*, but apples and pears

– whether from Morgan's orchard or anyone else's – were a lot harder than white powder to slice, dice and flush down the toilet.

They had nothing to fear. Grandad never showed his face again at Walpole Fruit Packers. After a respectable period, Dad was bold enough to do so. They were still prepared to do business. Ted lost his job, but not his liberty. I don't know if a fine or probation was imposed, the whole topic one that vanished from the family's conversation as quickly as it had burst into it, briefly monopolised it. I never saw Ted in the least abashed, so perhaps – for all the stress and grief the episode had caused – he was innocent and cleared of all charges. His subsequent account to his future wife was that he took the rap for a married friend who had more to lose.

The land demands its attention whatever else we may have on our minds. The first fruiting of the summer, the strawberries, was always at once the most arduous and the most profitable. I was involved from an early age, never forced to work more hours than I wanted, yet knowing like everyone else the minute you stopped picking you stopped earning. However hard I tried to stay upright, straddling the row to move more quickly along it, I would soon be shuffling along on my knees, like the women except at half their pace. If I crossed Mum, Nan or an aunt they would usually throw a handful of fruit into my chip as they moved along their own row or backtracked on mine to help me keep up with the rest.

Some people preferred 'plugging', removing the stalks as would be done for the trays going off for jam. 'Stalking' was appropriate if the fruit was to be decanted into punnets for sale at the shop. I was equally undistinguished at both – can't remember which it was that paid a ha'penny a pound more. I learned to work with more application as I grew older, as I had more use for spending money. The only time I ever heard a word of praise from Grandad was when I had managed to put in a full day in the fields.

'How much do you think he's earned today?' he asked Mum, arriving from our own field for an evening shift. She probably guessed low, then expressed delight and pride at what would seem an absurdly piffling sum today. To her congratulations he added his own comment, to the air somewhere between us. 'Yes, he haven't done a miss, has he?' (that was what I heard, he may have said 'amiss').

Far more congenial than strawberry picking was redcurranting. The fruit came off in heavy clusters in your hand. The bushes afforded an element of shade wholly absent on a strawberry field. It was never a crop any of our family grew, though various of us helped harvest it.

Mr Brown added a gang of pickers to his steady employee Uncle Sid at redcurranting time. His sisters Gert and Ivy would join Sid there, as would Mum and I cycling down Hall Road (something I was put off doing alone for a spell when I saw a rat tear across it in front of me, from one dyke to the other).

The atmosphere never seemed quite as frenetic as on the strawberry fields. Aunt Ivy's strawberrying days may already have been behind her, but she could manage redcurranting, at her own pace. Aunt Gert, nearly ten years younger than her sister, was more energetic as well as more talkative, closer to a same-generation friend for Mum than Aunt Ivy could be. Both were unfailingly kind to me. Along with Mum, at least in my early years at Mr Brown's, they would happily sub-contract. Instead of filling the big wicker baskets, I would work with chips, which one of my aunts or Mum would buy from me for sixpence. I don't recall Uncle Sid offering this deal, but then as a full-time employee he may have been on day's pay.

Mr Brown himself was usually present, a gentleman of patience and great courtesy. Not quite an albino, he wore a floppy hat against the sun, his face and arms bleached milk white in places; his age was possibly more advanced than Aunt Ivy's. He would compliment me on how cleanly I picked, with virtually no leaves in the basket compared to those more professional, who knew how to gauge an acceptable level of debris to speed their gathering of the fruit. We were given thick cardboard discs each time he weighed up for us, round like coins for which they were indeed tokens, convertible at the end of the day. Each would have its value marked on it in shillings and pence. They were possibly also differentiated by size and colour. There was no worry of fraud on either side.

Uncle Tom laughed when I asked, 'Is this real money?' of the handful of silver he gave me for my first chips of strawberries at Tydd. Mr Brown's payment methods may have been old-fashioned, yet it was more convenient to carry his tokens through working hours than accumulated coin of the realm.

Wheat was the Thorpes' other main crop. They owned a combine harvester, with which Tom would rent himself out to others as well as bringing in his own harvest. Never involved with cereals, I worked with them sowing beans once, as well as there and elsewhere with Mum on a potato-picker, sorting the spuds as they were churned up from the earth onto its conveyor belt.

Cousins 1959
Shirley and Tom's wedding with their nephews and nieces
(L to R) David B, Jackie, David H, Barrie, Teresa, Graham

As a very small boy I saw a few cattle in what on Tom's land was called the crew yard (father and son in my time had only one full-time employee, a lad called Peter they released before he was out of his teens). Uncle Charlie persevered longer with livestock: cattle, pigs, chickens, for a spell geese. I was given the opportunity to milk cows at his place, one I got out from under as soon as I decently could. It was more fun to run around the fields with Barrie and Graham, especially when Uncle Charlie was burning the stubble. 'Can't have a piss without a kid under your feet,' he complained one evening as we came round a tractor at him. Barrie's early inclination was to get involved in the farm, driving a tractor before he left primary school, but he was kept harder and longer at work on it than perhaps a schoolboy should have been.

'Wait for it,' Barrie said one night from the next bed in Newlands Road. Aunt Dawn had just brought us up a snack and hot drink before sleep. Unfortunately, in going for his, my cousin had upended the lot over his bedspread.

'Bloody guts couldn't wait,' came the outraged shriek from downstairs as she fetched stuff to clear up the mess. Barrie grinned triumphantly. Uncle Charlie made no reply audible to us. He was maybe happy not to be in the firing line himself. As a young husband, suited and booted to go out when Doreen threw a bucket of water over him, he had hopelessly asked Nan Dinah, 'What would you do with her, mother?'

As the summer wore on, in those years before I reached the heights of plums, apples and pears, the last earning opportunity was among the blackberry brambles. Uncle Fred's son, Bobby Goldsmith, had rows of these on the outskirts of the village past Churchfield Road. Fred himself had been involved in that line of business, generous as ever in giving away to village kids the runtish fruit that in a later generation would be rebranded and marketed as cherry tomatoes.

A sometime drinking mate of Ted's, ex-navy Bobby like his cousin lived at home with his parents, a bachelor gay when that meant actively heterosexual unmarried man. He longed to make a financial killing by building houses on his land, knocked back on that more than once by the authorities. While he waited in hope to turn the soil to more profitable use, Bobby had his family and others work it. I gave it a try, my last job of the summer holidays, with Mum who could make a good fist of picking anything. You could stand upright while blackberrying. The constant scratches to your hands were bearable – you were unlucky if a springing branch tore at your face. The problem was, I could not pick fast enough to make it worthwhile. I may have been an unwaged schoolboy, it may have been nineteen-sixty-something, the pay was admittedly lower than for strawberries, yet two bob, a couple of shillings, ten pence in new money was not a reasonable return for a long afternoon's work.

Just once on my first day of autumn term at primary school, from Grandad's, I sicked up my beans on toast, more from greed and haste eating them than any nerves about the coming academic year. (I would already have been down Isle Bridge Road on starting with Mrs Booley, when my cowardice has been documented.) I had no cause for trepidation before my last year at Beaupré and second in her class, having been ranked top of it during my first.

Our school reports came in an exercise book, wrapped in brown paper with a white sticker bearing my name on the cover. Each year a new page would be filled in by the class teacher, writing by hand on a printed pro forma, counter-signed by the headmaster then commended to the child's parents. They were asked to sign it (Dad's job), take care of it during the holiday and return it on the Tuesday early in September that marked the start of the next term.

Thirty-eight pupils in Harry Wiseman's class would reduce to thirty-four with Mrs Lawrence, then thirty-one with Mrs Booley. My main competitors for first place were usually girls. I got off the bus at Grandad's one evening, to find a stranger on a ladder in the drive doing something at a bedroom window. Grandad quickly introduced him by surname, as father of one of these, quickly because – he told me and Nan afterwards – he was fearful that I would immediately start bad-mouthing the poor lass if she had outscored me in a test.

I remember no academic rivalry with boys. Tom Russell was the only one to pass the eleven-plus for grammar school entry during my first year in top class, as Martin Linford had been twelve months earlier. John Goman's handwriting wasn't quite enough to get him through, while Lawsie was at the same stage as me, with a year to go.

The report card shows a broad enough curriculum, arithmetic and English occupying the top half of the page with their constituent elements. These were marked in numbers, whereas the bottom half – oral, history, geography, handwork or needlework (the latter scored through by Harry on mine), art, music and physical education – shifted to letters, discriminated on occasion by plus or minus signs.

Arithmetic was split into mechanical, tables and problems. For all Grandad's coaching, in Harry's class my 18/20 revealed 'one or two small weaknesses' in tables. In the English disciplines – English, composition, reading, spelling and handwriting – I usually scored high, a 14/20 for Harry in composition down to a 'very fair' exam, though he granted 'class ones usually very good'. He found my handwriting (9 out of 10, while the other English subjects were out of 20) 'Very good, despite being left-handed.'

Mr Wiseman nailed his colours to the mast on my future, just as he had in talking to Mum: 'David shows very good promise, especially in the academic subjects. He has an excellent memory and should do well in the future. Of this I am certain.' Like him, Mrs Lawrence described me as a keen reader with 'an excellent general knowledge' yet sounded the odd cautionary note: 'he must learn to do his best at all times' could have referred to problems – 'very good, occasionally careless' – handwriting – 'Classwork can be untidy' – or most likely art – 'Often does not try. Shows little interest.' Art and music were the only Cs on my card (C+'s mind), with the mitigation in one that I was 'not musically inclined'. Harry agreed on art ('does not show much aptitude'), while giving me a 'fairly good' B for music. Perhaps this was before Mrs Booley had outed me as a grunter.

I have no idea what 'handwork' entailed. It had ceased to be graded by Mrs Booley's class, which was no loss to me as a B student for both Mr Wiseman ('very fair', but at least he didn't blame my left-handedness) and Mrs Lawrence. 'Oral' is the other curiosity in those Beaupré reports, sub-classified into speech, reading aloud and drama recitation. Again I was stuck with Bs, Harry loyally adding 'Always keen to take part' to his 'V. good', so that must have been the year I gave my Mr Bumble. What my teachers were aiming for was something that has fallen so far from grace it must be next door to damnation: the ability of children to speak properly.

There was no need to qualify 'properly' in those days. Everyone knew it meant to speak the Queen's English as closely as possible to the way the Queen spoke it, or in her default like a television newsreader. Alvy Jones was a girl from the village. Harry Wiseman, living in Wisbech, was from the West Country. Mrs Booley spoke of one of her daughters – we heard often of both – asking to plant a chair leg in the garden when they first came to Outwell. Someone had told her our land was so fertile it would grow, someone from the concrete north they had escaped. The three teachers converged to speak in one voice, enunciating clearly in an accent belonging to no region of England, nor to any of the kingdom's working-class stock.

Mrs Booley was a tartar on this topic. Note the change in emphasis between Alvy's 'Very good but some words mispronounced' (B+) and her 'Good expression – but some vowel sounds need attention' (B). She is praising eloquence, while giving elocution equal importance.

Elocution lessons! Mum would sometimes threaten me with these when she chose to focus on my accent. I was roundly opposed, wanting to speak in the same way as my mates, not copy some old biddy of an (hypothetical) elocution tutor. The threat was never pursued. Perhaps it was never seriously meant, though it was consistent as an idea with her wanting me to have every possible chance to avoid working on the land all my life. My parents thought I might even become a teacher.

The rule of 'proper' English as described above would end soon enough with growing recognition of the importance of regional and ethnic diversity, neither then in evidence at Beaupré County Primary. In my final year (1966-67) there would be an influx of children from abroad, talking funny. Six American cousins of mine came to live in Outwell. Five of them left when it ended.

Chapter Eighteen

Matt and Jo

Nana Goldsmith and Aunt Shirley

Bobby Tambling, Chelsea's record goalscorer until overtaken by Fat Frank in the next century, was in his mid-twenties prime that season. At the end of it I would write his name in red ink with all the other players' in my 1967 *Valiant* album as number 10 in their team losing the FA Cup Final to Spurs. When it was still something of a treat for me to watch *Match of the Day* at all, on 17 September 1966 I saw him on it score five in a 6–2 win at Villa Park.

The programme that would outlast many generations of footballers made its debut in August 1964, so was still fresh for everyone. A single match was shown each week, far too rarely United. The novelty of that Chelsea win for me was not in Tambling's feat – I cared nothing for it – but that I was watching the highlights at Uncle Sid's.

At Wenn's Bridge there were steps leading down to the river, the lowest one visible under a quarter inch of scummy lawn. I used to think, given a credulous enough audience, you could put on a fair show of walking on water there, since the main channel was the same queasy green. Big trees – willows, I think – led down to the waterside and crept up behind the wooden bus shelter, heading to Wisbech, or in my earlier days just home from school to Grandad's. Opposite this, Uncle Sid's terraced house was within yards of both the Red Lion and his local the Swan. Not much further towards Wisbech, past the Sluice footbridge, lived Aunt Gert. A big driveway, leading down to someone's farm building, separated her small home from two or three cottages, in one of them my classmate Christopher Buzzard.

I had not suspected Uncle Sid of an interest in football. In any case, I was not there to keep him company. I had no notion of his wife Edna as any kind of aunt. She seemed harmless enough, big and shapeless in cardigans and floor-length skirts, muttering occasionally to herself. The true mark of her 'funniness' was that she showed not the least interest in me. There were no offers of sweets or biscuits, much less beans on toast or games of 26-card whist.

The reason for my presence – perhaps my first time ever in that house – was my new cousin Matthew, whom I was invited to call Matt. It was expected, or at least hoped, that I could be a good friend, in some degree a protector, to this gangly, crewcut, bespectacled boy, two years my junior. Well… up to a point, Lord Copper.

Sid and Edna's daughters, Sheila and Colleen, had both worked as nurses. Both had moved to the United States with American husbands. Aunt Sheila's adventure with a serviceman ended in tears, with heart-rending letters from her across the Atlantic to Aunt Gert. It seems he was unfaithful. She was now more happily married, living in London with Ed and their baby, also Sheila but always called She-she.

Aunt Colleen, not divorced, had returned from America to her parents' home with two children. Colleen was not 'funny'. She was 'highly strung'. I saw a friendly woman, trying against the odds to make Uncle Sid's place feel like somewhere children might comfortably fit. As lean as her father, she was another constant smoker, of cigarettes rather than the pipe he favoured. Her short dark hair and preference for trousers over skirts were mannish, while her figure would more usually be described as boyish – no curves to be hidden beneath the unflattering clothes.

She was back in Outwell while her husband did a US military tour outside the States, as he had once done in England. Uncle Don may have come to install his family on the way to Vietnam (or perhaps the Philippines; he had also served in Korea). I would not meet him until the following summer. Meanwhile, Grandad Sid would have to provide the adult male influence in the lives of Matt and his younger sister, Sheila Mary.

While Mum and Dad may have made some tentative commitment that I would play with Matthew, they must have known better than to imagine any such involvement with Sheila Mary. Apart from being a girl, she was little more than a baby to me, a pudgy one already wearing glasses like her brother. That feature would put them in a minority at school, if their being Americans had not already definitively done so.

My first impression of Matt was as a kid who could get over-boisterous, a tad disrespectful. I was trying to watch the football. I had a high idea of my own importance, not so much within the family as at school. This came not from any academic success, but my status as a footballer and one of the 'hard' boys in the class. Hardness was a quality most easily defined by negatives. People did not take liberties with you. They did not challenge you. It had nothing to do with strength. It was rarely if ever tested by physical or verbal confrontation. It was nothing, but it meant everything.

At Beaupré I clearly had to ignore Matt. There was no question of him joining me at playtimes. He got the message quickly. Sheila Mary made no attempt to seek me out there. I did not deny my kinship with them, nor was I ashamed of it. They were just in lower years.

Of my own classmates, Tom had moved on to Wisbech Grammar School, Henry, Fiddle, John and our captain Brin to Upwell Secondary Modern. My new deskmate was Lawsie (Robert Laws), with whom I quickly formed a friendship so close it would extend to Cibola. His house appeared on the map as Morroco.

Lawsie and I sat in the window file, as far back as we could behind two pairs of the high-ranking girls. One of those who would pass the eleven-plus was Lesley Seaman, next-door neighbour to Hank in Churchfield Road, a pretty girl who wore a calliper.

Polio had been a scourge in our infant years, paralysing from the waist down my Uncle Hugh (married to Uncle Fred's elder daughter Eileen, Mum's cousin) and leaving his older son, Martin, with a permanent limp. They fell ill at the same time. The boy, a year or so older than me, spent his third birthday in hospital in an iron lung. Lesley was similarly confined and paralysed for three months at an even earlier age. I don't remember her being singled out for special treatment by either staff or pupils at Beaupré. Children were routinely mocked in those days by their peers for being too fat or thin, but we were quickly taught that it was not acceptable to do so for other reasons. Another boy and I had to make a formal joint apology to Lesley at Mrs Booley's outraged insistence. She could not believe we would be so thoughtless and unkind as to call the girl Long John Silver. I suspect it was referring to her in that way rather than calling her the name direct, since Lesley was well able to stick up for herself.

I was not a teacher's pet for Mrs Booley, who could be as waspish with me as with anyone else. She was quick to correct a composition on our harvest festival. I must have forgotten to ask Mum for some tinned fruit or vegetables to take in to class.

'You've put here "some of us brought in offerings for the harvest festival". You can't write that, because you didn't bring anything. You would have to say "some of my classmates", or better "*most* of my classmates"…'

She would sometimes offer us a treat, as well as an example of how it should be done, the reading of compositions from past pupils. Perhaps I heard it more than once in the two years I was with Mrs Booley, so clearly do I remember one extract from something by one of Tom's older brothers or cousins: 'And this is the bit I really like coming up now… "the wily old tomcat"…' She would pause with a fearsome grin, expecting us also to delight in one adjective beyond the reach of the average ten-year-old.

Although exams were the main criterion, if not the only one, for determining our positions in class at the end of each year, great store was set by the star system. They were five-pointed, about the size of a modern penny piece, to be stuck on good work, or directly onto a wall chart. I remember there were different coloured stars, but not to what purpose. A constant source of grievance to me, one of which I never stopped moaning to Mum and Dad, was that Mrs Booley would hand out stars willy-nilly to girls in the class, for nothing more difficult than presenting her of a morning with an apple or a spray of flowers. It was rank favouritism on her part, gross crawling on theirs. I could not sink to it myself, yet how I grudged them those stars.

Relations with the opposite sex were not exclusively antagonistic or competitive. Boys and girls alike, the whole street it seemed, took part one mad summer's evening in a great water-fight down Isle Bridge Road. More than one adult got involved with garden hoses or buckets. It was normally part of our unwritten, unspoken code as boys to look down on or ignore anything that could be remotely construed as girlish. Unfortunately, this included girls. There was no problem with those generally considered unattractive, but any academic threat was the more perturbing if it came from a borderline crush. I had marked since my earliest days in Harry's class two favourites (sitting near Hank), but apart from showing off in front of them by fighting in the playground, their world was as separate from ours as the disciplines of needlework and handwork were kept at Beaupré. If I could dream, I never spoke to them except in mockery, to which they proved impervious. We had bravado, they were already developing self-confidence.

American girls were different.

I first saw my second set of foreign cousins in that bus shelter across from the Lion. I was going to Wisbech with Mum. Her cousin Ena was Aunt Gert's younger daughter, a tall, forceful woman, a regular smoker like Sid and Colleen (Aunt Gert was known to have an occasional puff). As Ena chatted to Joyce, her four daughters sat quietly beside her on the bench seat. I was the other side of the two women, in no way prepared to initiate a conversation. Nor was there one. Beverley, a year younger than me, came round to sit beside me. Joanne, who would end up in Harry's class, followed. Debbie was next, before five-year-old Sandra completed the migration. They sat like birds on a wire, the smaller ones swinging their feet backwards and forwards. All of them were looking to their right at me, all of them smiling.

Ena was in a similar state to her cousin Colleen, except her husband's posting at that point may have been no further away than Germany. Uncle Doug and Ena's daughters seemed to have alternated with the dark and lean genes – Bev and Debbie – and the more rounded, fairer look of Jo and Sandy.

It did not take me long to get to know them. Bev, the closest in age to me, remained perhaps the most distant, a great favourite with her grandmother. Debbie was virtually toothless, not from a backwoods raising (or an Everglades one – they came from Florida), but at that stage between milk and adult teeth. She was excitable, quick in laughter as in tears. Sandra was a doll, chubby features and the purest, straight blonde hair of them all. Joanne was the one who claimed me for her own.

With a freckled face and overbite, a brighter white blemish on one of her front teeth, Jo's beauty owed a lot to her snub nose and browny-green eyes. She wore her hair, light brown, long and straight in contrast to Bev's boyish cut and Debbie's mop-head. She and her younger sisters, as their confidence grew, would comb and brush *my* hair, as if I were one of their dolls. In truth, I had as little ability to resist.

While there was never anything sexual between us, nor pre-sexual fumblings, the younger girls led by Jo would plant kisses somewhat at random on my face, almost as if I was now not a toy so much as an adored family pet. They would cling to my legs when I sought to leave, them sometimes already in their pyjamas (which I was surprised to learn they wore over vests and pants). It was flattering, and for all that I maintained a surface indifference I was soon addicted to that flattery. I spent more time than ever before at Aunt Gert's, often not biking home until I needed to engage the dynamo on my Raleigh's back wheel to provide light on the road.

I wasn't the only one to feel the attraction of my cousins. Hank, Jim, Buzzy and others would hang around Aunt Gert's almost as much as I did, albeit without the privileged indoor access. You snooze, you lose. Jo worked hard for what seemed a long time to evoke some expression of affection from me, but I was too stuck in absurd thoughts of my image, of what my mates would say if I showed the weakness of liking girls. They had no such inhibitions. I thus found myself conducting a wedding between Jimmy and Joanne (Hank had a strange fondness for Debbie). I intoned whatever words I had picked up from television or films, enough to make a fist of it anyway as they stood before me in the driveway off Wisbech Road. I held my peace when I offered anyone 'knowing just cause why these two should not …' to speak up or else.

I should have seen it coming. There was a time when Jo would hang on my every word, enjoying the verses I had picked up from Grandad and sententious stuff I'd found in my own reading:

He who knows and knows he knows, he is a wise man – seek him.
He who knows and knows not he knows, he is asleep – wake him.
He who knows not and knows he knows not, he is a child – teach him.
He who knows not and knows not he knows not – he is a fool, shun him.

From listening soulfully as I declaimed this, how short a step it was for her to become the teacher.

'You know a lot of card games, don't you, David?'

'Well... yeah.' I'd probably tried to extend their horizons beyond rummy, which they insisted on calling 'gin'.

'Do you know fifty-two pick-up?'

All right, I'm sure you see it coming. Me reluctantly conceding that I probably did, but not under that exact name. Her hurling the pack all over the floor. 'There's the fifty-two, now pick 'em up.' It was her laughter that hurt the most.

I did not get the impression my two sets of cousins were close. Sid and Gert's houses were crowded that year, so perhaps there was no room for sleepovers or other mixing. Matt was the awkward outsider – as the only boy among them, and at school as one with a strange accent lacking any compensating sporting or social gifts. He proved useless at football. Worse, he was not interested in it. I think we may have taken him once or twice to see Wisbech or Peterborough play. My schoolmates lacked the family connection, and I do not remember Matt making friends among them.

Most of the gang were out there by Well Creek the evening before Beaupré's Sports Day of 1967, spread across both sides of the road. Matt was in one of his hyper moods, running around outside his grandad's house. I was on the riverside pavement, standing by or on my bike, talking soberly to Derek Upson.

I thought it was a honeymoon car passing, boots clunking together as they swung tied from its rear bumper. I was wrong. It was one of Matthew's shoes flying off as he appeared, crumpled against the kerb, behind the car. Apparently he had been showing off by touching vehicles as they passed, growing more daring until he literally over-reached himself. He was knocked unconscious. I saw blood trickling from his ear as he lay there.

Chapter Nineteen

Boys' Brigade

Aunt Ive, born in 1900, was of an age with most of the few regulars in the congregation at St Clement's. The Methodist chapel, that single-storey building on our run, with its own parking area which in later years would host car-boot sales, was an altogether more welcoming place. We had no thought of theology. We were all Church of England.

I had loyally kept (mainly) my promise to Mum not to swear. At night, before getting into bed, I would kneel beside it to race through the Lord's Prayer in my mind. I never managed a first prize for Sunday-school attendance, which would have meant not missing a single week in the year. My single third prize was what I thought an adventurous choice from limited options: *Pakala and Tandala*, a collection of folk tales from Albania.

My first book gift had been a Collins illustrated Holy Bible, inscribed to me (in letters now almost faded to illegibility) from 'GREAT-GRANDMOTHER GOLDSMITH, XMAS 1958'. It came in a leather cover that zip-closed over its gilt-edged pages, in turn snugly wrapped in tissue paper inside a hard box some four by six inches, again with gold trim framing the colour plate captioned *The Soldiers Take Paul to Antipatris, Acts 23:31*. This is also the final picture within the text, of more than a dozen with *The Adoration of the Shepherds, St Luke 2:16* as frontispiece.

As a boy I looked at the pictures in the St James, but never got into its text, let alone as conscientiously as Grandad Bailey had. Nevertheless, there was something about me that led Uncle Tom's mum to predict I would one day become a minister. I had a meeting with the St Clement's vicar on one occasion, to do with a school project, in his home at the top of Isle Bridge Road (on Rectory Road, right enough). On that same mission, one Sunday morning I took in consecutive church and chapel services, which Mum sanctioned while somehow making clear I should not let it become a habit.

Ken Russell, an uncle of Tom's, was a leading light in chapel, preaching in a houndstooth jacket. His Adam's apple would bob up and down on his tanned neck as he spoke to us without affectation, at no great length, from the pulpit. I have no memory of anything he said, only of his cheerfulness, a readiness to smile he brought to any conversation, without ever appearing to be a soft touch.

Except on special occasions, we children would not remain in the pews for the whole service. We would gather in a hall, off to the right of a corridor with smaller rooms, kitchens, toilets and suchlike on its left. Groups would be led by older teenagers or young adults. Led in what, I'm no longer sure.

Attendance at chapel picked up around Christmas – carols were somehow more fun than the usual round of Wesley hymns – Easter or harvest festival, and notably when the summer bus trip was in the offing. I thought I died and went to heaven on one of these.

The seaside would have been a logical destination, and perhaps we were there. I was in a hurry to get to something, running down a grassy hill. I was rated as reasonably speedy at school, but now my legs were moving faster than I could control. I pitched forward, over and over. Perhaps I was influenced towards a state of grace by being on a Sunday-school trip. Flat on my back at last, I honestly thought I was part of the skies above, not looking at them. The world stopped for me a moment. I was whole, unhurt. Nobody expressed any concern; it probably only looked like a minor tumble. From the inside it was much more, blind terror at being totally out of control, then what I can only call bliss as I came back to life.

If I was never forced to go to church, Mum and Dad were probably pleased on balance that I did – as long as I didn't take the religious bit too seriously. Linked to chapel, and something that lasted beyond primary school, was the Outwell company of the Boys' Brigade to which I was transferred in November 1966 after two sessions in the Life Boys, its Junior Reserve.

Apart from playing Subbuteo and generally hanging out together, Henry was my main companion walking up Isle Bridge Road on Monday nights (there was a Girls' Brigade too, which must have mustered on a different evening, for we never mixed). I don't think we had uniforms like our officers, beyond a belt Mum would have to keep polished.

Walter Sands was our captain, a ruddy-faced farmer whose Brigade hat covered a balding head. His sergeant Jack Robb, a raw-boned taller man, would sometimes preach in the chapel. I don't recall if we opened or closed our meetings with prayers. Walter, as behoved his higher rank, had little to do with us as individuals. Jack could be riled, but he could never be shifted in his faith. He would concede evolution, the Big Bang, whatever you liked, always coming back with 'And before that?' It was maddening to have no answer.

The couple of hours we spent on parade each week had a fixed pattern. When Captain Sands judged our high spirits on arrival to have abated sufficiently, Jack would form us into a line, dressing by the right. Henry had some sort of corporal status, which he never abused. With painful but necessary slowness we would be drilled in the about-turn, moving our toes half a compass point at a time. We usually did slow marching too; otherwise, we would have felt too soon the confines of the hall, the same in which Sunday school was held. We did not use the raised stage area, where all the chairs and other furniture were stacked.

Hunstanton beach – my turn next
David following cousin Mandy on donkey

I was never in the Cubs or Scouts, which may not have had an Outwell troop. Beaupré's one football match in our final year was against Upwell Cubs, whose star player was Martin Rayner. Stan interrupted his wife's classes one day to announce it, at the same time naming his selection committee, with Mr Linford no longer involved. 'We'll have David Bailey, Jim Wilson and streaky Hancock' (I've never known why he picked that word to call Hank). 'Put your heads together and come to me when you've got a team.'

I don't think it took us long. Stan's only query was Peter Goman at right back. He taught us the word 'nepotism'. Hank and Jim were quick to confirm Peter was in on merit, as a joint pick, and not because of his brother's friendship with me.

With the three selectors in the forward line, completed by John Chapman and Lawsie, Aidi was the only defender left from the previous year, promoted to centre half. 'Bail, when you pass it back to me from kick-off, see if you can get it in the air, cos I can kick it further when it's off the ground.'

Hank got two goals and Jim or Jonno the other in our 3–3 draw. Rayner may have scored a hat-trick against us. I ran all over the pitch. There was no follow-up of shared activities or further competition with the Cubs, probably busy earning their badges at similar disciplines to us in the Boys' Brigade. I never progressed to one from the preliminary qualification of certificates, as a wayfarer and for physical training. The absence of any others in Mum's carefully preserved stash, where the Cycling Proficiency Test pass was a document to be cherished, leads me to think I did not distinguish myself in other fields.

With knots I could blame my eternal left-handedness. I was OK on the difference between a granny and a reef knot. Slip knots, hitch knots, I forget the names of the others so plainly set out on the sheet of paper. Jack did not lack the patience, much less the expertise, to show us any of them. Henry picked them up readily enough, in the same way he would throw a cricket ball twenty yards further than I could manage. Nobody could show me how to tie them left-handed, and there I stuck.

Dad, with his history as a cornet player, was more enthusiastic than I when he heard we would be working towards a marching band. Trumpets, bugles, cornets, saxophones, clarinets, trombones – some of these were put at our disposal. I couldn't produce a sound, let alone a note. The only thing they trusted me with was the big drum, strapped around my neck and bellying out before me to be thumped every time the boy in front of me put his left foot down. I needed that kind of visual prompt, having no idea of keeping time in any musical sense.

If my drumming was put in a real parade once, it was no more often than that. The big one was Remembrance Sunday, or Armistice Day as some still preferred to call it. A wreath would be laid at the memorial in St Clement's yard listing the village's dead from both world wars. On one occasion we also went to Ely Cathedral, where as part of the much larger army our bandsman skills were not required.

Christopher Buzzard's life had begun with weeks if not months in hospital, from which he was not always expected to emerge. He was an only child, whose parents were friends of Hank's, so those two boys spent time together. Hank did not go to Boys' Brigade, but Jim did, with Buzzy after going round his for tea.

Despite these friendships with my mates, I was not at that point close to Buzzy. He could be contrary, hard only in endurance, sometimes seeming to delight in provoking aggression from which he never knew the right moment to retreat. Or was he simply spoilt? A connoisseur in that field, I felt the officers at Boys' Brigade let him get away with far too much. He was running around one evening, like a much younger child, when with a spurt of malice I stuck out a foot from my seat to send him sprawling to the floor. Knowing he would be restrained, he made a show of coming at me. I could not explain to anyone why I had done it, for all Jack Robb's kindly questioning. I felt he deserved it; that was the plain answer I didn't give.

While not a star at football, Buzzy made our Beaupré team against the Cubs at right-half, beside Aidi. He would now and then embark on a mazy, crazy dribble during which he could not be separated from the ball. He was a regular down the playing field, as in the four- or five-a-side games with which we always ended our evenings at Boys' Brigade. This indoor football was the highlight for us all. As Captain Sands rounded off the drills before calling parade's end, we were all jealously eyeing the clock to ensure we got a full half-hour, ideally more. A half-sized, soft rubbery ball would be produced from a sliding door under the stage; chairs were placed as goalposts, to be defended by Jack invariably and sometimes by Walter himself; off would come neckties, and away we went. The ball left smudges on the walls from our wilder shooting. We heard of complaints at that, rumours we would be forbidden to play. Our confidence that our officers would defend our interests was never dented.

Boys' Brigade was essentially a winter activity. We went carolling round the village at least once, with the officers threatening to send Henry and me home (which might have improved the singing) after we fell out about something and got into a brief scuffle. When summer came, Walter and Jack would have more than enough to do on the land to keep them busy through the evenings, so perhaps there was a break. As the days lengthened towards it, we would sometimes take our parade down the Rec'. One evening we ran the road from chapel to Gill's Bridge, back along the Norfolk side and through the village via Wenn's then Tuck's Bridge. This was deemed near enough a mile to be worth the PT certificate if we could cover it in ten minutes or less. Not a problem.

Odd times we would take the football outside too. Once we were joined by Walter's son Derek, who drove a St John ambulance in his downtime from driving a real one. He was our first-aid lecturer, with more success than he had showing off tricks with the ball. While the theory of artificial respiration was explained to us, without a doll a practical demonstration was inconceivable. We were shown how to do a fireman's lift, effective on people heavier than ourselves. We put splints and slings on broken legs and arms, respectively but not always efficiently.

Although I would not receive my Boys' Brigade First Year First Aid certificate until January 1968, I had already learned by that summer of 1967 that blood leaking from an ear could mean a fractured skull. You were not to scruple to rip up clothes to bind the head as tightly as possible. That seemed somehow too dramatic a step for my American cousin, lying in the street near his grandad's house. The adults were soon there anyway.

Aunt Gert was laid up in Wisbech hospital with an illness that would eventually cost her a kidney. Mum happened to be round at her house, hanging out washing with both her cousins, when someone brought news of the accident. They were almost close enough to hear the thud of impact, car on boy, boy on road. There was no panic or tears from the children gathered around, careful now to keep themselves off the narrow road on which traffic had not stopped passing.

Uncle Sid would not go in the ambulance with his daughter and grandson. Mum and Dad followed it in our car. I was dropped off at Maillebourne on their way to town.

Chapter Twenty

Passing On

'David, he's dead.' Mum's face was working as she put her hand on my upper arm. She blurted it out as if she had only heard a second before and half expected me to have the power to contradict her. Colleen had been given the news too brusquely by a hospital nurse – 'I've never heard a sound like the one that came out of her when they told her,' Mum said. Matt's skull was fractured. There were other significant internal injuries, we gathered, without ever being given specifics.

Mum and Dad (he had been very steady in the crisis) would stay with Matt's nearest kin. I slept at Maillebourne, in the same bed as Grandad. When I would do so as a younger child, he would insist on clamping my feet between his knees, so that I did not kick him in my sleep. Perhaps we went through the same ritual. We did not talk about the accident.

Aunt Colleen had seemed to me, if anything, calmer than usual when she asked me to tell her what had happened 'if you can, honey, and then never think about it again'. She declined the option Mr Booley gave her of having the Beaupré Sports Day cancelled. In the playground before school one kid from a lower class was running around chanting my cousin's name and crowing that he was dead. More overexcited than malicious, he was corralled by others and offered for me to punch.

We had heard Stan announce one other death from the stage at assembly, a boy I remembered falling over a football in a scrum and going home in tears, to which I ascribed the start of whatever killed him. I don't think there was any misplaced attempt at oratory for Matt. It was good of Stan to speak to me separately afterwards. I told him I had hit the smaller boy and why. He said he didn't have a problem with it. It is probably a false memory that he asked me to show calm and restraint, as an example to the younger children.

I don't doubt that for most of that Sports Day afternoon we kids were able to forget about Matt. It was the usual mixture: individual footraces from forty yards for the five-year-olds rising gradually to ninety for those in Mrs Booley's class, who also had a relay; monkey runs, egg-and-spoon, sack, wheelbarrow, flower-pot and slow-cycle races, with separate categories for boys and girls in all but the three-legged race for boys only, and the skipping, which none of us begrudged the girls. Parents were welcome and attended, without in those days expecting to participate. It was among the last days of the school year, if not the last, so the accident was not one we brooded about among ourselves. Outwardly my main reaction to my first lived and remembered human death was not to want to sleep alone for a few nights following it.

I was allowed to attend Matt's funeral, at Kensal Green in London. There was a service first at a local church, Wisbech for some reason. Aunt Gert was at neither. There was enough concern for her own life not to tell her of Matt's death until the funeral was past. With Aunt Edna's illness, Gert had been almost as heavily involved in the upbringing of Sheila and Colleen as in that of her own girls, Pam and Ena.

Matt had not been happy in England, had often (I was told) expressed a wish to go back to the States. Whether or not there was any thought of honouring this wish in his death, London was the choice. Uncle Don had compassionate leave, the only time I would meet him. If Matthew knew that his parents were separated emotionally as well as geographically, he never let on to me and I had it then from no other source. Don was older than his (still) wife, leathery almost bald head and thick-framed glasses. He said he'd heard a lot about me, his son really thought I was 'the bee's knees'. That may have been the title of a mawkish short piece I wrote in my later youth, a way of putting the event into a (barely) fictional context. While it did not go too easy on me, the story let me show awareness of having been – beyond the eyes of adults – a poor friend to my younger cousin.

Uncle Sid had a blue, closed-back van. Dad drove it, with me in the middle of its front bench seat between him and Uncle Sid. I suppose we were following a hearse also carrying the principal mourners. I had decided to draw a map to scale of the various roads and distances we would cover on the way to London. I did so, hunched over an exercise book with ruler and pencil, helped by Dad and the odometer. Uncle Sid sat mainly silent, flat-capped as ever but strangely bereft of his pipe. Aunt Edna was not involved, her only recorded reaction to say 'poor little boy' when given the news before returning to her own world and never again mentioning her grandson.

I remember a graveyard not just bigger than Outwell cemetery, much bigger than the whole playing field. It was a sunny day. Afterwards we went to Aunt Sheila's flat. The directions to escape London from there given by Uncle Ed, an Irish bookie, were held up ever after as models of their kind. A tun of pub names were supplemented by helpful local knowledge: 'There'll be a lady in the garden on the corner wearing a big straw hat, can't miss her'.

Ed seemed good fun insofar as one could judge on such a day. He and Sheila had a different sadness to face when their daughter was found to have spina bifida. At this stage She-she was a beautiful dark-haired baby in a cot, her disabilities not immediately visible. She would live to attend school for just one term.

On our way back to Outwell, without my map to keep me occupied, I hinted at one point I could fancy some fish and chips. 'You took the words out of my mouth, boy,' said Uncle Sid. We were pleased to hear him speak.

At the time of his grandson's death, Sid was doing up a bigger house for himself and Edna, on the Isle side further down towards Gill's Bridge. It was set back from the road, with a decent garden. His brother Will was involved in the deal, whether as vendor or in tipping him off to the availability of property on what had been railway land. Don helped him and Dad out briefly on the renovation. There was some thought their shared loss might bring Colleen and him back together, but it didn't happen. As her dad was hanging up the 'Mattville' sign in his new front porch, she left Outwell to move between London and the States, depending on the stages of Sheila Mary's education.

Aunt Ena would re-join Uncle Doug with their daughters, who soon had a little brother (I think Jimmy was born in the Philippines). Outwell would not see any of the girls for another ten years, when Aunt Gert would have to exercise closer supervision on visiting teenage granddaughters and their now less innocent suitors.

We were all moving on. Outwell had no secondary school. Those who passed the eleven-plus went to Wisbech Grammar (boys) or High (girls). A year or two later the authorities would dictate that Norfolk children should go instead to Downham Market. There was Lesley Seaman, catching a bus every day the six miles to Wisbech, while her brother John headed the same distance in the opposite direction. They could wave at each other from bus stops either side of the road, near where Matt had fallen.

Buses were hardly needed from the middle of Outwell to the secondary modern school at Upwell on its then site. From Churchfield, a left turn along Low Side brought you there in less than ten minutes. From Isle Bridge Road it was similar, crossing the footbridge by the British Legion virtually at the school's gates.

I suppose we may have been coached for the exam. My only memory is of Mrs Booley demonstrating on the blackboard how we should put our name in the top corner. Before starting the mocks, she walked her ranked files.

'What's this, Jeffrey?'

'I did what you said, Miss. I copied it down.'

'But your name's not Linda, is it? Is it, Jeffrey?'

'No, sir.'

'I was just using that as an example to show you all, I didn't expect… Cross it out and put your own name in, heavens preserve us.'

Jeffers was not the only one to do some crossing out.

I can't pretend the scholarship was a cause of stress, since I remember nothing else of the build-up to it or the exam itself. I was one of the children expected to pass, a small group occasionally taken out of Mrs Booley's classes towards the end of the year for some beginners' lessons in French. Her husband taught these, confiding to Mum and Dad at a teachers' evening that my pronunciation was not good; he feared I might not have an ear for languages.

Lawsie, pulled into the French class later than the rest of us, was off school the day the results were announced. He was prone to taking time off with colds and the like. I never had to miss school through illness. So there I was, absurdly patting the unoccupied desk beside me to congratulate my absent friend when Stan said Robert Laws had passed. He and I would go to Wisbech Grammar School. Across the Nene, on North Brink at Wisbech High, would be four new girls from Beaupré.

Six was a big number of pupils to pass the scholarship from Outwell. It did not occur to me at the time to ask why I had not been put in for it twelve months earlier.

'I didn't have any doubts about you academically. I just thought we would keep you for another year, another year to mature would do you good,' Mr Booley explained (even as an adult I never came to call him 'Stan' to his face). Well might I finish first of thirty-three in July 1967, aged '11 years 7 mth' in a class with an average age of '10½ yrs', when the year before, only a month above the class's average age, I was first of thirty-one. It was clearly an area where primary school heads had some discretion. I was not unique; at least one of the high-school bound girls was older than I. I don't necessarily disagree with Stan's assessment, which as far as I know he made and acted on alone – certainly without consulting Mum and Dad. An extra year of boyhood is quite a gift, after all.

There is little difference between the report cards of my last two years at Beaupré, no startling new gift unearthed, no major weakness eliminated. Using a calculator that would have been the marvel of the age if I could have transported it to Mrs Booley's class then – how many stars is *that* worth, girls? – I can tell you this: in the major skill sets of numeracy and literacy I went off the boil from 97.6% to 97.5%.

Yes, of course I'm showing off.

After noting 'some improvement' during my first year with her, in repeating its C Mrs Booley sadly concluded I was 'not very musical'. Art was stuck on B–, without comment in either year. Physical education wordlessly moved from B to A–. I kept my A for geography, which she cannot have meant to bracket with handwork when talking of my 'keen interest'. This had not been applied to my vowel sounds, as she deemed my speech still to need attention when downgrading 'oral' from B to B–.

All those successful in the scholarship were given a Collins Dictionary as a prize, to add in my case to the one for top boy, *The Book of Explorers* by Arthur L. Hayward. The Booleys' summary (it looks like Stan wrote the final sentence, below his signature) of my years at Beaupré, their farewell note read: 'David works intelligently and industriously. He well deserves his place at the Grammar School. We wish him every success in the future.'

Should I close there? I think not. Tolstoy titled his memoir *Childhood, Boyhood, Youth*. It would be too facile to say my childhood ended when I left primary school, and far from the Tolstoyan model, since he defined childhood as a time before he was conscious of his gender. I can remember no such time. I will write on to the point where my youth kicks in. I have two markers for that, one of which is when I began to keep a regular diary.

I feel no need to attempt my own summary of Beaupré. The leaving of it did not feel like a major life change, for all that Mr Booley had warned, in these actual words, that I would go 'from being a big fish in a little pond, to a little fish in a big pond'. There was no sense of privilege in heading to Wisbech

Grammar instead of Upwell. Henry and Fiddle had left the year before, but we still lived in the same road. Hank, Jim, Aidi, Buzzy and Stink would still be my mates, although I might now spend more time with Lawsie. I might no longer be able to sneak looks across the classroom at Angie or Debbie; on the other hand, what was not to like about being free at last of my female academic competitors? Before I moved into the all-boys environment of Wisbech Grammar there would be a foretaste of such a world during the holidays: Boys' Brigade Camp.

Chapter Twenty-One

Fen Rabbits

'My eyes are dim, I cannot see,
I have not brought my specs with me.
I left the-em in thee-ee lavatory.'

I didn't wear glasses. If I had, nothing would have persuaded me to fetch them from the Boys' Brigade lavatories in Wolferton Woods.

Our first job on arriving at the big field on the edge of woodland between King's Lynn and Hunstanton – part of the Royal Sandringham Estate – was to construct said lavatories. Latrines they called them, and they made Grandad Bailey's seem luxurious, almost decadent. I say construct, but no more than digging was required, of a long trench, away from the tents towards the treeline. I was too shy to use them for a squat until we'd been there two days, when nature would no longer be denied.

The Outwell regiment was represented by Henry, Buzzy and me. Our officers were not involved. The hierarchy had older boys entrusted with more power and responsibility than we were used to seeing. We knew nobody beyond our own group; there was some posturing. We were told that Gaywood was a hard area of King's Lynn. One kid from there swore he was going to beat me up before the week was out. The time apparently wasn't right just then. Buzzy quickly acquired a new moniker, known for the week and briefly beyond it as 'Kestrel'. Henry, as usual, got on with most people.

There were campfires at night, without singing of 'Kumbaya'. The songs we heard were more ribald, generally fixed on a topic of nearer concern to the older boys:

'And there was Spud, Spud
Pulling on his pud, in the stores,
In the stores.
And there was Spud, Spud,
Pulling on his pud,
In the quartermaster's stores.'

That was an indecent lead-in to the failing eyesight and misplaced spectacles. You could have Frank yanking on his crank, Billy playing with his willy, with easily imagined variants for Bob, Jock and Rick. 'So my ma came in while I was in the bath, and said, "What's that?" I said "That's my prike, Ma".' Either the deliberate mispronunciation or the fact it was a hard Gaywood boy telling the tale made us all laugh.

There is an understated Christian mission behind the Boys' Brigade. Our platoon leader was a well-meaning boy who subscribed to it. Keith (let's call him, I genuinely don't remember) did good work helping us to settle in the jostling new environment. He was in the same tent as half a dozen of us, me in a new grey sleeping bag and under canvas for the first time (I think we'd been expected to pitch the tents that taxing first day, when I could only try not to hinder more competent hands). His sleeping back provided a log-like support for that of another boy who joined us one night, casually jerking his thumb behind him to ask a mate if Keith would cause any problems. He was told no, and our leader slept on with great resolution. The next day I heard him asking an adult if he could move out. He wouldn't say what had upset him, beyond that it was 'disgusting'.

I was not bothered by the lewd talk after lights out and don't know whether it went further into social masturbation. Smoking would have been a more probable transgression to me, except that there was the whole of the woods for that. There was supposedly a girls' camp within striking distance, to which there was talk of a midnight expedition. If it happened, as with the case of the Beaupré tease-stripper I was not involved. The chance to flee it all was provided – perhaps deliberately – by a parents' visiting day halfway through the camp. The following year Jim Wilson would go home early. I saw the attraction myself, uncertain how I might come out of my impending scrap. In the end, pride would not let me say anything to Mum and Dad, much less get in the car with them when they left.

The fight never happened, as was probably also true of the raid on the girls' camp (if there was such a camp) and of Keith's worst wakeful shut-eyed nightmares. Whether or not he succeeded in changing tents, he was still our leader on the last full day's expedition through the woods.

One thing being tested was our orienteering skill, another our imagination. To this day I can study a compass for minutes without it giving me the faintest hint of anything, so I was happy to tag along within our detail. We had become so swiftly absorbed into our own community that I was surprised to come upon railway tracks, then a village post office. Nobody had any ideas for the strange and wonderful object we were tasked to bring back from our adventure. Keith ended up buying two stamps, which he stuck together. The resulting double-faced queen was not a winner for us. Whatever did win was not strange or wonderful enough to stay in my memory.

By the time we broke camp, we were on the best of terms with the Gaywood boys. Dad fetched me home, his first words to Mum on arrival 'for Christ's sake get this boy into a bath!' The fact I have no memory of washing facilities at Wolferton does not mean there were none or that I never used them. I suspect the set-up was Spartan enough to discourage any lingering.

Never having experienced showers before, I would not have been keen to get undressed among other boys, scruples that had to end quickly at grammar school. The showers there were communal, with PE teacher Keith Hipwell (Hippie) making sure you at least went in at one end and came out the other bollock-naked, no matter how thoroughly or cursorily you chose to wash yourself on the way through.

Showering after gym was one change of many in my new school life. The most startling at first was the movement. Instead of sitting at the same desk all day, once assembly and the register in our form-room were done we would scurry from one lesson to another, in different classrooms, sometimes different buildings, with different teachers for each subject. All according to a timetable pasted into the front cover of an exercise book, impossibly complicated yet memorised as quickly as if each of us had access to a form memory powered by thirty boys.

The intake was split into forms A and Alpha, no doubt so named to signify equivalent levels of academic excellence. Although we were assured the selection was random, Mum quickly concluded that mine had the pick of the talent. Each form ranged the whole alphabet: in 1A Atkins, Bacon, Bailey,

Bales, right through to W... W... Westhorpe, for whom each roll call must have been an agony of anticipation.

And wasn't there a roll call at the start of every lesson in those early days? Likely it was to discourage truancy, more likely to avoid some shrill-voiced first-former getting lost in the grounds and starting to cry, most likely to help the teachers get a fix on the names of their new charges. In some if not all classes we were made to sit in alphabetical order, which would be a further help for them (that put me in the front row, not ideal). They stuck to surnames, another change from primary school. We did the same amongst ourselves at first, not so much because we didn't know the other boys' first names, more so as not to be humiliated by them answering a cheery John or Joe with a Doe or Blow, which would at once put them – like teachers – at an advantage.

Apart from a couple of secretaries entombed somewhere near the headmaster's lair, and the dinner ladies, the environment was exclusively male. There were no female teachers, unless you counted the students who came over as French *assistantes* to help O and A level pupils with pronunciation.

At Christine Chappell's wedding 1964

'"Qu'est-ce que c'est sur la table", she said, and she meant the pen or something but she had these massive tits and she was leaning forward so Twoll had to say...' That was the sort of thing that scotched it for my generation; when we reached the higher forms, we found only weedy young *assistants* trying to grow their first moustaches.

The absence of girls in the playground or classroom was little remarked on by any of us, and Harry Wiseman had given me a good experience of male teachers. Like him, each of our new masters had a nickname, inherited rather than invented by us newcomers. As with the extra power of collective memory, we knew these seemingly without ever being told. I had no idea that the teachers knew them too.

Our form teacher in 1A was Mr Sleight, 'Basil' probably on the strength of no more than the initial of his first name (which was Brian). He took us for geography, one of the younger men with carefully groomed hair. Friendly enough, he was easily capable of quelling us, sarcasm his weapon of choice as it was with many of the others. We were all disloyal enough to laugh at the discomfiture of any of our classmates, which I suppose only encouraged the teachers to parade their lowest form at our expense.

Our history master Mr Skinner's first name was John, too boring for a nickname. He was Hank, slicked back hair of a wartime spiv making him look older than he probably was. He was not averse to 'slippering', not always with as much justification as when one of our class got it for hurling a javelin in the general direction of other boys while Hank was supervising us in games. The type of footwear used to paddle boys' arses – the cane was reserved for the headmaster – was never seen or felt by me; any such punishments were administered out of sight of the class. My alphabetical predecessor David Bacon drew a punishment, alerting the whole rowdy 1A to teacher's arrival at the Nissen hut by bellowing 'Skinner' too loudly to be ignored. His crime was not the use of a nickname but the absence of a 'Mr'.

We assumed Hank was a bachelor from the fact that his holiday snaps never featured anyone but him. There he was, projected on the blackboard, floating on the Dead Sea, explaining that he couldn't have sunk, however much he wanted to please us. Actually he didn't say that, any attempt at humour either alien to him or above our heads. He was honestly surprised when some minor miscreant, given the choice, said they would take standing outside during the director's cut of his summer vacation over a slippering. He let the lad off the slipper, but not the slideshow.

171

What were called the Nissen huts by staff and boys alike were not the classic metal, cylindrical structures but two or three rows of free-standing wooden, windowed classrooms outside the main building, on the way to the hall of similar shape – fewer windows though – where we all went for dinner.

A gaggle of masters would sit at the end furthest from the door, to keep order and maybe start proceedings with a grace. Boys were on tables of eight, moving in turn to fetch their food – main course then pudding – from a big serving hatch. There was always a buzz of anticipation if a second helping of chips became available, the desperate hope there would be enough to reach your table from the seemingly arbitrary starting point selected by the teachers.

A full single helping of chips would have been welcome to some boys. Although most sat with classmates, there was no reason why each year would have a number of pupils exactly divisible by eight. I found myself on a table of mainly second-years. It was not alphabetical order, for Cracknell and Holdsworth of 1A were with me. We had perhaps been at the front of the queue for the trough on the first day, which determined our seats for the whole year.

Although we may not have realised it immediately, we were not with just any second-formers. Steve was the lanky goalkeeper for the Under-13 XI, though like many keepers he fancied himself more as a centre-forward. Stu, his captain and one of the few viewed as equally hard in their year, was more stockily built, with shorter hair. To Stu's right, opposite me at the end of the table furthest from the window, was Stephen (never Steve), a boy smaller than most of us newcomers.

When the mood took them, Stu and Steve (more so) would have a bit of fun at the juniors' expense. Having established our names, they thought nothing of repeating an unfunny routine a dozen times in the same snatched meal.

'David?'

'Yeah?'

'Bailey.'

That was it. Their power lay in that you dared not fail to answer to your first name. Our amusements were limited in those days.

Stu and Steve would nick chips from our first-former plates. We all suffered from their depredations, but with my instinct to be a bully rather than be bullied I was soon pinching from my immediate neighbour myself.

Retaliation or armed resistance – a stabbing fork, say – against Steve or Stu was unthinkable. They operated more by distraction and misdirection than main force, so I learned quickly to extend my handwriting technique to eating: both hands around the exposed side of the plate, head down as close to it as possible, chips shovelled into mouth without pause until it was clear of the only thing ever thought worth stealing. More than one person would remark on my table manners as an adult.

One day Steve was staring at me from the moment I sat down. He had no reason that I knew to be annoyed. I couldn't meet his gaze, after trying a smile that drew no response. It was uncomfortable, embarrassing as well as intimidating… and it was all a joke, one more way of getting a rise out of us.

Steve was more volatile than Stu, who always maintained the reserve befitting a football captain with kids a year below him. They both treated Stephen with a degree of respect, encouraging us to believe in him as a little nutter, though he rarely spoke to them and never to us. Stephen did not steal chips. Every day, as we were about to leave the table, he would put an item of cutlery – knife, fork or spoon – into the breast pocket of his blazer, underneath the WGS badge. He never made any attempt to conceal it further; it was always sticking out in plain view as he marched out with his bantam-cock gait, fists clenched at his sides. I was going to ask him about the habit one time, until kindly warned off doing so by Stu. It was to be viewed as an eccentricity, albeit one with an edge to it like the braces keeping his trousers up. To comment on either might invite the third, a pair of bovver boots he wore all year round in flat contravention of school rules.

Although the council paid our bus fares, with a season ticket delivered each term, school uniform was an expense for parents. If there was any provision for state help, again it wasn't provided to Mum and Dad. Perhaps my set of white shirts, grey trousers, dark shoes and socks, school tie, badged blazer and cap was in part funded by Nana and Grandad. There might have been a market in second-hand blazers, but mine were always new.

It was clearly one of Dad's jobs to show me how to knot a tie. I hope he had an easier time than Jack Robb teaching me to tie a knot. It soon became routine to wear it, light blue and yellow diagonal stripes at six-inch intervals, with a yellow badge – something like a stained-glass window with a couple of figures framed in a locket – on a navy-blue background. The cap was what everyone hated, too easy a target for mockery or snatching by Queen's School boys, until that far distant day at the end of third year when it could be discarded. They all went into the Nene.

The rule was, whenever we were in uniform outside the school grounds, that uniform had to feature the cap. Our playing fields were at Harecroft Road, almost straight across the river from us beyond North Brink, except there was no bridge straight across. The pavilion was over half a mile away by road, walking up to Town Bridge (commonly known as Clarkson's bridge for the statue of Wilberforce's less famous anti-slavery confederate that loomed over the traffic lights), across it, through the Corn Exchange archway and left out towards Sutton Bridge. To make the walk worthwhile, games was always a double period at the end of the day, unlike PE, gym-bound in the school.

With competition from the likes of double maths, it is no surprise that games was our favourite extended class – at least when it was football and not cross-country, a brutal slog along the Peterborough Road, cutting across ploughed fields to find our way back to the school gates. A further bonus in our first year was that it fell on Friday. Small wonder we were anxious to be away, crouched forward over our desks like sprinters at the off, caps already in hand, anticipating the bell in more than one sense of the word.

'Sit down!' roared Joe, as the sound of the bell competed with 120 chairlegs being scraped back over the wooden floor. He waited until everyone had complied.

'Stand up.'

Warily, we rose again to our feet.

'Sit down. Stand up. Sit down. Stand up. Sit down,' he yelled at increasing pace, throwing us out of sync but stopping just before it became ridiculous. He was angry.

'Who do you think you are, you little Fen rabbits? The bell is for my convenience and information, not yours. *I* decide when class ends. If I want I can keep you here all afternoon. Mr Hipwell won't miss you at games. And if I ever see a cap out in this classroom again, you'll all be staying here with that boy till it's time to go home. Is that clear? Is that clear?' he turned up the volume again.

'Yes, sir,' we spoke as one.

By the time we reached the Clarkson Memorial, we were probably laughing at Joe's rant (I still struggled to believe, when I later saw it in print, that Mr Davy's first name was not Joe but James). None of us had laughed in the classroom, his calculated loss of temper being the first time we had seen him bare his teeth. Until then the school's Head of English and Senior Master – third in line behind the head and his deputy, the ancient yet formidable science teacher Mr Neale (Nobby, in whispers) – had shown us only his wise-cracking, benevolent side. No taller than some second-formers, his white tonsured hair put him firmly among the older teachers, yet he seemed more relaxed than most of them with us. He promised to give us one day a full lesson on swearing, how 'bloody' comes from 'By our Lady' and so on. That lesson remained untaught at the end of the school year, and I would never again be in Joe's class.

Within limits, which included respecting his own sizeable ego, Joe encouraged a degree of individuality, an approach to the line beyond which lay the 'cheek' of which other teachers lived in daily fear. It was not good form to volunteer answers in class. We all knew you should wait to be named unless it was a dolly, which might spare you embarrassment later. I could not help but feel Joe made a connection with me. When he set us the homework of preparing for a debate, half the class on one side of the question, half on the other, I asked if I could chair it. He saw at once that I had picked up on the rules of engagement he had given us, that the chairman is the only person who does not have to speak to the question.

'Yes, you can be chairman, Bailey. You do the homework though, I want a speech written for the ayes.'

It fell to Joe to drum up contributions for the school magazine. Apart from reports on all the sporting activities, outings and academic successes, *The Wisbechian* would have something of poetry or prose from each year. Perhaps he didn't have much faith in his Fen rabbits' capacity to produce a polished short story, or anything in verse not scurrilous, for he tried towards the end of one lesson to draw us out on interesting hobbies we might have. I was not the first to speak, but when I did it was at some length.

'And do you think you could get that down on paper?'

'I suppose so, sir.'

As we left the room at the bell – I was in the row nearest the door, behind Atkins and Bacon – it struck me. I had just told the whole of 1A that my leading pastime was playing with toy soldiers.

Chapter Twenty-Two

The Young Faithfuls

At Princes St bars with mates

When Lawsie came to the game, Cibola already had its history. With greater purchasing power than me, he quickly built up a sizeable army. He could not, however, develop his own Morgan or O'Reilly dynasties, because their age was past. Soldiers were not available in the same variety as before, which made the ones from discontinued lines, those of which I only had singletons myself, of greater value. He made a half-hearted attempt at a battle, more like a massacre of white plastic astronauts that came with a space station we both received one Christmas. Generally though, he was accumulating more than destroying, our common focus having shifted from war to sports.

There are many stories to be told of Cibola. One is already in the world as my young adult novel *Seventeen: or the Blood City Tommy O'Reilly Benefit Tour*, with my December 1967 article for *The Wisbechian* as afterword. The trilogy *Joe Kingmaker* is in manuscript, while the late incursion of Napoleonic soldiers to the lost cities may yet inspire *The 102 Days*. Not only did the world of Cibola exist; it was important from an early stage for its existence to be chronicled. The history of its football leagues reflects to some extent that of my friendship with Robert Laws.

A compendium of games – another Christmas gift – had provided stacks of coloured counters, cards and, for a game I don't recall, many solid balls less than a quarter of an inch in diameter. These would eventually split or chip, but until then were ideal for football matches, replacing soldiers' heads for balls as the smaller Subbuteo nets did their bodies for goalposts. The two teams would be lined up, usually in four-two-four or four-three-three, on a large enough expanse of carpet, not too plush to prevent the free run of the ball, ideally not too hard on the knees either. The office served admirably, using the whole of the floor not occupied by its bed (single). The spare room downstairs was better if Lawsie was round, as there was more space.

The clashing of the players over the ball, their careful passes to each other, the crosses to which a Pink Viking or an Ivanhoe (whether John or Alan) would rise to head goalwards, all had to be managed with some care. It was not unknown for a player to be seriously injured, potentially shattered if a later, more brittle model, when a knee or hand came down carelessly on him. If there was a way to manage a game with two people, Lawsie and I never found it. He rightly remonstrated when, in his living room, I moved Sir Crispin of Blood City to make a goal-line clearance, in a match he was officiating.

Cricket was a different matter. He preferred to bowl, I to bat, a better arrangement than one of us having to use a hand for each. The walls of the room made convenient boundaries, with catches given if the ball struck a fielder off the batsman's swinging body. Rather than rearrange the field every over, we simply had the batsmen change ends.

Few cricketers did not also play football. A census taken in the sports camp at Blood found thirty-nine of 122 Pirates were professional footballers, against only eight cricketers. As in the lives where we only proposed, cricket was very much the junior partner. Neither of us was any good as a player. I was allowed to open the batting with Mark Vincent once at grammar, as a sop from Gary Rider to both of us for being put in the 1A second XI. Even in those depths I was unable to shine; Lawsie made no more of a name for himself in Alpha.

Given their historical pre-eminence (albeit as first of one), it was fitting that the Young Faithfuls won the earliest recorded First Division Championship. A single loose sheet of paper records the tables for first, second and international divisions, of five, five and four teams respectively. Leading scorers are listed (the Ivanhoe twins joint top with eleven), as are cup winners Ajax, with the result of every First Division fixture in tabular form on the other side of the sheet. The season was 1966-67, one of the many in which United won the English First Division, coinciding with my last year at Beaupré.

Lawsie's house became a flourishing city within Cibola as Morroco. Who chose the name I am not sure, nor whether either of us realised it is in Africa not a town but a country. There is no contemporary record of its spelling, so I adopted the one above in *Seventeen* to separate it slightly more from our own world. Zanzibar was by now almost a ghost town (Hank had never built a big army of his own). The most exciting city was Casablanca (Maillebourne) but there could be no real challenge to Blood City in Isle Bridge Road as the capital. It went equally without saying that the league Lawsie ran that same season was the Second Division.

With only twenty games – twenty-five minutes each, thirty for internationals or cup finals – needed to complete the whole league programme, it would not last a whole school year. The only extant copy of the *Cibolan News* is dated Saturday 13 January, from which we can deduce 1968. It led with news of the Maffia killing Tiny Tim's brother and featured a list of its fifty top agents (number one was Long John Silver). The final international tables and scorers' list were published, as well as a pre-cup final interview with Long Horns, the Ajax manager talking to Casey Jones.

Like me, Robert was an only child. His mum always made me feel welcome when I cycled to their house, twenty or thirty men in the white plastic saddlebag behind the seat of my red bike. Joyce was tickled when, sitting together at a grammar school induction night for parents, Christine remarked that our new headmaster was 'a bit of all right'. They were both indulgent of what they probably called our hobby. Our exchanges with each other's parents never went beyond the formalities of hello, goodbye, and yes please when offered something to eat or drink.

I fear I may have casually given up Lawsie's name as a fellow enthusiast when spilling the beans in Joe's English class. Despite the magazine article (where he was not mentioned), neither of us took any flak from our schoolmates beyond a half-hearted teasing for a couple of days. There were either smaller fry, wider eccentricities to attack, or the whole thing was not as age inappropriate as I had feared it might be seen. I never took any men to school, as I had on at least one occasion to Beaupré. The Young Faithfuls' captain, Coluna, had to be rescued off the corrugated roof of the bike sheds by Stan himself – janitor Kelly Hite was too disobliging an old sod to ask – when he came to fetch us in from playtime.

I see now that my concern some pages back, over my age on leaving Beaupré, was due mainly to stupidity at maths. If there were kids in Mrs Booley's class aged nine to eleven, then why wouldn't I be older than the average in my second year? Any old road (as Uncle Bob used to say), at the end of my first grammar school term I was aged 12.1 against an average of 11.9. To be close to the norm, or at least not too far from it in the unfavoured direction, was important to us all. The opinions we formed of each other then would suffer little modification through the rest of our schooldays, beyond them in some cases.

Without much effort of memory, forty years on (as our school song, more famously Harrow's, has it) I could jot down twenty-five of the thirty names in 1A. Six I can say were from villages, including Stuart Lunn from Upwell, a hulking blonde boy we had certainly not seen in the Cubs' football team. Stephen Doughty was parachuted in from up north, with an accent Joe tried to make sound less mockworthy to us.

'I remember we had one lad from Yorkshire, a much stronger accent than Doughty's. He said to me one day, when I must have told him off for being late or something, see if you can guess what he meant – "Annocumbackinsuh, acumbussin".'

Sideways smirks at Doughty, who had no more idea than the rest of us – or if he did, wasn't letting on.

'All the poor boy was telling me was he'd come to school on the bus, not a bicycle. He couldn't be blamed for being late then, do you see?'

Many of the Wisbech boys were able to continue their primary school friendships, if not too far separated by alphabetical accident. Ramnoth Road was the biggest provider of pupils in our year, with rumours the teachers had given them a hand in the eleven-plus; from Peckover came another sizeable contingent.

Gary Rider, of Ramnoth Road, was a known footballing prodigy, named almost instantly captain of the Under-12 football team. Although our surly gym teacher Hippie could intervene if he chose, team selection was essentially down to Gary, the only pupil in those first weeks the rest of us would address by his given name.

I suppose there must have been some boys who did not play football before and after school, at morning, dinner and afternoon breaks. What I can't get straight in my mind is where they were. Every square inch of playground was part of somebody's pitch, with school doors and spaces between the wooden struts of bike sheds popular as goals. One of these was usually kept by a third former in a wheelchair, of which he made quite a weapon, and not just a defensive one.

Our longest series of games was United fans against the rest, which happily put me on the same side as Gary. It also shows the popularity of the team of the Holy Trinity – Best, Law and Charlton – at a school founded by the town's Guild of the Holy Trinity, in a part of England lacking any First Division team. For Sundays' *Match of the Week* we were fed so much Second-Division Hull City that Ken Wagstaff's striking proficiency (and prolificity) grew stale.

A teacher or two would be on playground duty, as alert to the chant of 'Fight! Fight! Fight!' as their charges were quick to form a ring around the boys involved. From the authorities' fear of property damage, we were restricted to a particular kind of ball, on sale at a window near the top of the sloping playground, alongside a limited selection of confectionery. Bigger than a tennis ball, in hard hatched plastic, single primary-coloured, a ball's life was limited on the rough paving of the playground. Pristine and with some degree of bounce it soon became scuffed; stuffed with paper once the outer shell had split, its days were numbered until someone sprang for a new one. There was no discernible pressure to be that someone, nor credit gained by the provider, which seems odd in a world where most other things were as strictly ordered as the customers in a barber's shop. Perhaps the order in the supplying of balls was of that same invisible, unspoken kind.

The games were generally played in reasonable spirit, with a tumble likely to rip your trousers. We may have sloughed off our blazers in spring or summer; otherwise, we had no option but to play in uniform. If there was sometimes a heady scent to some of us after the dinner break, our teachers must have been as inured as the boys; I never felt it, smelt it or heard it mentioned.

Each year generally kept to its own game or games. One day I kicked a ball on our patch back into the second-formers. I hadn't seen Steve chasing it. 'You cocky little twat, who do you think you are?' He booted me solidly up the arse and was gone. Hierarchy was all.

Apart from breaking up fights, teachers only came to spoil the fun if an outbreak of cockles and mussels occurred. Tom Russell never noticed us at school, which was understood and fine, until one day he invited Lawsie and me to join a growing band of his year-mates. He did me the favour of standing me against the wall, with my back to it. Half a dozen or more boys then formed a chain away from it. The first placed his head between my legs, clutching the backs of my knees. The others followed suit, grabbing the front of the next boy's legs, shoulders hunched at the back of his thighs. We had not been told what the game was, only that we wouldn't get hurt. Nor were we, in fairness. A line of yelling boys ran up to vault as far along the line of backs as they could, pressing further and further forward as they tried to break it. Tom had looked out for me. I was under no pressure at all, while the others risked being mashed to the concrete playground or, in the case of the first one, ground into the wall.

The change of mood that ended the football matches for (much rarer) cockles and mussels was as unplanned as the odd times in Outwell when someone would bring a bat and ball to the playing field for cricket. It was as short-lived too, drawing a prohibition in assembly against the 'idiotic and dangerous thuggery some of you seem to think can be classified as a game'. Pleased though we were to have been enlisted by Tom, I don't think Lawsie or I were sorry.

There was no problem in anyone at all playing football during breaks. It was a different matter for Hippie to guarantee an appearance in the Under-12s to every boy who cared to attend the trials. I don't remember how these went, but I was selected for the season opener on 21 October 1967 against Queen's School.

Queen's was the Wisbech secondary modern, as which it had many more pupils than us, albeit lacking a sixth form. Their equivalent of Gary was related to me, second son of Mum's cousin Eileen. Trevor 'Tiddler' Scott had been known, despite his lack of height, to go into battle for slights against his older brother Martin, lamed by polio. Martin, reportedly handy himself with his fists, may not always have been aware of these insults.

Trevor's nickname was nothing to do with his size. Family knew he had been seen as a toddler peeing on a headland, with someone thinking to tease him as a 'tiddler'. He and I were friendly, and I could brag on his footballing talent. Queen's was a regular on the fixture list, faced three times including that first one in the nine games the Under-12s played through March 1968.

I was excited enough to dream about the match the night before we played it. We all know dreams don't always come true. This one sadly did, in the form of a 0–0 draw. It was the only scoreless match I ever played in at school. As centre-forward I had to take some blame, along with John Burbridge beside me at inside-right. Burbridge would become Burby then Herby and, some way down the track, a good mate. Now I could only brood on the brown-haired kid from Alpha and Emneth (a village halfway between Outwell and Wisbech) picking a chance off my feet to blast it wide himself.

The school shirt was in big squares of dark and light blue, alternating like a fragment of a chess board. Neither Herby nor I wore it again for the Under-12s. His place went to Doughty, a powerful striker who perhaps started term a bit late; mine was occupied by a different pretender every week – Chapman, Matthews, Murray, Staveley, not Lawsie for some reason – as Hippie honoured his pledge to give everyone a game.

There was little consolation in playing for 1A against Alpha, or in matches for Clarkson's House team (red, they got that right for me) against Holmes', Crane's or Parke's. Those three earned their Houses in return for more tangible property, as seventeenth century benefactors of the school, noted Wisbechians whereas the red, blue, green and yellow Houses at Beaupré were named after heroes of Empire – Clive, Cook, Wolfe and Livingstone, respectively. Mr Hipwell's comments in my first grammar school report that autumn I chose to view as satirical: 'Good. He is a member of the Under-12 XI Soccer Team.' He could have written the same for every boy in the fucking year.

Chapter Twenty-Three

Foreign Exchange

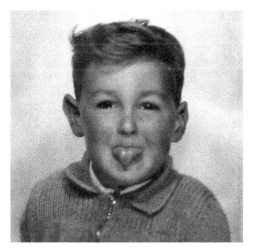

Giving tongue

I dreaded any of my Beaupré mates finding out I could not make the grammar school football team. Just as bad would have been for them to hear me called 'Bailey', the use of surnames in the village a mortal insult by now. Although the teachers persisted with these, the pupils did not. I soon became 'Bill' to everyone. I was surprised to learn that Dad had once been too, perhaps *his* dad since the song 'Won't You Come Home, Bill Bailey?' dates from before the First World War. I knew there was another Bailey two years ahead of me at grammar, but not until years later that he was another David Bailey. Our paths never crossed to confirm what he was called in the playground.

I had an odd shyness about revealing my new name to my Outwell mates, as if it somehow diminished me. It seemed I didn't need to say anything, for 'Bail' was soon gone for ever, the village taking to 'Bill' without any obvious input from the town.

It hurt me badly not to be a regular in the Under-12s, undoubtedly more than no longer to be top of the class. I placed third in each of that first year's report cards, of which I will spare you the exegesis I gave those from Beaupré. I do not lack the source material, all folded inside my primary school report book.

Class positions were based exclusively on exam results. In no subject did I come lower at the end of 1A than fifth, where I landed for geography, general science and physics. Science was the strength of the lad who came second, Stephen Wenn from Upwell. A head taller than most first years and nephew of the Outwell butcher, he would be called Charlie after him when we dropped surnames.

It was vexing in the extreme that top of the class was the same boy who played most regularly at centre-forward for the Under-12s. Ben Staveley was from Ramnoth Road, so I consoled myself that he was either a pet of Gary's or doing his homework. He had straight, fine blonde hair, and wore glasses to play. 'If you head the ball properly, using your forehead, they won't get in the way,' said Hank, who liked to pontificate on the game. 'I don't care if Murray was in dreamland right out by the corner flag. If I think that for one second, out of the corner of his eye, the goalkeeper might have caught the slightest glimpse of him, then he is interfering with play. Offside.' While unluckier boys might have specs smashed into their face by a stray ball or elbow, Ben – neither Milky Bar Kid nor Joe 90 stuck for long – kept his sports pair unscathed. He showed the same proficiency to come first or second in virtually every subject, earning the top spot on aggregate.

If Mum and Dad were disappointed at my third, I'm sure they hid it behind talk of big ponds and little ponds or finding my feet. While I was not the most outgoing of boys, many were shyer, so that settling into the Grammar was not too much of a trial. 'Energetic and decisive he has made a very good start in his new surroundings,' was Basil's view as form master.

Trying to impress Joe no doubt, I came second in English as in maths for Mr Carkeek. Thinning on top, Rex Carkeek had something of the slim dandy look of a Rex Harrison, sporting luxuriant flared sideboards, which were forbidden to the boys (a purely theoretical prohibition for 1A). While many masters would relax their cramming of us with facts, if not their discipline, at the dog-end of terms once exams were over, he would only unbutton to the extent of showing us mathematical puzzles not strictly related to the syllabus. I put one of Uncle Ted's to him.

'You've got a hundred pounds, sir, and you have to buy exactly a hundred animals. Sheep are a pound each, chickens a shilling and cows five pounds. You've got to have at least one of each, and you have to spend all the money.'

While I expect to remember the answer as long as I remember anything, I don't claim to have solved it myself. Mr Carkeek spent time enough at the blackboard in silence, chalk in hand and gown to the class, to give us hope he wouldn't either. He did, by trial and error I suppose; he did not come up with some quick and easy solution, so family honour was satisfied. If there was a point in history when those prices were realistic, alone or relative to each other, it will never return. For children of a brighter age the poser is no different putting chickens at 5p a beak.

Divinity was a new word for me, if not a new subject. I don't remember it ever being called anything else at grammar, so was surprised to see 'Scripture' on the report card, albeit only for our first year. The teacher Alex Stuart was a young ginger-haired enthusiast, as much in reffing our football as in the classroom.

The many hours spent at Sunday school and Boys' Brigade had nothing to do with my only unqualified first in class at scripture. The same can be said more emphatically of Stan's dabbling and my first place in French (is there a French word for 'eminence'?) by year end. Mr Booley may have been right about my accent, but Mr Wiseman was right to describe my memory as excellent, for me a key element in learning any foreign language. Though ye speak with the tongues of angels, if you can't master the vocab you will stay firmly earthbound.

Our French teacher happened to live in Outwell, down Beaupré Avenue. Mr Fuller's nickname, entrenched and unexplainable, was Henry. Once we had progressed beyond Messieurs Petitrond and Maigrecorps, he played to this by naming any French character in his dictations or illustrations Henri. Like Hank he was probably younger than he seemed to us, wearing a short back and sides and a parting in his hair.

Henry was not one to shout, maintaining discipline comfortably enough without recourse to the slipper, lines his last resort. One Saturday afternoon in Wisbech Library I came upon a boy from Alpha, seeking peace and space to write his repetitive penance conventionally rather than using three pens at once, gripped between your four fingers and secured by thumb. This was a skill more touted than mastered. If Jonno's lines were from Henry, they would be fifty in number, alive with alliteration: 'Projecting projectiles is a project not worth pursuing' was the punishment for a paper plane dogfight in the Nissen huts one day.

As with tables at primary school, much of our early French learning was by drill, repetition: *je suis*, *tu es*, *il est* and so on, with regular tests of vocabulary we were expected to acquire as homework. There was no whisper of language labs, but a chance to improve our accents was offered by Henry for the Easter holiday. Wisbech is twinned with Arles in Provence, a fact unknown about a place unheard of by me at that time. Every year exchange trips were organised, the English visit returned in their summer vacs by the French.

The trips were not limited to grammar school kids. I have no idea of the selection process, nor if the school subsidised its pupils in any way. Mum told me the cost was £25, probably then more than the weekly wage of an average working man. Dad wasn't working, yet I was told from the start I could go if I wanted. My education came first. That was the mantra, one I did not appreciate at the time.

It was no small undertaking. The only family in the generation above mine to have travelled abroad – Dad, Uncles Ted, Bob and Bobby – had done so in the forces. For their generation, Bailey and Goldsmith uncles and a grandad had not returned from France. Fifty years on, there was nothing to fear except what Mum may have dreamed up for herself.

Organisation of the logistics was smoother and more competent than that of our generals in the Great War. There was at least one meeting in a schoolroom at Wisbech (not the Grammar), where we watched a slide show, were allowed to ask questions and told £5 was the most any child could take as pocket money. Exchange controls were in place, albeit at a somewhat higher level. The motive was more likely to avoid the accompanying adults being given larger sums in custody to dole out to their charges 'or in case anything happens, you never know over there'. It meant also nobody would be lord or ladying it over their fellows in conspicuous consumption.

Mum and Dad struck up an acquaintance with the parents of Alan Lindsay, the only other grammar first-former on the trip that year. He was top of the class in Alpha (not a huge achievement). With hair so blonde it was almost white and a frame that would have been spindly with a bit more weight on it, Alan was saved from anonymity by his skill as a footballer. Playing left-half for the school team, without saying much more on the pitch than he did off it he was a fearless tackler, with a good left foot that helped give balance to the side. He was a Clarkson's Housemate of mine, the mainstay of our defence.

Alan had the window seat beside me on the bus as we waited at six in the morning to leave the Horsefair, wishing our parents would do the same rather than hang about for a final wave. There was no culture of hugs and kisses in those days. There might be a clap on the back from Dad, a lot of verbal fussing from Mum, reinforced by tentative dabs at my arm.

'I wonder if my French will be good enough,' worried Alan. 'I can count to a hundred… I think.'

I told him I was sure he could.

'Un, deux, trois, quatre…'

I told him several times more, as he laboured along like Mr Jones doling out precious redcurrant coins one by one: 'quarante-cinq, quarante-six, quarante-sept…' I couldn't believe he would go all the way through until he did, arriving modestly at 'cent' after a bit of a wobble around the eighty mark. It looked like it would be a long trip.

Chapter Twenty-Four

Letters from France

Rue Rouget de l'Isle
with Christian 1968

It was indeed a long trip: coach to Victoria then trains to Paris, with the cross-channel stretch from Dover to Calais by hovercraft. We overnighted at the Hotel Alhambra near the Place de la Bastille, with a guided coach tour of the capital the next morning: Montmartre, Place de la Concorde, Arc de Triomphe, most of the big sights in short, including the Eiffel Tower without time to go up it before catching a train from Gare de Lyon for the ten-hour journey to Arles in the Camargue, less than thirty miles from the Mediterranean. On our return we would take the overnight sleeper train back to Paris.

Apart from Alan, with whom I casually lost contact as soon as we changed transport, there were a couple of other grammar boys on the trip. Fourth-former Phillip Mott – his surname was comical, for a reason I didn't quite understand – had a fringe of hair almost as thick as his glasses. He lived in Beaupré Avenue, too remote in age for me to have heard of at primary school. The other was Stu, noticeably more friendly to me amongst the exchange trippers than he could allow himself to be at the school dinner table.

Very apt to be attracted to girls, I still lacked any idea of how to talk to them. Motty and Stu were prepared to pursue their interest further, competing for a while to gain the attention of one in our group on the long train ride south. I think it was a Christine, possibly older than any of us, to whom Stu was getting as close as he could, using me as a mascot.

'He may only be a first-former, but he's sound. He knows what's what.'

Up I piped like a performing pre-schooler. 'I know what a leiblem is.'

Puzzled, Stu gallantly continued to back me. 'See, I told you he knows all the words.'

'What is it then?' Christine was more forthright.

'It's a girl who likes other girls.'

'That's a lesbian, you twerp,' she was not unkind enough to say. She did put me right though, while her pitying smile at Stu cut me to the bone. I felt worse for showing his trust in me to be misplaced than for looking like an idiot.

The trip was between 9 and 17 April 1968, including the Easter weekend. Assigned to our host families on reaching Arles after ten at night, any further contact between the English party depended on the extent to which they took part in the formal programme organised by the twinning committee. This included receptions and sightseeing tours, not just in Arles but the surrounding countryside. We visited Daudet's windmill, of which I have no recollection.

My exchange partner was Christian, aged fourteen at the time to my twelve and significantly bigger. He was handsome in that curly-haired, hollow-cheeked, leather-jacketed Gallic way for which I can't think of a film star example.

All my parents' pre-trip correspondence was with Christian's mother Angeline (we always called her 'Madame'). Mr Fuller kindly provided them with translations from her French. She proved to be smaller than me, with a short haircut of jet black; her cheekbones were high enough to threaten its fringe, a prominent nose making her face all sharp angles; she might have been witchlike with another foot of height and without her constant smile. Christian took me to visit his father once during my stay, at some place of work with a lot of gleaming agricultural machinery. He gave me a John Deere keyring.

We would always think of Madame as a nurse, which suited her though in fact her self-introduction to us by letter was as a secretary in a health clinic. She had no trouble keeping us and her other two children in order with a mixture of brisk efficiency and motherly clucking. With Christian the oldest, she trod the fine line of letting him feel like the man of the house without burdening him with those responsibilities. From the first, she treated me like one of her own children in the most unaffected way.

I had not been studying French long enough to be fluent, far from it. I suspect Christian had more English than he was ever prepared to use. Angeline had none. Yet we managed fine. Our main contact was at mealtimes, when it was simple enough to get by with gestures if all else failed. Madame had asked pre-arrival for as much detail as possible on my culinary tastes. Wishing only to be polite, Dad (all correspondence was one of his jobs) had written no more than that I preferred savoury food to sweet. She soon had me at work on a detailed list, probably one of her kids' English vocab sheets, ticking or (predominantly) crossing out each item. Mum had not quite dared to say I must not be served salad, but such items inevitably drew an X.

In Provence, breakfast was not a poached egg on toast. We all had bowls – a blue-ringed pattern on them – of café au lait, probably strong on the milk and weak on the coffee. That was OK, dunking into it bread which would hardly have submitted to a toaster. The baguettes, fresh from the bakery each morning, were on the table with a knife beside them throughout every meal. There were varieties of jam at breakfast, but I would not normally smear anything more than butter on my slices. Madame would be buzzing around with a cup of black coffee, usually busier serving others than feeding herself, as insubstantial in weight as in height.

Dinner in the evening was a more problematic meal, partly because I never knew quite where we were in it. It was disconcerting to be served a plate of peas with no accompaniment other than the trusty crusty bread. How proud

I was to learn they were called petits pois, never dreaming they would be sold under exactly that name in English supermarkets before my hair turned grey. The meat we had was probably of better quality than we bought in England, where we never had steak. Unknown being bad – see also salad – I did not fully enjoy the steaks I was given in Arles, feeding a good part of them to the family cat. Seeing my conservatism, Angeline may have fed us more chips (frites) than her kids normally got. I enjoyed the egg and bacon with which she would sometimes open the meal, the eggs fried on top of the bacon not curled beside it and – here's the Gallic touch of genius for you – the ketchup squirted onto it *in the very pan*, so it too came hot to the table. There was an epic egg and potato salad, the better I had to concede for the oil in which it was steeped.

The only true conversion she made – it was Damascene – was with *tomates farcies*. The huge local tomatoes could be bought already stuffed with their mince at the local butcher's, ready to go into the oven before being eaten with bread. I can pay them no higher compliment than to say I did not miss potatoes when they were served.

Food was important to us all, without becoming an obsession. I don't remember anything of our midday meals, perhaps bread and ham – I never ate cheese – taken between Madame puttering off to work on her moped and returning in the evening. We were left to amuse ourselves all day, which we did easily enough with a football between us.

Number 2, 'our' house was the first on the right as you turned into Rue Rouget de l'Isle from the town-centre side. I did not know I had absorbed the fact until a few years later, in an end-of-term French quiz, I was able to name for bonus points dear old Rouget as the writer of the Marseillaise. Opposite us, presumably Number 1, was a blank house wall, to which a smaller garden one was connected by a sheet-metal door, set back from the street above a stone step perhaps a foot high.

The door was our goal. Christian, a Saint-Étienne fan at a time when they were France's most successful team (a bit like being top in Alpha), said he followed cycling more than football. I understood the words, but the sentiment was incomprehensible. Cycling was not a sport. At football we were unevenly matched, yet not enough so for me to give up. We would play one against one, banging the ball at the keeperless goal. He would always win, by a margin like 15–11; if young Michel played on my side, the balance tipped and Christian would never win. We spent hours in that way, mainly one-on-one. Michel may not have had the interest; nor did he have his brother's obligation to entertain the visitor.

We were close to a main road, which led straight towards the centre of Arles. Passing in tree-shaded areas outside cafés what to us were old men playing boules (which I was happy to take as an exact physical as well as verbal replica of bowls, having no more interest in either French or English version of the pastime than in cycling), it was only a fifteen-minute walk. I was shown the places where Van Gogh set up his easel, marked by stones rough and heavy enough to prove nasty stumbling blocks for the unwary. If I was also shown churches and museums, nothing of them remained with me. When we got into town, it was usually to meet Christian's friends.

Moving among these older teenagers – I don't know where they had left their English visitors – was like being back with Geoff Chappell and his mates around the Monopoly board. I could display my precocity with a few hard-learned, well-turned phrases in French, just as I had early understood the orange and dark blue sets are all you need to win. Still, much of the conversation and all the jokes will have passed me by.

Christian became much less serious, or perhaps just less bored, when we were sitting in a café, more than willing to play the fool with slapstick French clowning. His best friend was Jean-Paul, improbably tall, brown suede-jacketed and smoking as if he'd already given up on his teeth, which were yellow verging on green. And yet… and yet beside him, hanging on his every word and often on his arm, was the most beautiful girl I'd ever seen.

Although Ani was a year or two older than I, physically mature, her body was not voluptuous. It was her face that won me: dark brown eyes, a tanned Mediterranean complexion, teeth as bright as her boyfriend's were grimy, most of all a smile she was ready to bestow on me from time to time.

I fantasised about kissing her lips, on purpose but as if by accident, in that exchange of pecks on both cheeks I was struggling to come to terms with as occurring between males. The attraction was sexual as well as romantic, and it hurt badly to see her kissing Jean-Paul in more than greeting. That pain had to be endured as the admission price to gawp and wonder at her.

Christian moved with equal familiarity from male to female friends, without having a girlfriend in the only sense I could understand the term. Perhaps he fancied one of the English girls. There must have been some organised group outings. Didn't we go to the Roman aqueduct at Avignon?

The bullfight was at the option of each host family, probably for reasons of cost more than conscience.

Until the Arles trip became a possibility, I had assumed bullfighting to be exclusively Spanish. In fact it was popular enough to sustain a circuit in southern France too, a proper one on which the bulls bled and died rather than one of tilting in play only. If there was already a strong feeling in England against bullfighting, like foxhunting it was not a topic that had ever come up in Outwell.

Some of the English kids spoke of having gone to see the matadors in training, rehearsal or whatever the proper term is, meeting and greeting them. I was happy enough to go to the main event, without any idea of whether our seats were soleil or ombre, plebeian or pricey. One square yard on a stone bench in an amphitheatre was much the same as another, though I might have thought differently in the height of summer.

I was predisposed to favour the bulls. If there was no outright disapproval of the spectacle, there was a residual English feeling that they got a raw deal. This was reinforced as the picadors rooted with their lances into the creature's flanks, while it tried to get through the mattress-like padding to the underbelly of the horse. The toreadors with their banderillas (how the swot in me loved all this new vocab) did not seem heroic as they left their beribboned blades in its neck. The matador was seen to be taking on a sadly depleted animal, one perhaps already sensing the end. All that was true, and yet from the second bull onward I was cheering for my own race. Some of this was the influence of the crowd. More was empathy outweighing sympathy. I could only imagine myself as the human in that ring.

Although I would not have missed the bullfight, I would not clamour to attend the next day, or regret its absence back in England. I bought myself some bullfighter figures. I hesitate to call them soldiers, since they would end up on my bedroom mantelpiece, too effete with their berets and swirling capes to mix with the Zunis. A bronze bull in aggressive stance, one front foot raised in readiness to paw the ground, took up residence on the living-room mantelpiece, the most expensive gift I brought home. I had plenty of photos too, in the fashion of the day as slides, which meant I never saw them again after one interminable evening in Wisbech, when everyone got a chance to project the ones they had taken at a closing meeting of that year's exchange group.

As I came back for my last term in 1A, my knowledge of French greatly improved, Mum and Dad must have wondered how Outwell could offer Christian the sort of experiences Arles had given me, when the summer holidays brought the return fixture. I wondered what I could offer when we met again to impress Ani, a girl still totally unaware of her impact on me.

Chapter Twenty-Five

Big Fights

He had a curious technique for hitting Mum.

It was usually his bouts of illness that led to trouble. When he was well, things were fine, affectionate even, between them. His pet name for her was Liz, or occasionally lollops. Seeking to copy this endearment at some point I was corrected to that from 'trollop', as I had innocently misspoken.

One day I was attracted by a simmering row to stand at their bedroom door. He was in the bed, she sitting on it at the side nearer the door, by the fireplace.

'You're a hypocrite,' he was saying when I began to listen.

'What did you call me?'

'You heard. Hypocrite.'

Perhaps she made him repeat it to give her time to formulate a response. This came as a crisp slap to his face. He sat quickly upright in bed, pulling her towards him. Once he had her head immobilised against his stomach, bent towards his lap, he applied himself to smacking the back of her neck. He used palms rather than fists. His look was one of concentration as much as anger. She cried, there would be a period of separation within the house, then reconciliation. 'I'm a rotten bugger,' he said once, which she immediately protested was not so.

I would not consider myself a mummy's boy, yet my sympathies were all with Joyce. Allen never spoke to me of their rows. She still insisted they were a normal part of married life, with the faintest hint that I was perhaps over-reacting. Certainly, we heard shouting and screaming from neighbours at times. There was a separate world behind closed doors to that of the streets, where at least the semblance of harmony must be maintained. It was a community where everyone knew each other, and the walls between terraced houses were not soundproof.

The fact of Mum forgiving Dad so readily, so often, did not incline me to do so. The violence could have been worse, of course it could. The slap and the sting of her tongue showed it was not all on one side. At the time, I lacked that perspective.

The rows were, as I grew older, increasingly the exception to a rule of relative contentment. Mum was not entirely unhappy to have Dad at home. Once in a while he would try to extend his horizons, as for instance when he developed a friendship with our next-but-one neighbours on the other side from the Chapmans (now a different family with the same surname as the Chuffers).

Beyond the Churchyards towards Isle Bridge Road, set at right angles to our house, lived Ernie and Violet, always Mr and Mrs Betts to me. This marked not just their seniority – they were of my grandparents' generation – but a lack of warmth on their part, kindling none in me. Ernie would normally nod when we passed, he usually on or with the bike that took him to land work somewhere. Violet was a borderline frightening figure, shrewish and dwarfish in features as well as stature, with a shock of white hair over thick glasses.

Violet was, as I grew older, increasingly seen outdoors only in her wheelchair, pushed if not by Ernie then by Sid Cole. When Mum referred to him as their lodger, the word was always in inverted commas. Any present or past sexual relationship she implied between Sid and Violet did not seem to affect his relationship with Ernie. Both men wore flat caps, yet there was something more urbane about Sid, a slightly less worn and grimy look to his clothes. Dapper he was not, except in comparison to Ernie.

The three of them would use one of the village pubs, perhaps more than one. Violet was often at her most boisterously disagreeable on their return. As her independent mobility reduced, their drinking became more housebound, only Sid still venturing forth – he did always have a smile for me. Dad began spending time in their house during the afternoon.

Mum had no need to worry about him becoming a drunkard. I never saw him seriously affected by alcohol. He was probably in the best shape of any when he returned to our house in Princes Street one night with my uncles Tom and Brian. While Tom tried to put the lead on the arse end of Nick to walk him, Brian sat on the stairs. He told me seriously, more than once, that I mustn't tell Grandad George about this. It went down in family history as a mildly comic incident, the night they had somehow been caught unawares by the strength of Newcastle Brown Ale.

If Dad was drinking anything with his new friends, it would only have been the odd bottle of beer. Mum was always concerned with village and neighbour perceptions. She may have used these as a none too discreet lever, she may have used the cost of that bottle of beer (though it would have been far worse for him to accept one from them without paying his way); whatever her tools, the flirtation soon ended, and he was back to the blank afternoon television screen at home. To be scrupulously fair, he may have reached the conclusion unprompted that this was better than sitting with three bibulous septuagenarians while he waited for his wife to come home from work.

Mum took the feeding of her family seriously. I would get breakfast in bed, usually an egg on toast, before she went off to work. In my blazer pocket there was always a bar of chocolate or packet of crisps. While I was scrapping for my chips at school dinnertime, Mum would be biking home to put a couple of rashers under the grill for Dad.

As I opened the back door, home from school at around quarter to five, I developed the habit of announcing my day's doings to Mum in the style of ITV's then *News at Ten*. 'Boing,' I would stab at Big Ben, 'ten out of ten in maths test.' She was properly interested, amid the preparations for tea. 'Boing – only sixteen out of twenty for divinity – but the best in the class.' It was always good news I gave her.

Three-seater

197

Almost as soon as the headlines were over, at five, we would sit down to our cooked tea. I was never reluctant. Dad would only be late to table if he was engrossed in a chore, one that fell to him such as mending a bike chain. I would then be treated to Mum's glances at his plate, the second call that tea was ready, the pursed lips through which she offered to put it in the oven, unable to settle to her own meal until at last he came in, notching her vexation up one more level by washing his hands where the pots were already waiting for her attention as soon as we finished eating. The thought of anyone happening upon unwashed dishes was anathema to her. Dad and I were both touched when the council put a new sink in the kitchen. Mum was so proud of it; for the first few days she carried all the plates into the wash-house to do, never mind our teasing.

Our meals would be meat and potatoes with one green vegetable, tea to drink, maybe a rice pudding from the oven for dessert. Perhaps we had chips sometimes in the week, as we invariably did on Saturday. Before bedtime I was always offered supper, always accepted it. Crisp sandwiches – Golden Wonder, cheese and onion – were a favourite, with hot milk as the drink for one spell, in 1969 because I remember *Judge Dee* being on television.

I could never understand the older generation's preoccupation with the news (unless it was my news). They would watch the teatime bulletin without fail, then the BBC at nine and/or ITV at ten. The weather forecast being at the end meant the whole programme had to be endured.

I was never forced to miss a favourite programme because it clashed with something Mum and Dad wanted to watch. Our tastes in some things (Benny Hill, Frankie Howerd, both enjoyed more by Dad than Mum) were similar. *Coronation Street* was an automatic choice on Mondays and Wednesdays at seven thirty. If I did not follow it slavishly, I always knew what was going on there. Our set was black-and-white; we had BBC and ITV, not BBC2 from its launch in 1964. The only downside to this was that I did not catch the early series of *Monty Python's Flying Circus*. Maybe I took a dislike to that gang in part as a defence mechanism, not having been able to parrot their sketches the next day at school as we would with the fabulous Marty Feldman.

Dad had his regular armchair nearest to the television, by the bay window, cigarettes and ashtray close by though used sparingly – less than a whole packet of ten a day, perhaps. His legs would be extended towards the fireplace, crossed at the ankles, with the top foot constantly twitching from side to side in a wholly unconscious motion. Mum would occupy the other armchair, with me on the three-seater settee against the wall to the other downstairs room. If it was a cold night with a fire going, Mum would sometimes suggest 'pulling the settee up'. She could not prevail on me to join them on it, sometimes holding hands for heaven's sake, except for one (later) photograph where my beaming face belies the defensive body language of tightly folded arms as I sit between them. It must have been if not Christmas then some family occasion, to provide the photographer and the glass of sparkling wine in Mum's hand.

If my parents were not on the settee, it was mine to share with the cats. You need not tremble for these. I got on fine with black Smoky then her sons Willy and Wally. One of those was impertinent enough in his youth to have a wet dream right there beside me, milky fluid flooding the fur around the base of his penis.

Without any threat from me, Willy and Wally were lucky to survive. More than one litter was drowned in the outside toilet, between coalhouse and kitchen. Malky Smith from two doors further down, an uncle of Henry, was enlisted to put the blind creatures, born in our airing cupboard and catching us all unawares, into a potato sack for dispatch. Since they were shoved under the bowl's water level anyway, the flush must have been to drown whatever sounds they made in death. This was clearly a man's job, one Dad took on himself for the next batch.

Smoky died from natural causes or on the road. I have no memory, and Mum's on enquiry did not stretch to the existence of the cat and her young. Willy and Wally took to spending days and nights away as they grew up, no doubt searching for the waking stuff of feline wet dreams through the village. One day we must have given up on their return, spared at least any view of them as roadkill.

I too was spending less time on the settee, with the advent of homework since the first weeks at grammar, two or at most three subjects a night. I did this at our bureau, which we had moved in from the back room for that purpose. It stood between the kitchen door and the one leading to the hall and sitting room, against the wall so that, when I had pulled down its writing surface above the two drawers, my back was to the television. There was no need for my parents to limit their viewing, as it did not distract me.

I never considered skipping homework; nor, as far as I recall, did many of my classmates. It wasn't unduly onerous, though I smart at the time I wasted on some of the history for Hank Skinner. He liked his essays presented with imaginative 'artistic' flourishes. As avid for high marks as I had been for stars from Mrs Booley, I took it upon myself one night to use a different coloured pencil, in a sequence of say half a dozen, for each *letter* in the essay. Imagine going back to your earliest days of wielding a writing implement, before joined-up script. The effort was ridiculously disproportionate. Dad had more success for Hank with his sketch of a Viking longboat, which still drew a lower mark than Paul Dewey's with a pattern of different-coloured waves crashing over it.

Allen would also, at least in my first year or two, look to support me at maths. 'Don't cry, I'm only trying to help' were his exact words once when I could or would not be convinced of the proposition he was making. Maybe it was flawed, and I was right to stand by my guns. Standing by his chair, I had not realised I was indeed on the point of tears, not from any physical fear – he never hit me, rarely shouted – but from some strange mixture of frustration and embarrassment.

Mum's forte was revision. She was always ready to take me into the kitchen (so we would not disturb the television, rather than the reverse) to hear me regurgitate pages of notes taken in history, geography or divinity. She would sit on a hard chair, while I ran single-net football training sessions for a few soldiers on the floor. My learning method was simply to read through the notes enough times for them to stick. I could get them nearly word for word without feeling resentful at the time needed to do so. It made it easier for Mum if I did not deviate from the text in front of her. We would go through French vocabulary and maths theorems in the same way, the latter with their triumphant QED sign-off. She tried to keep with me in algebra, genuinely wishing to understand how it worked. I was amazed at how readily she accepted, how diligently she worked through a load of 'homework' I set her – forty questions at least – which would have had the whole class in revolt had Rex given it to us.

We were keyed up to protest on Wednesday, 29 May 1968 when one of our teachers – maybe Basil, but I prefer to credit Joe – mentioned the H word. Tension soon became hero-worship when the assignment given was to watch United in the European Cup Final – *without* the need to write anything about it for school the next day.

While Dad's spell of attending local football at Wisbech or Lynn, with or without Uncle Charlie, was long past, they were both with me at Fenland Park one day in my early teens for an open day. Kids had a chance to beat the Town's keeper from the penalty spot, which Charlie congratulated me on doing.

Allen would usually watch *Match of the Day*, without my obsessive interest. Once I called him a goal-hanger, as he set off for bed when the programme's last one went in – a late equaliser for Sheffield Wednesday – without waiting for the credits. He paused, suspecting an unacceptable degree of cheek, before carrying on his way. Mum would usually be in bed already. She was, however, very much present (along with Dad, Uncle Charlie and Cousin Barrie – Aunt Doreen stayed home with her younger children) the first time I saw United in the flesh. They were at Nottingham Forest on Saturday, 28 October 1967, days before my twelfth birthday, the best and most imaginative present I would ever receive. The Trinity were all there, just before the King began a suspension. Nobby Stiles was the only absentee (through injury) of those considered the team's top stars; I like to think I also missed Tony Dunne.

While we lost that cold day in Nottingham and would not retain our league title, we had the holy grail of the European Cup at last within our reach, if not yet our grasp. I had loved Tommy Gemmell's thunderous goal for the Lisbon Lions against Inter the year before, in days when Celtic's links to United were strong and true. In 1968 we faced the mighty Benfica of Lisbon (Sport Lisboa e Benfica), Eusébio and all. Their centre-forward's nickname in those days was 'the Black Panther', his name always appeared without the accent (Eusebio), and he was rated second only to Pelé (Pele) in world football.

Benfica were humbled at Wembley by a sadly Lawless United. Denis is my all-time idol, yet Bobby – his baldness, as well as a certain quality of aloofness, making him seem almost of a different generation to the others – and Georgie had more than enough firepower to carry us through. If none of us guessed it was the last hurrah for that great team, it was one to cheer us through many of the hard years before we reclaimed our birthright at the top of the world.

As the great televised sporting experience of my boyhood, the United–Benfica final was at the opposite end of the scale to one I had keenly anticipated three years earlier. Part of the excitement in watching Ali (we still knew him better then as Cassius Clay) was the outlandish hour he would hit our screens. Dad probably had to intercede for Mum to let me get up at two or three in the morning of Wednesday, 26 May 1965 to watch him fight Sonny Liston.

Mum missed this rematch between the two men. She was in the kitchen to make tea, having ensured that I was warmly enough blanketed. Before the kettle could boil, Liston was down and out. I'm not sure we bothered with the cuppa before going back to bed.

Boxing was of less interest to me than wrestling, which I know some would not deign to classify as a sport. It was, however, undeniably entertainment, experienced live just once by me as a boy. On the only occasion I recall socialising with Grandad Bailey outside Railway Lane, he met us in King's Lynn. His younger son Brian remembered their trips to any local fair when he was a boy would always end in the boxing tent. Although Grandad would not pay money to get in the ring as a challenger to the fairground champion, he did put on the gloves from time to time among a group of mates.

The principal wrestling villain of the day, Mick McManus, was not on the bill that night in Lynn. We saw his tag partner and undisputed second in that league, Steve Logan, beating his chest and flicking his long, greasy black hair styled like a Red Indian's. Despite a row between Joyce and Allen before we set out, the evening was a success (and not just because it dissipated that atmosphere between them). I never saw any sign of an uneasy relationship between Allen and his father, though I recall little direct interaction between them either. Another recollection by Brian was of them going out together a few times for a drink in the Bridge. He heard (there were twenty-one years between the two brothers, so he could not have seen it) both that Cecil hit Allen as a boy and that he was upset to see him go off to war. 'He did love him,' my uncle offered, somewhere between hope and conviction.

My own sporting endeavours changed with the seasons and the school timetable. From football we progressed, in the worst of winter, to cross-country running. I was among the best half-dozen in our year, with stamina a greater attribute of mine at football than speed. Gym facilities did not extend much beyond the odd vaulting horse and medicine ball. Despite the close watch kept on the more dangerous weapons by the likes of Hank, I had a go at the discus as well as the javelin. My upper-body strength was minimal, and I did not excel at any of the track events. Still, I was never among the outright spastics, as we unaffectionately called them (we called everyone spastics, the fashionable term of all-purpose mild abuse for a spell). I did not need an excuse note for gym from Mum, such as a couple of boys brought in every week. Exasperated in his science class at the insolence of one of these, a tubby lad with a sharp tongue, Tommy Trinder asked rhetorically what was the matter with him. Stephen 'Till' Tyler almost got the slipper for answering: 'He's just had his period, sir.'

Rugby was not offered. Basketball was only for higher years. Some of these privileged creatures enjoyed access to the tennis courts at one end of Harecroft

Road. The school did not have a swimming pool, which unfortunately did not mean we were spared swimming. In the middle of April – summer term was reserved for cricket – we had to trek through town, past what few vessels still docked at Wisbech to the open-air municipal facilities.

Few of us could swim at all, let alone well. As we were sent into the small wooden cubicles to change, considerations of safety and hygiene were in any case higher priorities for our teachers than developing the next generation of Olympians. We were enjoined to use the toilet and blow our noses thoroughly before going anywhere near the water. The usual rules against horseplay, spitting, bombing or fighting were reinforced by the threat of a slippering, nobody caring to provoke Hippie by asking if that applied also to petting. The town pool's own form of punishment would only have spurred us on to deviant behaviour, ejection from the premises being our fondest wish, preferably before we touched the freezing water. Mr Hipwell gave his coaching tips in a tracksuit from poolside.

The stress of first finding a day with temperatures above, say, fifty Fahrenheit, then ensuring thirty boys' safety against the perils of cross-town traffic, drowning and hypothermia, meant our swimming lessons were few and far between. It cannot have been that the pool was ever overbooked. Its days were numbered, with an indoor complex including gyms, bars, squash and badminton courts available to us before we left the Grammar, along the Harecroft Road from the school's own sports fields.

The annual swimming gala was a muted affair. The few capable of staying afloat hardly had time to dry themselves during the afternoon, pressed as they were into every race. In contrast, Sports Day at Harecroft Road saw the whole school turn out, whether sporting or spectating. The competition was between Houses more than forms. My own role was more limited than the year before at Beaupré. I may have done a four hundred or eight hundred metres, individual or relay. What our headmaster chose to notice, walking round the running track with teachers or bigwigs, was my unscheduled fight with Eddie Gilroy.

Chapter Twenty-Six

Kraut

You know that old-school kind of school photograph, a strip perhaps four feet long and six inches high, where every pupil is captured? The photographer would slowly pan his camera from one end of the serried ranks to the other, giving an enterprising and nippy lad the chance to twin himself. By standing at one end and, as soon as the camera left it, scuttling behind the back row of boys to the other, he would appear twice on the print. At Wisbech Grammar in 1971, one otherwise blameless boy (Steve Allcoat) opted instead to frame a discreet V-sign at the lens. For all he might have argued it was only the way he happened to be standing, arms folded across the chest in an approved manner, the offending digits were smudged over in the version for sale to parents, at a cost of 50p to his dad and a call on the headmaster for him.

The staff photograph of May 1969 provides no such wide-angle challenge or opportunity, with only twenty-five figures. The outliers in the seated front row are two female secretaries or administrative assistants, beside urbane David 'Decker' Morgan, Head of Geography, and Rex Carkeek, whose gown shows a splash of colour – mauve I have to remember, as the photograph is black-and-white. Head of Classics (though he had no Greek) Ralph 'Taffy' Roberts and Joe Davy are closer to the centre on the outside of Mr and Mrs Neale – he first appointed teacher there in 1928, his wife school secretary since 1943 – respectively. Between the Neales sits the man named as Headmaster on the crested white envelope frame: D. S. Anderson, M.Sc., Ph.D.

The only 'doctor' among the teachers, Douglas Anderson did little teaching, a single class for me, subbing for Tommy Trinder at general science in my first year. He was as new to the school as we were, appointed in 1967 to replace an ailing A.O. Chesters, headmaster since 1940.

WGS staff 1969

I never knew Mr Chesters, from all I heard a kindly gentleman. I can hardly claim to have known Dr Anderson based on our handful of direct interactions – spotting my red socks in the corridor one day he told me I needed to 'shape up and conform' – but I suspect 'kindly' is a word few of my schoolmates would reach for to describe him. His nickname was 'Kraut', not ex officio but more likely a perception of the chill efficiency we had all seen a hundred times from German officers in war films.

During our first year I had no more contact with Eddie Gilroy in 1A than with Kraut. He was one of the handful of Catholics, mildly envied for being excused morning assembly. They were taken elsewhere; to do what, I never had the curiosity to ask. Whatever we were scrapping about on Sports Day, it wasn't religion.

We didn't get to the stage of trading punches. It was more of a wrestling match, albeit one with real hostile intent (unlike some of those we watched on TV). Obviously, Kraut didn't know us by name. He had Mrs Neale for that. We were ordered to separate at once, to reconvene outside his office on Monday, the next school day.

I doubt the summons made my News at Five broadcast. While it was useful to satisfy parental curiosity and draw praise, I dreaded their sympathy or concern in moments of trouble. Dad would have taken a robust view, seeing fighting as a normal part of growing up and probably adult life too. Mum would have pegged the other boy sight unseen as a bully, for standing up to whom I deserved no censure. I felt no need to involve either of them. Although

205

I was liable to fret and puzzle over forthcoming trials, this was done within the confines of my own head.

Screwed up to the sticking-books-down-trousers point, it was almost a disappointment not to have a caning to shrug off to classmates when I left the head's office with Eddie that Monday afternoon. Kraut may have realised this. Beyond stressing our role as representatives of Wisbech Grammar School, especially on public occasions, he did not let us take up too much of his time. Without deliberately avoiding each other – we stand side by side in the 2A form photograph – I don't recall that Eddie and I ever spoke again.

Apart from a 'Good!' on the first term, the head added no more than his signature to my three (termly) 1A report cards. I like to take any positive comments on them at face value. Still and all, I cannot help thinking there was an element of denial if not delusion in those of our art and woodwork masters.

John Hall stood over six feet, with wavy hair. He wore a sandy corduroy jacket, this mild deviation from the standard staff dress code of suit and – where earned – gown, the only hint he might be a man apart, an artist. We saw little of Wombat's own work. The nickname was of uncertain origin, no stereotypical Strine accent, so perhaps suggested by his habit of gliding around the room behind his pupils as they hunched at easels, trying vainly to reproduce a bowl of fruit. He was unfailingly encouraging, professing to find in every daub if not a likeness an 'interesting' approach to the subject. My reports went in order from 'a promising term' to 'continues to do well' to 'generally pleasing' as he cannily eased my grade down from B+ to B–.

I got a good mark for one essay in art, English composition more in my comfort zone than painting. I was never in danger of having a piece displayed on the walls of the spacious, perhaps skylighted studio. My favourite of those that were, the only piece of art I have ever coveted, was of Denis Law and Ian Ure being sent off for fighting on the pitch. This had happened on 7 October 1967, leading to the six-week suspension Denis was about to begin when I saw him first at Forest. I remember the bright red of his shirt against the green background as he went after his bigger, lumpen countryman. I had some hopes that at term or year end the works would be offered for sale, but if that happened it was without me knowing.

Our woodwork master Edmund John Summerhayes (always John to family and friends) was called 'Chippy'. In those days I thought the nickname peculiar to him, not generic for carpenters.

It was accepted but no cause for envy that Rex was better than us at maths, Basil at geography; we might be persuaded the occasional abstract splashes we saw from Wombat were evidence of superior talent if anyone bothered to push the point; their skills were not, however, ones readily transferable to our daily lives. In Chippy's case, the mastery was self-evident, a craftsmanship beyond that of our own dads in a field where they might have felt able to compete on equal terms.

Perplexed at my clumsiness, Chippy asked if I never helped out with any woodwork at home. I replied that Dad and Grandad (only Grandad, had I been absolutely truthful), tolerant of my incompetence, preferred to do it themselves rather than let me have a go. Chippy would still, after saying they should encourage me more, single me out himself from time to time: 'Bailey's not impressed,' on catching me yawning or otherwise inattentive as he demonstrated a tenon and mortise joint; taking a damp rag he had asked me to fetch from the sink, wringing it out to form a substantial puddle on the floor, without comment. Asking me a question once when we had inspectors in class, something about cutting with the grain, at my clueless reply he told our visitors: 'You wouldn't believe it. Academically he's one of our best pupils, but when it comes to anything practical…'

Chippy had his own academic side, taking some English classes (as did our gym and divinity masters at different times) to support Joe. Like Joe, he did not take any nonsense from his pupils. I witnessed him reduce one, a second-former a good deal taller than the master, for bullying. 'So you didn't hit him yourself? You were just lurking in the background looking menacing, were you? In my book that's just as cowardly.'

Lawsie told me how Chippy had handled some swearing in class. 'What did you say, Gregory? I could understand you calling the lathe a "useless fucking tool" if it was designed for fucking. But it's not designed for fucking. Please don't refer to it as a "fucking tool" again.'

Even divinity master Colin Gough was heard to cry 'fuck' in momentary frustration on the football pitch (he later said there was 'nothing wrong with a bit of robust Anglo-Saxon'). Nevertheless, I found it almost as hard to believe that a teacher would swear in front of us as I did when Barrie told me Uncle Tom had used the same word in casual conversation with him. In my boyhood I never heard Tom, my grandparents, aunts or other uncles (except Ted, in a traffic snarl-up) or my parents use four-letter words. Perhaps the men did among friends or workmates, but it was much rarer in mixed company anywhere. 'Bloody' was still swearing, 'bugger' a smidgen stronger and 'pissing' the worst I ever heard Dad rise to under provocation from Mum.

Chippy's joshing made me feel not picked on but noticed, treated as an individual. He did not disfigure my report card with anything less than a B, writing at year end of 'a good term in both Practical and Technical Drawing'. As far as practical went, the only piece I finished in all my time at grammar was a toothbrush rack. Mum promised to have it fitted to the bathroom wall, so we could all use it. We never did, the one job she did not badger Dad to get done. The only thing I ever took home from Wombat's art classes, an ugly green pot about the height of a pint beer glass, with a neck that would not allow entry to more than a couple of flowers, could at least stand unsupported. It did so for forty years unused in my boyhood bedroom.

Basil's valediction as 1A form master read: 'I hope that his alert approach and willingness to work hard will continue. He has been a good pupil to have, and has thoroughly earned a good report.' For my part, it would be good to return in September 1968 as a second year, no longer at the bottom of the food chain.

Although I had left Beaupré school, I was still with my village mates. I still went to Boys' Brigade, if not perhaps Sunday school. Rec' or playing field was still our ground for football at weekends, holidays and evenings when there was sufficient light after school. I was pleased to bring back from Norwich a new game for us: Flash.

Norwich was altogether a significant place in my childhood, as in my family's history. I knew what to expect of its castle and museum: the dinosaur in the entry hall, a sabre-toothed tiger behind glass, two Robert Goldsmiths on the Great War Memorial wooden scroll. I knew that Edith Cavell was an heroic woman whose remains rest in the cathedral grounds. After getting to know Uncle Bob and Aunt Grace on their visits to Outwell at fruiting, I was offered the chance to spend a week or two of my summer holidays with them.

My courtesy aunt and uncle were on the Catton Estate, in ground-floor council accommodation. It was my first experience of living in a town, and of anyone living in a flat. By my second or third of what became regular visits they exchanged it for a slightly bigger one, first floor with a tiny balcony, less than a mile away in Sleaford Green.

Bob and Grace did not have as big a family network as we enjoyed in Outwell alone. Without living parents and never parents themselves, Bob's brother Bernie did live in Norwich, their sister Dora having emigrated to North

America. Bernie was taller than Bob (or perhaps just thinner), with greying curls. I joined the two of them and a couple of other men once in a small-stakes card game ('I want to see that snow over here in my pile,' Bernie said when I was reduced to changing a florin) at the house he shared with wife Doreen and a daughter Sandra, somewhat younger than me. The brothers would fall out over a visit to England by Dora, from which Bob felt he had somehow been excluded. Not a man to let a grudge go unnourished, he never spoke to Bernie again; still, he would religiously send birthday money to Sandra until she was eighteen.

Aunt Grace hardly had enough relatives for a decent feud. There was an aunt who lived the other side of Mile End Road, where Grace would call at least weekly, and a cousin gone to Australia, who would appear only every few years.

It was as well I was a quiet boy indoors, since Grace was paranoid about any noise that might disturb the neighbours. I had brought all my miniature soldiers, to arrange in battle lines in the grate of their open fire, unused in summer. The horses would stand better there than on the carpets. One Mongol leader, a red one, sat his white charger with a club raised from his right hand at waist level, lolling back in the saddle to accommodate a pot belly, a fine detail.

I soon learned to tease Grace to the limits of her patience and beyond, something I would never try with Bob. They both had broad Norwich accents – I was always 'boy David' to her – as did the only neighbour I met. Irene would bring a daily newspaper round once her own flat had finished it. The favour was returned when Bob brought an evening one home from work. He was reduced there in his later years mainly to making the tea after a site accident, for which he received compensation. It was rumoured to be a goodly sum; nobody had solid figures, least of all Grace. Either he bore the damage to his back with fortitude, or the pain had receded to leave him marooned in the junior role. I never saw any sign of disability.

Nodding to me as he came in, Bob would return his knapsack – a canvas satchel he would sling over one shoulder – for Grace to pass on the paper and replenish his docky bag (the term Dad used for the container of your pack-up) for the next day. He would spend time in the bathroom before sitting down to tea; outside work he always liked to be clean-shaven and smart.

Despite smoking eighty to a hundred Embassy a day – the ceiling above his armchair was patched as yellow as his fingers and teeth – Bob did not use cigarettes as a substitute for food. No smoker, Grace would snack on biscuits and cakes during the day. Her food plan in the evenings was a rigid alternation between fry and roast. If we had sausage, bacon, egg, beans and chips with plates of triangular-sliced bread and butter on Tuesday, Wednesday would bring meat or meat pie in gravy, with Yorkshires and roast potatoes (which she called baked potatoes). Although food shopping was her task, Bob kept his eyes open as he cycled or walked through the city. He was proud of stewing steak he produced from somewhere for our Sunday dinners, gaining the impression from my politeness that I viewed it as a great treat, when in fact I would always have preferred the cheaper chicken.

Just as we had owned a budgie at Princes Street, Bob doted on a canary. 'The Canaries' are Norwich City FC; my uncle's was called Joey. The bird would perch on his hand to peck lumps out of his forehead, Bob all the time muttering endearments and encouragement to it. Perhaps larger pets were not allowed in their first flat, since I don't remember the parade of Scottish terriers, each more spiteful than the last and all called Scottie, until they moved to Sleaford Green. Grace would walk these, except for first thing in the morning and last at night, when she would be too nervous to take to the streets with the vile-tempered mutt of the day.

Although it would be close season during some visits, on others I did go to Carrow Road to watch the Canaries (once wearing my United scarf almost forced by police onto the post-match train to Manchester). Complimentary or concessionary tickets during his spell working at the ground were not enough to make Bob a regular or enthusiastic follower of football. Horse racing was a different matter.

I think he had a flutter (as women would put it if they viewed the addiction as supportable) every day. At weekends, on Saturday at least, he would be up at his usual unearthly hour, sitting at the kitchen table with a packet of cigarettes, a cup of Camp coffee and the racing form spread out in front of him, biro in hand. He would go out to place his bets, return to bed then watch racing on television through the afternoon. On Sundays he would return to bed in the afternoon as well as the morning. He kept his betting close, unwilling to tell me which horse he might be on in any given race. He showed no emotional involvement in the programme, however excited the commentator might get.

Grace made no complaint or enquiry about Bob's betting, since he never left her short on housekeeping and was always able to find a lump sum if something major for the flat was needed. Her main recreations were knitting and bingo. She would take me to visit her aunt, making much of how my curly hair was wasted on a boy.

Bob took me once to the swimming pool along the Mile End Road, heading into the city. He had perhaps been tasked with this by Mum and Dad, as the only adult in our family who knew how to swim. It was not a success. The pool was indoors and heated, so there was not the ball-shrivelling agony of Wisbech to be endured. The problem was simply my fear of the water. He would support me with arms under my chest or back, so that I could keep my face dry. Nevertheless, it was blind panic the first time I swallowed a mouthful, no matter that we were in the shallow end.

I did not learn to swim in Norwich, but I did learn Flash. Near the flat was Waterloo Park, which seemed vast to me at the time. There were broad avenues with flowerbeds raised on either side. There was the usual kiddies' playground. I found no marked-out football pitches, but there was grass, with the mesh fences around tennis courts making viable nets.

As he would have a kick-about with me once or twice in Grandad's yard, I knew what to expect when Bob took me to the park with a football. He would go in permanent goal, too stiff ever to dive but saving a surprising number of my shots. It was a salutary lesson, seeing how often I failed to beat a stationary keeper, either putting it too close to him or missing the target altogether. He encouraged me to go up to some other lads and ask for a game, one of those things that may seem the easiest in the world to an adult but can be quite an undertaking for a kid. I could not back away from it with him there, and they did let me join them.

There were not enough of us for a full-blown game, so I quickly picked up Flash, which pits two or three outfielders against a keeper. Passing the ball around between them, the players can only score by doing something flashy, a back-heel, a scissors kick or, less exotically, a header. Fancy tricks and flicks on the ball were then actively discouraged by teachers and coaches, and hardly featured in the English professional game.

Flash (which would now probably be renamed Showboat, featuring rabonas, scorpions and I don't know what else) gave moves that would normally be classified as 'fannying about' a limited legitimacy, was relatively good fun if you were short-handed and retained a competitive element. The goalkeeper, who 'scored' if the attackers put the ball wide or over the bar, often won by being the first to three or five.

I can't say I made friends with the Norwich boys. After playing once or twice, as I walked over again, I heard one tell another, 'Say it's your ball and he can't play today, we're already picked up.' So it was done. I never approached them again. Never mind, Flash gave us many subsequent hours in one of the Swifts' goals, with lasting kudos to me as its discoverer.

Trips to Norwich would continue but change through my teenage years, as I grew old enough to hitch-hike there and go out drinking with Bob, playing darts or crib with him in a variety of local pubs (excluding one he had vowed never to revisit after once not being offered a Christmas drink there). At this stage I was dependent on public transport or Mum and Dad, with whom my travel horizon would soon extend to Scotland, to share a holiday with my French pal Christian.

Chapter Twenty-Seven

1000 Bornes

At David Goldsmith's wedding 1967
(L to R) Nan Dinah, Shirley, Joyce behind Mandy, Allen, David, Uncle Bob King

Grandad would employ whatever casual labour was needed at fruiting, whether wives of Ted's friends from Wisbech or women from the village. While he needed enough to cover the fields before the fruit rotted on the leaf, going over them two or three times in a season, he could tolerate some who were slow or put in fewer hours (witness Aunt Grace). At the end of the day, he only paid them for what they picked.

One year two ladies unused to land work presented themselves. Mum had doubts about their staying power and indeed Mrs Claxton did not last long. The other was Anne Fuller, who lived in Beaupré Avenue with her husband Laurie and only child Stephen, a couple of years younger than me.

Anne's work at Grandad's may have pre-dated mine for Laurie aka Henry in 1A French classes. I would imagine Mum was reserved yet keen to show the family in a good light to avoid any possible repercussions for her son at school. Dad would have been more natural in his friendliness, while the law of obliquity shielded Anne from any direct conversation with Daub.

There was perhaps a feeling in our family that teachers, if not necessarily of a higher social class than us, might think themselves to be, a greater sin in a wife without the professional cachet. If Anne had any awareness of this, any misgivings about it, she soon won everyone over. Totally unaffected, willing to work hard in the hot sun for little reward – good money by land standards could be made, but not by a novice – she was the sweetest of women. Mum never had a bad word to say about her, a rare accolade.

The acquaintance already established through Anne no doubt gave Mum and Dad the courage to seek help with the translation of Angeline's letters, undertaken pro bono by Laurie. When Christian eventually arrived in Outwell, we naturally had to introduce him to Mr and Mrs Fuller. I had my misgivings. I was morbidly conscious of never wanting to appear a teacher's pet. As usual, in my grand self-absorption I imagined that a twenty-minute chat on the Fullers' small back lawn would become the scandal of the second year when we returned to school a few weeks later.

Laurie was probably sensitive to this. A reserved man by nature, he made no attempt to be over-chummy. Christian was continuing where we had left off in Arles, expecting me to make any conversational running in French. Laurie tried him in our language before speaking fluently to him in his own. My teacher was clearly on the easiest of terms with Dad as he told us all of a comic mistranslation he had seen. Christian frowned in puzzlement at the phrase 'un cabriolet jeune homme', explained to us as 'a hansom young man'.

It soon grew old for me to be asked a hundred times a day whether Christian was all right, if he was enjoying himself. I sort of knew what Mum meant; while always scrupulously polite, he rarely laughed or showed great animation with us. As in France, he was far easier among his French friends, with whom we linked up a few times on bus outings organised for the whole group. I could hardly wait for these myself, for another chance to see Ani.

Dad had almost blown my cover: 'He… like… Annie… very… much,' he gurned at Christian from his chair in our living room. 'Allen,' Mum warned him as she came in from the kitchen, but the danger had already passed. As always when addressed by either of my parents, Christian looked to me for a translation without seeming to have listened to them at all. On this occasion, as on various others during his stay with us, I either fudged it or fobbed it off as superfluous, which he accepted readily enough.

With Ani it was the hackneyed good-news, bad-news scenario. My heart leapt to find Jean-Paul abandoned to his suede jacket and unfiltered Gauloises. He was not a bad bloke really. But this Sylvain… so undistinguished I hadn't noticed him in Arles, pallid chubby face, weedy physique, did he have a club foot or something, gimping along? What could give him any kind of romantic appeal to a girl like Ani, bursting with rude good health?

I totally muffed my one chance to talk to her à deux, *tête-à-tête*, whatever. We were on a bus either to the seaside or the dreaded Wisbech swimming pool. I was sitting alone in a window seat, a few rows from the rear. She had, as usual, been the centre of attention in a laughing group across the five-seater bench at the back. Pretending to take offence at something, or perhaps just wanting to cool down for a few minutes, she came to plonk herself down beside me. Well, 'plonk' is the right word for the lack of ceremony, but I must not suggest any lack of grace. Before settling down she sat very upright, breasts jutting forward in her T-shirt as she arranged her hair with both hands behind that slender neck, at the same time favouring me with one of those smiles.

I had already had many conversations with her, some quite lengthy and intimate. It was a different matter when the chance arose face-to-face, not in my imagination with a French dictionary open on the bureau. I knew I had to say something, engage her somehow.

'Vous savez nager?'

'Oui. Et vous?'

The enquiry itself was bad enough. Of course she knew how to swim. She was French. Furthermore, had I anticipated the obvious counter-enquiry, it could only force me to admit my inability to keep afloat. Worse by far was the fact that I had addressed her with the formal 'vous', not thrusting an immediate, more intimate 'tu' at her. She replied in the same register. Did the smile now have something of tolerant amusement about it? Instead of a suave potential suitor, did she see me as an odious little swot practising his French?

That conversation went no further. It was another, overheard again on a bus – possibly the same one after she had gone back to the cool kids – that finally crushed my hopes. I had to swallow, however reluctantly, Sylvain's primacy, though I was never reduced to joining in the chants of encouragement when he and Ani were snogging in public – 'Allez, Sylvain, allez Sylvain, allez' their French friends would chorus, Christian among them. I thought at least, through her friendship with him and my attempts to talk to her in her own language – however feebly – she might have an affection for me slightly above that for the other English boys. Perhaps someone else thought so too, for it was in answering a girlfriend that Ani casually delivered the *coup de grâce*: 'Des anglais, je préfère Barry.' Barry! Oh, he was all right, laughing and joking with the girls somehow without good French, but to prefer him of all the English boys, where would that leave me in a hypothetical pecking order? I conceded defeat the same way I had allowed myself to dream, without anyone noticing.

Already before Christian's first visit, Madame had been writing to my parents about a second one the following year, organised independently of the twin-town trip so that both legs of the exchange could take place during the summer holidays, when she would be able to take time off work. On his first visit we stayed in East Anglia, on the second in late summer 1969 going to Scotland.

With the spoilt kid's casual sense of entitlement, I did not realise that a family holiday including a French guest would be a major undertaking for my parents, both financially and as an experience, since as far back as I could remember we had never been away anywhere together for more than a day trip. Grandad George at that time had a blue Wolseley, by no means new but much roomier than our black Morris Minor. It was also more powerful, so its loan was necessary to make that of his small touring caravan worthwhile.

My memories of the holiday are little more than snapshots, with some details of the itinerary thrown in by Mum. I remembered we went to Filey, a big funfair there probably part of the local Butlin's. We saw a show, variety compered by a middle-ranking comedian of the day. I liked the dancing girls with their high-kicking, spangled legs, picking out a favourite on whose I focused exclusively during their various returns to the stage. One part of the evening we could never decide on: was the violent row between a floor manager or stagehand and some of the cast genuine, or a piece of business to keep the audience entertained? We would not be there a second night to find out, as more than half of our trip northwards lay ahead.

One peril to be negotiated, of which my parents had perhaps been forewarned by George, was Sutton Bank in Yorkshire, billed as a one-in-three gradient. Traffic was heavy on the ascent, and at a sharp curve – to the right I think – Dad lost revs, to the point where he could no longer advance towing the caravan. I don't know how help was summoned. There must have been contingency plans in place by the authorities, which eventually helped him reverse downwards until we could take another route avoiding the steep hill. As we were stranded on it, while careful not to tax him outright, Mum was mortified and moaned to me in the back seat how she had known he wouldn't be able to make it. There was no swearing or panic from him. As stress went, it did not compare to driving a lorry under German shellfire.

At the Edinburgh Tattoo I noted down the motto 'Nemo me impune lacessit' to put to Taffy Roberts ('Nobody messes wi me, Jimmy' would be a rough translation). The big marching bands were more to my parents' taste than mine. Any enthusiasm I had for the spectacle – which it undoubtedly was – faded with the light as the chills of evening came down.

We were lucky to hit Glasgow on a weekend when my favourite Scottish team were at home. After an initial foray including Mum to scout out the ground's location, on Saturday, 30 August 1969 Dad took Christian and me to Parkhead. I wrote an account of the match for a school essay the next year, refuting the tight and unfriendly Scottish stereotype because someone had helped me get closer to the touchline and given me a 'bawbee' (thruppence or sixpence). We saw future United legend Lou Macari come on as a sub in a 2–2 draw with St Johnstone, to join Lisbon Lions Gemmell, McNeil, Johnstone, Wallace and Chalmers.

In retrospect – at the time I took it ungraciously as a given – I admire my parents' ambition in mounting such a full programme. I don't remember any disasters in terms of not finding an overnight spot for the caravan, indeed have no memory at all of any of the sites. The most vivid recollection, no doubt because it became ingrained, was of many hours motoring in Scotland, mostly on minor roads. I took a lot of flak for failure to appreciate the allegedly marvellous scenery all around us, which left me totally unmoved.

Christian and I may have done some reading in the back, but our main pastime was 1000 Bornes. I had learned this addictive card game in Arles, bringing a set home with me (English versions were available in later years if not already then). Suitable for two, three or four players, it is a race to cover a thousand miles/kilometres. You need a green light to start, and 'defence' cards to respond to all manner of mischief your opponent(s) may inflict, from simple but effective red lights to speed limits, flat tyres, accidents or running out of petrol. There are many satisfying wrinkles to the game, one for me a whole new vocab including fencing terms (*coup fourré!*). It kept us occupied for hours, setting out the cards on the broad shelf between back seat and windscreen (seatbelts, front or back, were a thing of the future), to duel in rubbers of five. The bonnie banks and braes passed us by as Mum bemoaned the waste of money in bringing us to such places when we could not even be bothered to look out of the window.

The only thing Christian jibbed at during the whole trip was the sea. I guess it was the Firth of Forth or Clyde, for convenient caravan parking within striking distance of Edinburgh or Glasgow. It was a beach, anyway. I gave it a go, entering the water to paddle and splash around. It was no different from Yarmouth or Hunstanton in temperature. I now accept that the Mediterranean is in a different league. Then, as Christian looked at me like I was demented, I probably thought he was a wimp.

Apart from 1000 Bornes, we took a football across the border with us. While my French was not good enough to enable Christian and me to converse in any great depth, we rubbed along well enough at our shared pursuits. He appeared robust yet watched his health. When we visited Uncle Tom and Aunt Shirley at Tydd, after playing in their yard we were all surprised to see him pull on a jerkin or jumper when we came in sweating. He explained he was nervous of catching a chill, having been laid low by pneumonia at some point. Luckily, he hadn't mentioned this to Mum until now, almost at the end of his stay.

One of the final communal activities of the first year's twinning visit was a party at someone's house in Wisbech. Although I did not know the boy well, we were invited, along with many others (if not everyone) in the group. There was music, slow dancing – smooching – towards the end of the evening, which I probably watched from the wall. I remember lusting after a French girl, Louise or Monique, with an impressive bust, once again in vain. Ani must not have been there. When Mum and Dad came to pick me up, I was evidently enjoying things enough to plead for another half-hour or so. They waited patiently outside before knocking again. As we drove home, they asked me why I had not passed on the invitation from the boy's parents for them to come in when they first arrived.

Among the documents Mum kept from my first trip to Arles was a small sheet of squared paper, headed WHERE THE MONEY'S GONE. It showed five francs saved of a total sixty, the balance split between PRESENTS (33.50, of which half went on Mum and Dad) and OTHER THINGS, ranging from 'Cokes and other Drinks' totalling eight francs, through five soldiers at a franc apiece to '1 French Newspaper' at forty centimes. We noticed when Christian was with us on the return trip that he had been careful not to spend a penny of his own money. Although he was not expected to pay for anything with us, Mum found it odd that he had not bought any gifts for his family (or, to be fair, anything for himself).

In writing to thank us after his return, Madame explained that Christian had been looking out for her. He was proud to be taking his five pounds equivalent spending money home intact. Sadly, he lost his wallet somewhere on the way, setting his good intentions to naught. She had not asked him to make the sacrifice any more than I had been asked for a detailed accounting of my holiday money. It seems we were both conscious, he more nobly than I, of living in households where money was tight, with mother the only earner.

Chapter Twenty-Eight

Golly's Girl

WGS class 2A 1968-69
Bailey is third from right, back row

Back at school in 2A we had new teachers, new subjects and sometimes new classmates. We were split into two sets for French and maths, while the new Latin class comprised the top halves of A and Alpha based on their final reports for the first year.

It was not long before we were wading – line by line, locution by locution, word by painful word – through the muddy fields of Gaul in Caesar's wars. Ralph 'Taffy' Roberts was a strict teacher, yet one who could sometimes be persuaded to reminisce at length on a variety of subjects, including his war service in Liberia. We were delighted when he went into one of these digressions, a respite from everyone in turn translating a couple of lines. Homework was usually to prepare a slab of Julius' lapidary (Latin *lapis*, stone) prose, without knowing which chunk of it any one of us would be asked to shoulder. Perhaps Taffy indulged us as much as himself, sensing we needed a break from this chain-gang labour every so often.

At the bottom of our second-year report cards, below physical education (where Mr Hipwell kept up his alternative narrative that I was a member of the Under-13s football team and showed promise at cricket), music had been added. John Watkeys, a barrel- or at least Watney's Party Seven-chested Welshman, had a powerful singing voice, handy since 2A provided minimum supporting volume in our joint attempts at making song. If there was the option of studying an instrument, it held no appeal for me. Judging by my reports from that year, Mr Watkeys had some trouble fixing on the extent of my musical gift. From an 'A– Good' (perhaps an essay on music, as once in art) in autumn term, I was dumped to twentieth place in spring ('Fair, but could do better'), to rally by summer to an unplaced 70% and 'a good year'.

My performance remained solid in maths and English, for both of which we had different teachers this year. Ernie Clark for maths was 'Lurch': tall and angular, his walk had the stiffness of film Frankensteins and the TV character who supplied his nickname. There was something simian about his face; perhaps the deep-set eyes, the rough and pocked skin, the loosely marshalled sharply filed teeth, the sparse hair on a great domed forehead; perhaps the overall impact of these features – nobody could have called him a handsome man. His hands often trembled, except when he was at the blackboard scribbling equations and calculations at bewildering speed. He did sums in his head before we could begin to work them out on paper. He was hearing-aid deaf, which made him suspicious. Not always, when he turned sharply from the board ready to hurl its wooden-backed cleaning brush, had anyone mocked him. He was never to be cheeked to his face, which was at its most frightening when he worked it into a smile.

'Morrie' Bluck was diminutive almost to the point of pixiedom. Even his boss Joe Davy stood taller. He lacked Joe's years, and most of his authority. I had not come across Morrie in first year, and he left at the end of my second, to be seen once more, when by quite a coincidence we crossed on the Royal Mile in Edinburgh during our summer holiday with Christian. He greeted me in a friendly way there, though I must have tried his patience many times in class.

Oliver Twist was one text we worked on in English with Morrie. I may already have known some Dickens, though it was a tad optimistic of Nana Goldsmith to gift me *Great Expectations* in April 1959 (says the inscription, written by Mum to 'David Geo Bailey') when I was not yet four. Apart from comics, which I continued to receive weekly, I steamed through many of the books then popular with children. Sometimes I must have appeared a more serious child than I was. Mum feared I would be disappointed that a volume I had taken from the town library (there was also a lending one at the grammar) was not about the historical William the Conqueror. In fact, I enjoyed the schoolboy hero's adventures in that title and many others by Richmal Crompton, who I was faintly let down to discover much later was a girl.

I read the Billy Bunter stories (he featured regularly in *Valiant*, as well as the Frank Richards books), indignant at his blatant thieving and lying; the Jennings books, from which Mum cast Staveley as Darbyshire, the speccy swot to my impish hero; and Blyton's *Famous Five*, never her *Secret Seven*. I went through a spell of collecting the Biggles series by Capt. W.E. Johns, my parents and family always willing to spend money on books and me keen enough to own as well as read them. In a vexingly undated Lion Brand thruppenny (that's 3d not 3p) Memo Book is a neatly numbered list of seventy Biggles books, with ticks against twenty-two of them.

The same little red book contains a list of 'Books I have Read': *Tom Sawyer, Huckleberry Finn, The Gauntlet, Chalky, Doctor Who and the Zarbi* (yet I was not a serious fan of the TV series), *Treasure Island, Wells Fargo, The Crimson Rust, Perilous Dawn, Thanks to Jennings*, and *Jennings' Diary*.

While there were one-off favourites, I did enjoy books where I knew there was a further stock available from the same author should they please me. Dennis Wheatley, whom I later championed against Staveley's favourite Alistair MacLean, was prolific (and proficient) enough for extended borrowing from the lower shelves of Wisbech Library where alphabetical order consigned him. He had several different series going on: the ruffles-and-rapiers Roger Brook, the saturnine spy Gregory Sallust, and the one who fought the Devil and all his works. The propaganda for reincarnation in each novel played well with me too.

Asked by English teacher Bill Trotter in our fourth form to list and critique our reading, none of us was as prolific as Paul Dewey. I filled almost half another red exercise book with eighty-three titles, including seventeen by Wheatley, ten by the lesser MacLean and five C.S. Forester Hornblowers including the one owned by Mum. Set texts in English, French and German were there, along with Hemingway, Steinbeck and Harold Robbins.

Aunt Shirley had been so impressed by a Billy Graham revival meeting in her early life that she never swore again. Perhaps you had to see him live. I rated *My Answer* five out of ten with the following comments: 'In this book the famous evangelist gives answers to more than three hundred questions which have been put to him at one time or another. Since few of the questions apply to the reader personally this book becomes intolerably boring after about a hundred questions have been answered.'

Wheatley was certainly the author I enjoyed most for a couple of my teenage years. I knew he was not considered a serious writer in the same way Dickens was, but as the above review suggests (and all the others I spared you), I lacked the critical apparatus to assess, much less articulate, why.

Although the first book in the second reading review was *The Old Curiosity Shop* (8+/10), aged twelve or thirteen I was young for Dickens. On the back of the dust jacket of my *Great Expectations* in the Regent Classics series, beneath the silhouette of a cove in a topper, it is one of eleven amongst the thirty-eight volumes listed with a blue cross against it. If these were the ones I owned, they show a predictable enough boy's taste for adventure tales: *The Last of the Mohicans*, *Ben-Hur*, *King Arthur and the Knights of the Round Table*, *The Three Musketeers*, *Kidnapped*, *Treasure Island*, *The Black Arrow*, *Robin Hood and his Merrie Men*. A hand-me-down from Uncle Ted, 'E Hills' and 'Outwell' firmly scored through above 'D Bailey' in Mum's hand, *The Coral Island* (R. M. Ballantyne) looked a better fit to Dad's collection. My feminine side went only as far as *Black Beauty* and Alice's adventures: Louisa M. Alcott (*Little Women* and others), Susan Coolidge (*What Katy Did* and did next), a couple of Brontë sisters, Austen and Eliot went unchecked, as did Moby-Dick (surely abridged).

At whatever stage my reading of Dickens was, it was good fun in Morrie's class to whale into Stephen Doughty as he knelt on the floor in front of me – Nancy to my Bill Sykes as we hopelessly attempted to dramatise a scene from *Oliver Twist*.

Such a liberty with Steve would have been unthinkable offstage. We were friends, in the same playground football match and sitting on the same table at dinner. There I was opposite Michael Westhorpe (Wes), whose stuttering was less disabling than once. Stephen Murray (Smuzz), a red-headed Spurs fan with a lot of football knowledge despite that, sat near the window. Next to me, as he would be in various class and school photos taken over the years, was David 'Spud' Plater.

I don't recall any one moment when my friendship with David began. He came from one of the Wisbech schools that was not Ramnoth Road, supported Leeds and played in goal. This eccentricity was perhaps his only one. He was a middling scholar and unremarkable physically – straight brown hair, slim build, some freckles. He did not owe his popularity to the sweets he brought in every day and was happy enough to share, though that would not have hurt. His good opinion somehow just mattered to people.

We were all hitting puberty during our first and second years, the physical evidence being 'waking up wet'. At dinner one day, Wes was the first to claim having done so, perhaps avoiding that particular phrase with its potential to trip his stutter. I had already enjoyed the odd nocturnal emission, without mentioning it at the time or now in reply to Wes' question of us all. I don't recall it having come as anything traumatic or surprising, which could only have been due to foreknowledge gained outside my home, where there was never any birds and bees discussion.

Our sex lives were limited to our dreams, as recounted to each other over dinner (without going into *too* much detail in case we were getting something wrong even in our subconscious). Our shared fantasies were not of girls our own age, of whom we saw few to none by day. Pop and television stars were at our mercy by night: Lulu, Cilla Black, Una Stubbs as Rita in *Till Death Us Do Part*, all wore skirts far shorter than were common in Wisbech or allowed in High School uniform.

Talk was all we shared in sexual matters. Statistically, I suppose some boys in our second year were gay. If so, it would have been latent not blatant. I never saw or heard of any such activity anywhere in the school. Attitudes towards it were much different then, as perhaps they were to masturbation. On that I can only speak for myself. I had no moral objection to it. I looked forward to my wet dreams and enjoyed them guiltlessly. There was just something too strongly pejorative about the word 'wanker' for me to wish to become one. It seemed shameful to me only in the sense of admitting defeat, a refuge from the real thing. Without claiming any great precocity, I had full sex before I ever masturbated (once I *had* had sex, I was by no means as strict with myself).

One female who did impinge on our daily routine was Golly's girlfriend. An Eastern Counties bus, usually a single-decker, would come to pick us up from school each evening before starting its normal route from Wisbech to Welney. Civilians could join us at the Horsefair. We were not aggressive or rowdy enough to offend paying passengers.

224

There was a hierarchy within our bus group, determined by where you sat. The pinnacle for an individual was beside driver 'Puff' Bell (his brother Jim and others might not countenance it), on the gate separating him from passengers, leaning against the machine that would spew out tickets at his command. Prime position for a group was the long bench seat running across the back window. Tom Russell was in evidence both front and back, where Twoll, a lairy fourth-former with bushy yellow hair, was the loudest if not the leader. I only saw him challenged once. For some reason he had not been able to get his normal seat. Just ahead of the back row were Aggie and Tadge, a kid so small he was viewed almost as a popular mascot. Twoll lumped himself onto their seat back first so that he could look towards his mates, squeezing Tadge up against the window.

Aggie, a year above me and a good footballer, showed a reckless bravery. Maybe he had remonstrated verbally before I saw him cup his hands from behind under Twoll's chin. Using his knee as a lever into the bigger boy's back, Aggie forced him off the seat. He took the resulting punch to the side of the face without raising his hands, having made his point about Tadge getting crushed. When Twoll sat down again, it was elsewhere.

Golly was smaller and more affable than Twoll. If his nickname came from any shortening of 'golliwog', there was no visible reason. He was white as the bread we all ate, with straight hair. Alumni of the school were all WOGs (Wisbech Old Grammarians); one such was met by the school travel club on a 1968 trip to Paris. He had acquired the nickname 'Golly' after being held up by the hair in front of the class by his Latin master – not good old Taffy, but whoever held that post in 1927. The Golly on our 360 bus was the only boy we knew at that time with a girlfriend, one of flesh and blood in our world.

Lawsie and I always sat together, mainly talking Cibola. Whenever Miss Golly – we never heard her named – got on our bus (which was not every night), she would have to run a gauntlet to the back, kids flicking up her navy skirt as she passed to pinch her plump thighs or reveal her knickers – that bright red was certainly not school uniform. Busty and with a mane of black hair, she accepted these attentions as her due, continuing with a smile but without pause or comment to the back. There Golly was rumoured to have his hand inside those red knickers as she sat on his lap. I never quite dared to stick out a hand of my own to pinch or flick. Lawsie said he had a mind to, but there was no way I was giving up my aisle seat with its better view.

Lawsie had the window seat because I got off the bus before him. He probably saw first my parents waiting and signalling at the request stop by Maillebourne one December afternoon in our second year. I did not realise anything was amiss until I had alighted to join them. Mum as usual came straight to the point.

'David, I'm sorry but your grandad's dead.'

Chapter Twenty-Nine

Friday the Thirteenth

Baileys at 1950s wedding
(L to R) Aunt Margaret, Uncle Jack, Mum, Dad, Uncle Brian and Nana Bailey

I hope my relief was not too obvious to Dad when Mum quickly clarified that it was Grandad Bailey who had suffered a fulminating heart attack, coming to the end of a day on his land covering up potatoes for winter. I pictured him lying on his back against a slope of spuds, tarpaulin tightly in his hand.

Mum and Dad had waited only to break the news to me before heading to Sutton Bridge, leaving me in the care of my other grandparents. I was more shocked at the thought of death than deeply upset. Grandad Bailey had been a remote and somewhat forbidding figure, right back to when I had spent a lot of time at his house. More recently, while we would have visited them over each Christmas season, and I did bring him and Nana Bailey a gift back from Arles, my only recollection of seeing him is the night at the wrestling.

Dad, the oldest of Grandad's children, was well-suited to take the family lead in a situation like this, a status Mum would have wanted to see respected. There was no question of any will. Everything would go straight to the widow Elsie who, as her husband had been, was on regular medication for angina.

I noted before it that the day chosen for the funeral was one of ill omen as a Friday the thirteenth (of December 1968). Grandad had died on the ninth, the day after his sixty-seventh birthday. Although I had not seen Nana as a widow till the day of the funeral, there was nothing unusual to me in her wearing black. I had no conception of offering my sympathies, but she found time in the kitchen as everyone prepared to leave for a few words with me, squeezing my hand.

I was perhaps taken to the funeral by Aunt Shirley, with Mum and Dad amongst the principal mourners. I remember Mandy being with us, aged four and giggling in the car either because she didn't realise what was going on, or because she kind of did and it made her nervous. I was pleased to see my cousin Susan, despite the circumstances. More deeply affected by the loss than I, she recalled us walking into St Matthew's together. My own memories of the Sutton Bridge funeral do not go beyond Nana collapsing in the front row as the coffin was carried in.

It was only back in Railway Lane that I learned Elsie, aged sixty-four, had died. The organist happened to be the village doctor; he had told Mum at the scene there was nothing to be done for her mother-in-law. The service went ahead. Dad was not given the full story till it was over. His father's coffin was placed in the grave, but the ground was too frozen for it to be covered that day.

I am told I saw Nana propped in a chair in the living room. I remember wanting to be outside, standing at the bottom of their garden. I found my way to Princes Street, nearly a mile away, to Uncle Norman and Aunt Maud's. Norman went quickly to Railway Lane to reassure my parents I was all right and could stay as long as I wanted, did not have to return to what was no longer my grandparents' house.

The flight to our old home street was a buried or forgotten detail Mum gave me years later. Grandad George made it over from Outwell through dense fog to fetch me back. I stayed at his that night, though Mum and Dad eventually returned to Outwell to sleep. She said I missed school the next day, amending that at my insistence the funeral was on a Friday to suggest I missed football. But I wasn't being picked for the school team at that time…

The cawing sound Nana made, on and on, as she fell at the front of the church, I was keen to establish as the 'death rattle' I had read of as always signalling a person's last moments. I was in bed that Friday night when, thinking how she had squeezed my hand, I quickly pulled it back inside the covers, fancying a sudden chill had struck it. Those are my two solid memories of the day.

In Sutton Bridge, I was later told, the remaining members of the family (my cousins, like me, had been taken away by their other grandparents) had one of their best nights ever together, full of laughter as they reminisced. Much of the laughter was probably close to hysterical, naturally enough after the day's initial stress and shocking close. The events at the funeral made it onto the local television news.

There were four new orphans. Margaret was always spoken of as highly strung. I can imagine Aunt Jean's natural vivacity could turn quickly to tears of either merriment or regret. I picture Brian as mainly silent, not necessarily because he was the most heavily hit (he was certainly that, in terms of impact on his daily life), but because he was usually so in any group. So much younger than his siblings, he perhaps heard stories that night of a father and mother he could barely recognise.

I never saw Dad cast down by the double loss, nor heard him mention his parents subsequently any more than he had before. Mum, as if anxious to ensure I knew the filial pieties were being observed, assured me he had been crying in bed every morning. There was no thought of me attending the second funeral. But what worse could have happened?

Nana Bailey had all her Christmas gifts ready and wrapped before her husband's death. I don't remember what mine was. Instead of going to Shirley and Tom's for Christmas dinner, as had become our custom and would remain so throughout my adolescence, my parents and I ate it in Outwell. Mum and I walked through the deserted village at her suggestion, to fill some time after the meal – excellent, in no way inferior to Shirley's – before we got in the car to my aunt and uncle's home.

After the 'Christmas bust-up' of family legend, Mum and Dad had re-established contact with Doreen and Charlie, taking the first step to visit them and being welcomed by one of Aunt Dawn's epic Sunday teas. The breach between her and Shirley was wider and more deeply poisoned. They would perhaps never be fully reconciled, and at this stage were definitely not on each other's Christmas card lists.

My most valued presents would go with us to Tydd St Mary, less than a mile beyond the turn-off to Sutton Bridge on a road more often taken by us than the one that led past Nineteen Trees to my earliest remembered home. More gifts would be exchanged there. Nana Dinah and Grandad George were always present, one of the few occasions when he could be persuaded to leave Maillebourne.

I recall no fuss about George becoming a pensioner aged sixty-five in December 1968, unless it was obliterated from memory by what happened to my other grandparents. George would never lack for work to do around the house and garden, while the roadside stall would become almost a full-time occupation. He never reached the size of business (declared size of business, I should say) to have to trouble the taxman. He never formally employed anyone, for all that my original idea had grown into something profitable. The proof of this for Mum was that he allowed Nana to keep both their pensions for her own use, without needing to budget any of it for domestic bills.

Food was one of our main occupations and delights at those Christmases. I tried not to overdo breakfast, to be sharper set for dinner, served up around one. We went straight to the main event: turkey, roast and mashed potatoes, chipolatas and home-made stuffing, sprouts inevitably, the peas I preferred, the Yorkshire puddings I adored (individual ones, then a bit of a novelty) and a big blue plastic pitcher of gravy, which – Shirley confided much later – she was always nervous to see me get my hands on first. Tom was an active and generous host, loading plates with meat, greed smiled upon to the extent of third helpings for me of my favourite elements. I would do my best with the mince pies and/or Christmas pudding and custard/brandy butter/cream, but the main course was my joy.

As during our daily lives, the meal was plain and simple. There was no lack of will or funds to supply whatever food and drink we wanted; it was simply that we had never been taught to look for fancy sauces on either our meat and potatoes or our puddings. Even cranberry sauce may have been a step too far – it certainly was for me.

The family did not have the habit of alcohol with meals. Wine was unheard of, beer for pubs, whisky only for Tom and his dad on the Christmas evenings. Nana and Grandad might have a shandy, while if the women tried anything it was likely to be a Snowball, Cinzano or port and lemon – something of only middling potency at any rate.

Escaping from the dinner table before the adults, Mandy and I would have some time in the back lounge to enjoy our gifts in relative peace. I was delighted to receive 'Two Little Boys' by Rolf Harris from Nana, a Christmas number one in 1969 unlikely now ever to be heard on the radio again. I had only a couple of other singles in my collection: 'A Boy Named Sue' by Johnny Cash, and the Byrds' 'Chestnut Mare', which I loved and felt I had to buy because it got too limited airplay to tape. In 1970 I subjected Mandy to Rod Stewart's *Gasoline Alley* album. The younger women would clear up the dinner things, helped by Uncle Tom, before everyone joined us. For years Grandad's Christmas television treat was Billy Smart's Circus. There was no great fuss about the Queen's speech, if it was watched at all.

Some of the gifts or games would need a degree of assembly, taken on by Tom or Grandad. Mandy and I would be indulged with adult participation in our projects when they were not maddeningly distracted by household chores or the banalities of grown-up conversation. Ted was the fiercest competitor. Playing chess in the dining room one Christmas afternoon, he felt he had been distracted from my killing attack by his mother talking to him. His resignation scattered the pieces over the table before he stormed to the downstairs toilet in the freezing corridor leading outside to cool down.

One game I clamoured for in my earlier Christmases at Tydd featured Shirley's wedding ring. A bowl of plain white flour would be upended on a plate so that it stood like a pudding. The ring would be stuck in the middle on top, leaving a semi-circle above the surface. Each player would then cut a piece of the pudding away. This was easy enough at first, but there always came a point when someone would set the ring falling. If you were that unlucky soldier, you had to retrieve it from the floury plate with your teeth, hands clasped behind your back as you lowered your head for it. Usually it meant a dunking of face into flour, however much everyone promised they wouldn't touch you and however much I pleaded with my aunt for a pass.

The table was laid again for tea, Christmas crackers and a big cold spread, always with elaborate trifle desserts. These, of little appeal to me, were favourites with Tom and Mum. I was as greedy as could be with crisps, Marks and Spencer cheese and onion from their big bags I only ever saw at Christmas. Otherwise, I would feed mainly on cold meats and salmon, going to the salads only to pick out the thin slices of hard-boiled egg.

In many ways my favourite part of Christmas was the evenings. Once the table had been cleared again, the fires made up in both rooms by Tom carrying in hand-shovels of coal, we could start the card school in the dining room, using the main table without its cloth.

I had a respectable repertoire of card games: knockout and classic four-hand whist, variants of rummy, Newmarket, sergeant major, cribbage in development, with a rudimentary understanding of brag and poker. The one we always played at Christmas was Nap.

Best suited to four players, using the twenty-four cards from ace through court to nines with five to each player, there is bidding to take from three to five tricks. Winner of the bidding chooses trumps, taking the top card face up on the discards if they are 'with', a lower bid than 'without'. Taking all five tricks is 'Nap', which clears the central kitty of accumulated stake money as well as the tributes from your opponents also payable (for smaller amounts) on successful calls of three or four.

Double stakes are paid for 'Napoleon', when the caller must lead with his or her lowest trump. Such a bid can only be made if there has already been a Nap call, and is most likely to succeed if you hold only A,K,Q of trumps. I won once at Grandad's without holding the ace, leading him to wonder at my nerve. I confessed I had seen the ace at the bottom of the discard pile. He decreed this sharp but legitimate practice, any fault lying with the dealer (Nan immediately came under suspicion) who had left the card visible at some point.

Tom always had a big pile of coppers ready for our Christmas games. Stakes were modest, a ha'penny for three, penny for four and tuppence (or perhaps a penny ha'penny) for Nap when I first started playing. Moving to the brave new decimal world in 1971, to change this to a penny, tuppence, thruppence was an inflation-busting increase of 140% at the lower end of the scale, which was quite enough for Grandad.

Ted played higher stakes or other interests elsewhere, usually drifting off after a few hands. If he was going to a pub on Christmas night, it was not one anywhere near Tydd. It was the only day of the year when Tom's dad did not go out for dinnertime and evening sessions. He and Tom's mum never joined us for Christmas meals, though we always saw them at some point during the day. He preferred to stand in the doorway leading outside, as if fearful of being trapped indoors I always thought. His one exception was on Christmas night, when he would join us for Nap and his whisky ration. It may have been at Christmas he introduced his grandson David and me to that drink, nasty stuff when you're aged seven or eight. I had forgotten it – not from alcoholic amnesia, we didn't have *that* much – until Mum mentioned the episode years later, without any hint of disapproval. Perhaps it was a cautionary move, in the same way kids showing an unhealthy interest were told to smoke as many of a packet of cigarettes as they could without being sick. That one was not part of my own sixties education, but I have heard of it often enough.

Deprived of her bingo in the same way Old Tom was of his normal social outlet at Tydd Gote, Nan Dinah was always keen to play cards. Nap could accommodate five players (by adding the eights, when it became tougher to take all the tricks, with a corresponding increase in average kitty size), and so it would for Ted, Mr Thorpe or, on Boxing Day, Uncle Len. Grandad, Tom and I were ever-presents. Shirley would take the odd hand if one of her menfolk, husband or father, had to go for a 'sit-down' when farting fit to gas the dogs would no longer answer.

Mum showed no interest in cards, and I imagine Dad preferred television, for I never saw him play. Maybe he was too embarrassed at the thought of having to interrupt the game for his own less protracted but more frequent visits to the toilet. We would play on until bedtime, long after Mum and Dad had driven back to Outwell, me always anxious for one last kitty. I usually ended up ahead in money, Tom and Len sometimes coming unstuck through recklessness, Nan Dinah always losing from lack of basic technique. George would become exasperated not only by her mistakes – 'How long have you been playing this game, woman? You must of *knew* he had that' – but by how she would casually appropriate more money from his pile when her funds ran dry. Christmas Nap was not something on which to waste her double pension.

Shirley and Tom had four bedrooms. Mandy was long abed in one, Nan and Grandad would take the main spare, leaving me the room at the top of the stairs. Shirley was by now past tucking me in at the end of each day, with her formulaic 'Night night'.

Rising on Boxing Day I would enjoy the treat of *two* poached eggs on toast before my parents returned. Dinner was the same full meal as the day before, perhaps with a supplementary joint. The big pans of bubble and squeak would come into play only on subsequent days.

On the twenty-sixth a portable card table had to be pressed into service at dinner for extra children. Tom's sister Joy and her lorry driver husband Len were there with children Jackie, my drinking buddy David and Mandy's contemporary Lorraine. Jackie would before long lead the charge in swelling the Boxing Day crowd further, as our generation accrued boyfriends, girlfriends, husbands, wives and children, not always in that order. His grandad would again treat teenage David and me to drinks, pints now at Tydd's lunchtime Five Bells.

The two or three days further I stayed between Christmas and New Year were much quieter. There was not a huge amount for Tom to do on the land, but he would at least want to be outside again. Mandy and I got on well together, with more leisure and space to examine our Christmas acquisitions. I drew the wrath of Shirley on one occasion.

'There's a boy here, I'm going to take all his favourite toys and break them,' she announced to the three of us over tea one night. Mandy had felt bound to tell her the prize Christmas doll Tiny Tears was in my custody when the fireguard had burned the hair off the back of the wretched thing's head. Tom, without contradicting his wife, let me know the offence was not that serious. One evening he and I took a centre-page pull-out from the *Mirror*, adding up huge columns of figures to calculate the number of people in the world from the individual country statistics. Our answer did not quite tally with the total we found too late on the outside back page of the supplement.

Tom and I would watch *Match of the Day* together if one fell during my stay. I usually benefited at least once from his dad's largesse on certain nights returning from the pub. He would appear in the doorway, without crossing the threshold as he handed wrapped portions of fish and chips to Shirley. She would give up her fish to me, I only twigged much later, contenting herself with some chips as Grandad Thorpe could not have been expected to remember I was there or to treat me if he had.

When I returned to Outwell after the 1968 Christmas, the death of my paternal grandparents seemed already to have shrunk as a major life event for me. In fact, after the hysterical euphoria on the Friday night of funeral and further death, its longer-term ramifications would become the biggest threat yet to the marriage of Joyce and Allen.

Chapter Thirty

Howling at the Moon

Uncle Fred would not live to see the first man on the moon in July 1969. The last time I saw him, reduced by lung cancer, smoking on the makeshift bed in their living room in Churchfield Road, he kept up his unbroken record of sending me on my way with a cash gift. His January funeral was another I did not attend, at Norwich crematorium. Aunt Peg had the support of their four children, including Bobby living in Outwell if not actually with her. After passing her driving test, she would be seen around the village in a bubble car.

My first-year form and geography teacher Mr Sleight had ceded the first of those posts in the order of things. He taught us geography until Christmas, when replaced by Mr Barrow, immediately christened Desmond from the first line of the Beatles' song (as performed by Marmalade) 'Ob-La-Di Ob-La-Da'. Neither Basil nor Desmond was as important a presence in my life as my second-year form master would become.

Harold Robinson was one of the older staff members, a classicist by preference who took French and English at Wisbech Grammar, only the former with me. Tall with spectacles and spectacular jowls, he exuded a quiet benevolence on which people were rarely tempted to trespass. His only nickname was the innocuous 'Robbo'. His end-of-term treat was to read Maupassant short stories to us, translating them from the French as he spoke.

Outside the normal run of exams, Robbo tried us one day with a huge test, seventy-five questions. Staveley was beaten only by an aberration on the gender of 'pomme', which pursued him through two or three of them. The prize Robbo awarded was as unusual as it was unexpected: a silk map of France, given to men parachuted in during the war, that would fold away to occupy the tiniest space. He never claimed it was his own, but the round of applause when he handed it over at the front of the classroom was more for him than the recipient. I have it still.

Robbo was one of the teachers who contributed to a collection I made for Boys' Brigade, shyly approaching each of them at the end of class over a week or so. Some gave nothing, some a sixpence, Taffy a half-crown with a reminiscence about his own former membership of the Brigade. The two leading contributors, tied on two and tenpence ha'penny, were Tommy Trinder and someone unexpected like Blocker Blackwell, oddly both having the same amount when they tipped out the change from their trouser pockets.

My shyness was to avoid any appearance of being 'in' with the teachers, anything like a pet or arse-licker. I was the more conscious of this as Dad's friendship with Laurie Fuller had by now brought us also into regular contact with the Robinsons. It was no doubt one of those 'secrets' I blew up in my mind, the need to keep these relationships unknown to my schoolmates (who could not have cared less). Both teachers were scrupulous in observing all the proprieties, using my surname in class, whereas I was David at the Fullers' on New Year's Eve, or at Heacham with the Robinsons.

Mr and Mrs Robinson, Margaret or Maggie, lived at March with sons Charles and Robert. She also taught, not then as a regular at WGS. I was not in any of her scripture classes when she did – she and Robbie (as he was known to family and friends) shared a Christian faith.

Robbie never learned to drive. Maggie, in the process, enlisted Dad to give her lessons. Charles was in the same year at March's grammar (the Neale-Wade) as I at Wisbech, so it must have occurred to them that we should be friends. Given that unpromising start of being thrust together by our parents, Charles and I got on well.

Making himself serviceable to the Robinsons, in whatever ways he could, became one of Dad's enthusiasms. Robbie was not the most practical of men. He or Charles, perhaps both, were working on a ham radio the first time I visited their house, an interest alien to me.

Mum was suspicious. To me the idea of any woman finding Dad attractive was ludicrous, though his easy manner may have brought him successes in his youth and did not go unremarked during his marriage. Apart from the traveller's suspender-twanging incident with Aunt Grace, at a family wedding Aunt Eileen's husband had both hands round his throat with bad intentions. Wheelchair-bound Uncle Hugh made a living as a potato buyer.

He had enough upper-body strength for Dad to need the rescue of Bob King. It was all put down to drink.

I did not know there can be causes other than sexual for jealousy. Although Maggie was slim with a pretty face and good legs, Mum's unease was probably more at the social difference between the two families. She always maintained, not in words but by attitude and actions, that we were as good as anyone – rightly so, I felt it too. She may not have liked to think of her husband acting as chauffeur to this middle-class couple, however willingly he did so.

My only mental picture of Mum at the Robinsons' is of her sitting in their dining room clutching her handbag. Dad and Maggie were the conversationalists. Robbie, always kindly, was abstracted much of the time, little given to small talk beyond mnemonics, aphorisms or riddles for us children, ones that had seen much classroom service: 'Je suis ce que je suis, mais je ne suis pas ce que je suis,' he would declaim; the term for a military policeman REDCAP held the key to those verbs followed in French by a direct object, not a preposition as in English. In others he seemed almost to have lost faith, muttering them to himself at the blackboard: 'Ce que… one born every minute.'

There were differences between Charles' home life and mine. For a start, he was not a spoilt bastard. One morning while I was in the bathroom Robert, barely of school age, knocked on the door to ask if I wanted a tune. Thinking this some new accomplishment he was anxious to parade, I agreed. I was miffed to have to open the door for it, until I found him innocently holding out a packet of cough sweets. I took a Tune, cherry flavoured.

Robbie set both boys the example, to which they were clearly inured, of doing the dishes, place-settings and the like. They used table napkins at every meal, folded and scrunched into wooden ring holders. These were as new to me as the chores. I did my bit as requested or instructed, without fear of either habit ever taking root in my own family.

I suppose the sharing of household tasks was not an eccentricity. The absence of a television was another matter. No wonder they were fiddling about building their own radios. Yet I should not give any impression of crankiness. We were not marshalled into games of charades, shared Bible readings or any other combined family activities. Free to amuse ourselves, we sometimes mogged along to the nearby park, playing tennis on at least one occasion. Otherwise, we would mooch around the house.

The Robinsons had a caravan at Heacham, a quieter satellite resort of Hunstanton. They would spend not just a week or two, but most of their spring and summer holidays there. Given that length of stay, each day was not full of excitement or treats. One was that at breakfast we boys could pick from a Kellogg's Variety Pack instead of pouring from a family box of cornflakes. It was a relaxed atmosphere, Robbie playing cricket with us and saying I should put myself forward at school as a slow left-arm bowler.

I saw at Heacham with the Robinsons Chippy Summerhayes and family (and separately bachelor Tommy Trinder). I knew Chippy had a life outside school, a gentler one, once reminded by him to take care not to step on cracks in the pavement. He was hunched over his toddler daughter Claire, near the post office in town, as they were carefully avoiding them.

The relationship between boys and teachers was often adversarial. It was not the thing to find anything good to say about any of them. We lacked context, any idea of their lives beyond the classroom. And we were boys, immature. Acquaintance with the Robinsons, as well as subsequent life experience and knowledge, gave me occasion to reassess my opinion of various teachers, usually in their favour. I did not know in woodwork class that Mr Summerhayes had left school himself at eleven to help support his family, and had a serious heart condition. It was at least rumoured that Mr Clark, so casually labelled Lurch, had been a Japanese prisoner of war. He never mentioned himself that part of his life, the ruin of his constitution. Both men died before their time, Chippy tragically as he rose to give his speech at Claire's wedding.

If in earlier parts of this narrative I have focused too much on the warts of teachers, let me not forget the all. Chippy ran a woodwork club for interested pupils up to three evenings a week, and with Mr Skinner gave up part of his summer holidays in different years to take groups of boys on travel club trips not only to Paris but Belgium and Holland. So Hank did not always travel alone. At various times within a couple of years he took pupils pony-trekking on Exmoor, to Grimes' Graves, the Houses of Parliament and Wimbledon for the tennis. Other teachers active and generous with their time were Mr Hipwell (twenty-two boys to the All-England Athletics Championships) and Mr Sleight, with various geography field trips as well as Scout leadership.

Apart from both taking kids on theatre visits, Mr Davy was behind the sailing club, while Mr Bluck was producer of the dramatic society's plays during his six years at WGS. In the 1969 *Wisbechian* my name appears twice in the cast list of his last one, an ambitious staging of *The Mysteries* pageant in

Wisbech parish church. Others from my form – Lewis, Lindsay (as Eve) and Wenn – had more glamorous parts in the production than 'Blind woman' and 'Mary Jacob', which were taken by the school's older David Bailey. My theatre days were over. Mr Robinson was assistant producer, with support in different areas from Messrs Carkeek, Fuller, Hall, Summerhayes and Watkeys.

In my later years at the school, after it had gone mixed, like many boys and girls I came to see the kind and gentle Mr Clark behind his grim appearance. His local press obituary notice in 1977, confirming his terrible wartime experiences and courage, had a colleague speaking of him as: '… probably the most liked member of the staff.'

I did not take Charles to Cibola. If there were cards or board games, they did not match the memorable rivalry of 1000 Bornes with Christian. Our schoolboy slang cannot have been that different, but his language was inventive and enjoyable to me. Sometimes it was crude, as in referring to the TV wheelchaired detective Ironside as 'Iron Bollocks', which struck me as hilarious. A phrase he assured me was in common use at Neale-Wade was 'knicker-jarring', meaning shocking or discomfiting. 'Ah, that jarred your knickers,' he said once to his dad, to crown an unexpected reply he had given him. Robbie could not condemn it as profanity, only bemoan it as puerile, asking plaintively, 'But what does it *mean*?'

It was not one-way traffic from Outwell to March. Charles came to stay with us one Easter holiday, when Grandad employed us both in his greenhouses pricking out bedding plants. He had made a tool that would put twenty-four holes in a tray of earth, into each of which we would deposit one tiny plant pulled from a clump of them. Jimmy Young was on the radio, Mum working beside us at a much faster pace.

As already mentioned, I envied Charles his piecework rate against my profit-sharing arrangement. There was a tenuous link in my mind with the story of the village idiot, which Daub had set me to ponder one day. Every time he meets someone new, the locals play the same trick on him. 'Here, Brian. Do you want thruppence or sixpence?' The 'idiot' takes thruppence… thruppence every time.

His parents put no restraints on Charles watching television when he came to us. At one point a Hammer House of Horror series of films was running on Friday nights, late enough for Mum and Dad also to be already in bed. Probably inspired by my reading of Wheatley, I had developed an interest in the occult (as he always called it). I had to give up on my bedroom as hopeless for conjuring the Devil. He would not come anywhere near a right angle, I read: mantlepiece, wardrobe, chairs, sundry parts of the bed frame, I would have had to haul all the furniture onto the landing before I could even start drawing the circles and pentagrams. That he would fear a representation of the cross made some sense, but to see this in the angles of my bedside table, frankly I thought Old Nick was looking for excuses not to come.

Christopher Lee had no such trouble encountering him on screen. I persuaded Charles that we should sneak downstairs to watch one of the films. He was less enthusiastic than I had expected, finally bringing with him a stack of comics. As we watched, undiscovered or at least undisturbed by parents, he confided these were in case he needed to take his eyes and mind off the screen.

In Charles' place, I would not have revealed a fear of horror movies to a friend at any price. I did not suffer it, watching and reading the genre avidly, ready for Stephen King when he began publishing a few years later. My second-form contribution to the December 1969 *Wisbechian* was a ghost story, one I am too ashamed of ever to consider reprinting. It was too good for me. If it beat competition to gain its place in the magazine, the credit was due to the anonymous author of a comic strip. *Mr Gregory and the Ghost* shows I changed from the original the protagonist's name – it was Mr Hand and I have sought in vain to track him down. I did not change much else, reproducing not only the storyline and twist in the tale, but I fear whole chunks of the text, particularly towards the end when I lacked the skill to ratchet up the suspense as the professional did.

Although we were not in touch outside the times we visited each other, my friendship with Charles continued throughout our schooldays. Like all Dad's enthusiasms, the adult counterpart could not remain full bore for long. Maggie did after all pass her driving test (with fewer failed attempts than Aunt Peg). Again characteristically, there was no falling out and everyone remained perfectly cordial when they did get together. The first half of 1969 would have given Dad more occupation than normal anyway, with the affairs of his doubly bereaved family.

There was not much to divide between the four children of Nana and Grandad Bailey. Brian, not allowed to take over the tenancy of Railway Lane, would move to Walpole Highway, within reach of Jean for meals and the like (their mother had asked her always to look out for him not long before she died). With a decent job on the draglines and rumoured to be close with his money, Brian at twenty-four had saved enough to buy his cottage down Mill Road outright for £1,000, living at his sister's for eighteen months while taking advantage of some council grant to renovate it. His snoring turfed cousin Stephen downstairs to sleep.

Brian sorted, there was the apple of Grandad's eye to rehouse. Out at work all day, Brian could hardly keep Judy, their snot-nosed brown-and-white Pekingese. Jean and Margaret did not want her, so she ended up with us, an affectionate little thing, already aged seven or eight. Dad soon came to dote on her turned-up nose and what he called her 'knickers', long hair hanging down the backs of her legs. If these were beshitten (not infrequently the case), it would be Mum who cleaned her up. That did not stop her too becoming besotted, albeit without the baby language with which Dad sometimes teased our new pet.

I liked Judy well enough myself, happy to sit tickling her belly as she lay flat on her back across my lap. I was walking her up Isle Bridge Road on one of her early days with us, when a man got out of a car maybe a hundred yards up the street. In build and from the back of his head he reminded me strongly of Grandad Bailey. What surprised me was that Judy too seemed to notice the resemblance, pricking up her ears and straining at the lead.

For a while it seemed the pledges to keep in closer touch exchanged that night of Grandad's funeral would become as much a reality as Judy's presence with us. Brian came round to take Lawsie and me to the pictures with Dad to see the Western *Mackenna's Gold*. ('I'll pay for David but I'm not going to pay for his mate.') He took to visiting us of a Friday evening, sitting on the settee with his big red farmer's face and appalling teeth. Mum gave Dad fair warning that his joshing references to my other bachelor uncle, Ted, whom he sometimes saw in Wisbech, were going too far. Not that he spoke of the Walpole Fruit Packers job, of which he was almost certainly unaware. He may have intended a show of respect for the older man. At any rate, one evening Mum turned, elbow on the edge of her armchair, to interrupt him.

'Brian, has my brother Ted ever done anything wrong to you?'

'No, he's always been all right with me.'

'Well, can I ask you to stop talking about him then?'

After that, with Dad silent, there was nowhere for poor Brian to go but home. He had not seen it coming and had no idea how to respond, apart from a deeper purpling of his face. That was the end of his Friday night visits.

Mum once told me, in all seriousness, that she had heard of an only child falling out with himself over an inheritance. Money was the cause of the rift between her and the other Baileys (nobody bothered to fall out with Margaret, who might hardly have noticed if they had). Mum deemed me old enough to explain the point of contention.

Joyce had always considered Jean and Susan to be unfairly favoured over the Baileys' other children and grandchildren respectively. Wed on Peter's specially requested leave around Armistice Day in 1955, Jean had begun married life alone in her mother's house. Susan was born in April 1956. When her brother Stephen followed in May 1957, it was difficult for their mother to cope with both; as a result, Susan spent her early years practically living at our grandparents' house in Railway Lane.

I don't know about Stephen, but I never felt any resentment towards Sue or that in our grandparents' eyes compared to her, in Mum's words, 'You and Stephen were nothing – him even worse than you'. (I recently heard a similar sentiment expressed more pithily in another context – 'I'm it, you're shit.') She told me Grandad roundly cursed us two boys once when he ran over a chip of

Santa's grotto – my turn next
Cousin Sue on Santa's lap

strawberries on his land, for all pre-school Susan had sweetly confessed she was the one to have put it in harm's way.

Mum might resent but had to accept that Grandad Bailey had loaned Peter and Jean a few hundred pounds at some point, when her own husband had never received any such help. It may have been for Peter to buy some land. Joyce would not forget, when he was already a farm manager and Dad was out of work, that Grandad and Nana Bailey would take all manner of delicacies – 'sandwiches, cakes, fruits, salad with radishes' – to tea at Jean's, but arrive at our house empty-handed.

The proposal, apparently agreed by all parties as fair, was that three quarters of the loan amount would be deducted from Peter and Jean's share of the inheritance to recompense her siblings. Mum explained she was not acting for any benefit herself, but in defence of my interests. If a house could be had for a thousand, even a hundred pounds would have made a big difference to her household economy.

Dad did not make it happen.

I assume there was a period of goodwill when Jean confessed the loan – how else would anyone have known? Mum would not have felt able to intervene directly, and perhaps Dad reassured her that things would be done to her satisfaction. I can understand him not wanting to hold his sister's hand to the flame, especially if the debt had been incurred by her husband.

For the only time in their marriage, Mum moved into the spare room. She returned after two or three days, oversharing that this was at Dad's middle-of-the-night plea. I am confident in my memory of this matter, for all Joyce years later said she remembered nothing of any loan or dispute. She stated that they 'didn't get a penny' from the estate of Allen's parents, swore she knew nothing of the financial side at the time of their death.

Given that even the one-sided version of the loan saga is conflicting, it may not have been the reason, or not the only one, for what would prove a rupture lasting several years between Mum and the Bailey side of the family. Everything was still amicable when we went to Jean and Peter's house that July 1969 night of the moon landing. For me it was Scottish scenery all over again. My cousins and I, whose relationship never changed, were called from our own amusements to watch an historic television moment. My only inspiration from the whole event was a few lines written years later, under the title *Howling at the Moon*.

Most nights we'd walk Nick down Robb's Lane,
Nan making cocoa for us home again.
One time, while waiting for the pup to pee
George looked up at the moon then down at me.

'They'll tell us if it's really cheese up there,
Them Yanks with all their fancy gear.
Man on the moon – who'd have dreamt it, Jim?'
(That never was my name to anyone but him).

Thirteen years old to me 'space race'
Meant nothing but the look on Grandad's face.
'You know it's really something new,
We'll all be going in a year or two.'

But not before he died, five years back now.
We buried him, my nan lives on somehow.
I had to take old Nick to James and Blore,
The vets, she couldn't cope with him no more.

I can't say why, but I won't let
Our boy Jim have a dog as yet.
He haunts me for one, 'When, Dad, when?'
'When man walks on the moon again.'

Chapter Thirty-One

Learning to Swim

Merry Xmas
Cousins Mandy and David with Nana Dinah and Grandad George at Tydd

At the end of my second year in grammar I had inched up to second place in the class rankings, still behind the stubborn Staveley. Robbo's note as form master spoke of 'a lively and enquiring mind and an admirable determination to do well', while Kraut offered a 'Well done!'

Over the summer of 1969 the counterpart of Christian's trip to Scotland was a wonderful holiday in France. Independent of the twinning committee, my mode of transport was different. Mum, reconciled to me flying, remained nervous of my change of plane in Paris for Marseilles. I have no memories of my first flights (other than helicopters or light aircraft at the English seaside), aside from a compliment on my French from a woman across the aisle.

I would coincide with the family's annual holidays, taken under canvas at Saintes-Maries-de-la-Mer, south-south-west of Arles on the Mediterranean coast. If I had any misgivings about this, based on my camping experience with the Boys' Brigade, they were soon put to rest. The tent was already there for one thing, a roomy structure towards the top of a slope among many others. We were almost at the dusty path that led down to the beach, 'Bon appétit!' from each bathing family or individual returning in the evening as we sat outside to eat. There was no trauma over toilet facilities either; fixed installations that must have been perfectly adequate from the fact I only remember the showers – taken cold from preference rather than any perversity of heating systems, as sometimes at grammar.

We had a football with us, naturally. Our one game ended badly. We were in a pick-up match with strangers, including young adults. Something happened between one of these and Christian. I could not understand what was said, or perhaps could not hear it as I was on the other side of the dustbowl pitch. Christian was clearly giving the man some verbals, despite being just as clearly physically outmatched. He took one punch on the jaw, and kept right on talking until he got another. Back at the tent Madame tended to the injury, more swollen than bloody, letting it be known it was not the first time she had done this for her older son.

It was too hot for football anyway. Our days' focus was always the beach. Although her facilities were presumably more limited, I noticed no great difference in Madame's cooking from that in Arles. As soon as we had finished breakfast we would make the steep rocky descent to the small cove, there to spend all morning in the sea. After lunch it would be the same, with the selfsame prohibition Mum would have made on entering the water before our food had at least an hour to go down. Returning in early evening, we would shower the salt and sand away. Every day I could see my whole body browner against the white patch covered in public by my red swimming trunks. There was no question of any sun cream. Perhaps Madame rationed my exposure at first, perhaps being in the water all the time stopped my skin drying out and cracking. Whatever the reason, I did not burn or peel at all, just tanned like a negative print of Good King's snow, deep and crisp and even.

Within our small group there was no emphasis on water games. I would stand up to my waist in the sea, pretending to make glorious square cuts or sumptuous sweeps with my linked hands as the bat, spraying water instead of a cricket ball. Christian would be swimming much further out or exploring on shore. Michel, with fairer skin than any of us, perhaps wore a T-shirt even in the sea. Madame would keep Dominique, who shared my birthday a year older, protectively close; the girl would enjoy splashing about in the shallows in her one-piece costume. I had to remember that this guaranteed sun, sea and sand was their Hunstanton, what they knew every year, not something brilliant and new as it was to me.

It was in those shallow, docile waters that I dared to swim. It was not so much a question of 'learning' as having the confidence to thrust and trust myself horizontal for the first time, not seeking to plant my feet on the ground (though knowing I could was a big part of that confidence). It was only a few strokes at a time, a clumsy doggy-paddle. But I was swimming, and I was proud of myself.

We fetched water from a tap on the site. Once I saw a woman there in a bikini, half an inch of thick black pubic hair visible between belly button and bottom half of the outfit. I stared hard enough, unable to stop myself, to make a Frenchwoman self-conscious. There must have been some kind of shop too, for every day I would buy myself a big bottle of orange Fanta. Madame allowed me to keep this in the top of the small icebox she had brought along. I would drink it at meals, or at odd times during the day when thirst made the trip back from the beach worthwhile. 'In the Ghetto' was often on the transistor radio, a song I liked without knowing it was by Elvis.

The others had red wine at table, watered to a greater or lesser extent, Michel asking only once if he could have a glass of my pop. I said yes without any problem, but he never asked again. I assume his mother had a word, saying it was mine, since I bought it with my own pocket money. That was my opinion, however fake-readily I'd poured Michel a big glassful.

We reached and left the campsite with the help of some family friend rather than by public transport. We did once visit an inland town or village. It was not too far for me to walk back alone the next or a subsequent day. I had seen soldiers there I wanted, cowboys and a set of blue-bibbed matelots. The attraction was that they were not figures I had seen in England. The need for the second trip, quite a hike in the hot sun, was either indecision or a lack of money at hand on the first.

Although I was keenly aware of the attractions of women, as the poor drawer of water found out, I don't remember the Saintes-Maries as a place of much female beauty. I would tell you if I had seen any topless girls. (I was a boy who used to notice such things.) It was more a resort of families and children than older teenagers and younger adults, who would have had no place to hide on that small beach. As casually as I could, under the cloak of a general enquiry, I had asked after Ani. There had been some kind of scandal, going off the rails, involving a boy (how could it not, I thought). My air of unconcern was effective, since Madame made no big fuss about Ani's sister coming down to see us one day.

Josette worked in the clinic with Angeline. Her smile and features were Ani to the life, though as a woman of twenty-six she had a fuller figure. Sitting opposite her at our dinner – candle-lit, as usual, not in her honour – I gawped like a fool, thankfully at her face. She would smile at me every few minutes, careful not to do so every time she caught my eyes on her (which would have been every time she looked in my direction). She was to stay the night, the only one we went for a swim after dark. We were all there, undressing on the beach. I had some hopes that Josette would have no swimwear, hopes entertained beyond all possible reason. It was not too dark to confirm she was definitely wearing something, top and bottom, as I followed her into the sea. She was equally discreet preparing for bed in the tent. If my mooncalf behaviour was noticed at all, nobody commented on it. I can only say Josette's smile snatched my heart at once from the scandalous clutches of her little sister.

There was a final French schoolboy exchange, this time with Christian's younger brother Michel. It would have been impossible to repeat the magic of the holiday at Saintes-Maries. I don't think we went there but to another beach. I have memories of the Arles outdoor swimming pool, an altogether more pleasant experience than the one in Wisbech. One boy approached me in it to try to strike up a friendship, or at least a conversation. Unable to understand him as well as I wished, vexed by his persistence, I threatened to hit him and he went away.

Mum's fears of me flying alone would have been put in the shade if she had known I was tootling around Arles and to the pool on a moped. It was much hotter during my summer visits than in the first one at Easter. Madame had to get strict with me about having the bedroom shutters in Rue Rouget de l'Isle closed at night. At least until the lights were all out, we had to keep mosquitoes from entering at the cost of any breath of air.

Even when my exchange partner was Michel, in France Christian remained my main companion. He was if anything more relaxed with me now that he was not officially responsible for my well-being. Because it was allowed, I started hacking my way through unfiltered Gauloises. Christian reassured me after several polite requests that I could smoke wherever and whenever I wanted ('tu fumes où tu veux, quand tu veux').

I doubt Michel would remember as fondly his holiday in England as I did mine in France. I struck a false note from the start. Meeting him at the airport, for some reason I was wearing a cowboy hat. In a misplaced attempt at friendliness, I plonked it on his head. He took it off as soon as he decently could.

Michel did not inspire the same affection in Mum that his brother had (Dad kept his own counsel). His cheerfulness and ready laughter on occasions came with sulkiness, tearfulness on others. He had no inhibitions about spending his money, which was soon gone. He resented me making him pay his own admission to *Carry On Up the Jungle*, which just the two of us went to see.

This year we went to Yarmouth, caravanned in the village of Caister-on-Sea, close enough for me to walk one afternoon along the seafront to look at the dirty postcards in the town. These used the same type of humour, sometimes the same jokes, as the *Carry On* franchise. I had left the caravan after some minor spat with Mum, who was crying and planning to call the police when I returned later in the afternoon. I was not sympathetic to her distress, feeling it to be an over-reaction.

Holidays were a time of stress for Mum. Returning from one, she told Shirley I had nearly ruined it for everyone, in a non-specific way she did not explain to me. On this one I heard her whisper something like 'Again? Twice in one day?' to Allen in their bed, the only intimation I ever had (one more than

249

I wanted) of my parents' sex life. Yet on another day she was wailing, 'We've already spent fifty pounds and we haven't *done* anything.'

Perhaps Dad was not as comfortable in a stationary caravan as he was driving, notwithstanding such perils of the road as Sutton Bank. The van was too cramped for him to escape his wife's nagging by going to bed. One evening instead he went out to sit in the car. Michel pulled the caravan curtains back to look out, gleefully asking what he was doing. That would have been another black mark against him in Mum's book, albeit not as serious as his failure to buy a gift to take home to his own mother. Joyce may have ended up buying one for him, so strong was her sense it was the right thing to do. She wanted to make the holiday so good that it ended up – as did all the males with her – unable to carry the weight of her expectations.

While Michel relied as much as Christian had on me as interpreter, a service I was happy enough to provide, I imagine there was still for my parents a sense of being on their best behaviour while he was with us. Dad going to sit in the car was embarrassing, but at least not frightening; the next day there was a special effort to leave the site and do something together (we must have visited the funfair and taken in at least one show during the week). We were on holiday, after all, with less chance for positions to become entrenched to the point where the only resolution was violence.

Back home one day, without visitors, when I can only estimate I was between fourteen and sixteen, I could not tell at once what had happened when louder noises than usual drew me to Mum and Dad's bedroom. She was standing in the doorway, an ugly gash over her right eye, from which blood was welling and dripping onto the carpet. Dad seemed to have been standing beside her, looking to see the extent of the injury. They had been rowing, of course. She was trying at once to brush him away and reassure me. He moved to get back into bed. I threw myself at him, punching him in the mouth.

I always thought of my dad as physically weak. He could not have weighed eleven stone. Still, he was a deal stronger than I, pinning my wrists to the bed. I had not attempted a second punch, nor did I struggle or speak. Mum was crying harder than ever. 'Stop it. Stop it. I don't want you fighting over me.' Dad released me soon enough, not hitting me back, though he did swing sharply around as I left the bed. I had moved suddenly enough for him to think I was resuming the attack.

Mum had followed him into the bedroom, arguing. As he slammed the door to keep her out, its jamb had caught her in the face. He had not meant to cut her that way. No matter, I did not regret my action. It was not a case of losing my temper either, the footballer's 'red mist' descending to make me lash out. I had been thinking for some time of putting down a marker. My one punch was it.

Did it make any difference? It ended that row, without lasting ill will on either side. If anything, Dad was proud of me. Soon after, we were at Hunstanton with Shirley and Tom. As we walked across the caravan site, Allen was talking to Tom, shooing me away as I tried to listen. I don't know how he set up the punchline, but he spoke admiringly of me giving him a fat lip.

'Did he, by Christ?' Tom laughed, not altogether comfortably. Without taking undue credit for my calculated show of aggression, I know Dad never hit Mum again.

Chapter Thirty-Two

Worlds End

Baby aged one – sunny

The ball came to me outside the penalty area, with my back to goal and a defender tight on me. I flicked it up, turned and volleyed it into the top corner. Herby may have got fingers to it, but it was in from the moment it left my boot. Think that goal of the few the French cheat scored against United. Hippie happened to be standing beside me as I turned back towards the centre circle. 'Not bad. Could you have done it with your left foot?'

As it happened I *was* two-footed, but could not get into the Under-13s any more than I could the Under-12s. The teacher might have argued the latter went through the season unbeaten without me. The Under-13 results were less impressive: won seven (including a 6–0 against Upwell made for me), lost seven.

For a time I was excluded from the playground games as well. I had taken to messing about with Spud, who was keeping goal at the steps leading up to the big doors for the gym/assembly hall. We would be laughing and joking until the ball came anywhere near, when I was expected to find a way to put it past him. Every so often we would pick up new teams. I realised both captains were ignoring me long after I would normally have been selected. Towards the end, with a guilty grin at his counterpart, Gary Rider pointed at me, on the cheap as it were. The next time I was out, looking for a game around the corner against the wheelchaired keeper.

If Gary remained skipper in our third year, I was not sad that Mr Hipwell had left. I liked his successor Brian Yates much better, and not (not only, at any rate) because he could honestly report that I was a regular member of the Under-14s.

Doughty left the school and a vacancy in the forward line when his parents moved. They did not go far, as I faced him a couple of years later in village football. When he tried to say hello before kick-off, I was a dick to blank him. It was a ridiculous attempt to copy the Scottish King ignoring club team-mate Nobby's friendly greeting before a Home International. There were other changes from the original Under-12s, some kids now working on Saturdays (WGS published rules were against this if it stopped you representing the school), losing interest in football (inconceivable to me then as now), acquiring other interests (girls had started to feature) or suffering dumb bad luck. Alan Lindsay was so keen to impress in the annual county trials that in the first few minutes he flew in horizontal to a challenge on Barry Lynn, breaking his own leg.

Early teen years were a time when total reinvention was possible. A mouse might grow over the summer holidays to roar his way into the team or become one of the hard boys. Gary Rider, below the average height in 3A, shot up in our later teens. He would play with distinction hundreds of times and score over a ton of goals for Wisbech, also turning out for King's Lynn (as did my Beaupré mate Jim Wilson).

I was unremarkable in height and build, a bit taller than average and a bit slimmer maybe, but not deviant enough to be called anything based on the way I looked ('coon', mentioned earlier, never gained any traction). Having a regular place in the team was enough to boost my confidence, so that I could relax and justify my inclusion.

With a selection of the six school teams playing at Harecroft Road of a Saturday morning, including the First XI which Beaupré hero Martin Linford had penetrated at an early age, Yatesie (I was stunned one day to hear Martin call him Brian) had to rely on his captains for substitutions and the like. From bobbing along the touchline, insinuating to Gary that he should bring me on for Staveley, I came to be a secure member of the starting XI. Yatesie always seemed to have noticed good work during his half-time chats, even if you thought he had been two pitches away with his back turned.

We wore the school shirt as far afield as Cambridge, with other fixtures at Fakenham, Soham, Peterborough (Orton Longueville) and March (Neale-Wade – no danger of facing Charles, not a footballer). There were orange segments at half-time, buns at the final whistle in one or two of the other schools. I would always end the morning alone with sit-down fish and chips, at a shop on the Brink approaching the Horsefair. We were not playing in any sort of league, which was as well since I guess we continued to lose as often as we won.

I was now a goalscoring midfielder, or linkman as we were called for that brief time, not an out-and-out striker. My main gifts were good ball control and that powerful shot with either foot. They did not include speed, heading or tackling. The only aggression in my game was what Yatesie once referred to as 'uncouth bouts of fisticuffs', having declined to send me off with a lad from Downham Grammar who I felt had been going in a bit too hard. Something similar happened in a House match against my old cutlery-snitching tablemate Stephen. Again, I was only trying to be like Denis Law.

Although I had not yet seen United live again, I was close enough to Spud to be invited by him to Stamford Bridge one weekend, taken by Mr Plater to see Chelsea against his son's favourite Leeds team, at a time when both were as good as they ever had been, much better than they would be in many of the years to come.

In the Cibolan leagues I administered with Lawsie, his Continentals and Westerners had been promoted in successive seasons (1966-67 and 1967-68), leaving my Amalgamated Unions and Blood City squads to move to Morroco and battle in his lower division. There was also movement of players between teams. This had been the case from the start in my world, with fees on paper only. With Lawsie's deep pockets on the scene, they became real money, stars such as Alan Ivanhoe changing owner as well as team. The ten shillings fee for Hulk was a record. Mum was concerned at its provenance when she found it in my school pockets, wondering where I could honestly have come by such an amount. She was soon reassured on that score, if not entirely on the ethics of the transaction.

Possibly thinking it time I stopped playing with soldiers altogether, Mum said a friend of hers (unnamed), sitting behind us on the school bus, had reported they were all we talked about. I had no reason to deny it, or to suspect till much later the existence of the 'friend', with Mum perhaps on a sly fishing expedition to discover whether soldiers remained our major bond.

Like partners in a marriage where the spark has gone, Lawsie and I continued to sit on the bus together every evening, our main if not only topic of conversation indeed Cibola. I did not always behave creditably in seeking to maintain the ascendancy of my cities and teams over his. It was one thing to bring new footballers back from France. I made a more important find by sheer accident. On the way out of Wisbech towards Outwell was a general store at Newcommon Bridge, opposite the Royal Standard. I must have been hitching home from town when I went in the shop (if not already, we would soon be going in the Standard on Friday nights). There towards the back was a whole box of some of my legendary figures, many O'Reillys and other Arab stars. They must have been old stock, for as a further bonus they were on sale at something like half the normal price.

I did not have money with me to buy them all. There was the further problem of not wishing to flood the market. The most prized soldiers were those who had no replicas (which we would refer to as brothers or nephews – not sons because they were all expected to play football together). I refused to tell Lawsie where I was getting my new men. He could walk all over town without finding them, so unlikely an outlet was Newcommon Bridge. He offered to buy me one for every one he got himself. No deal. I don't think I made any excuse. What excuse could there be, other than self-interest? I was the only one to draw from that well.

We never quarrelled. After the 1968-69 season his two teams returned to Morroco, as did mine to Blood and Casablanca. The Amalgamated Unions, who had not flourished with him, came back to win my league. That sent a message. The next season, 1970-71, I used the windfall of players to expand my league with new teams Sun City and Casablanca Kids. Records exist for just two campaigns with the eight sides. If the Cibolan seasons had corresponded with the English football league, this would have taken me to the end of fifth form, which I don't think was quite the case. On the other hand, I never made a conscious decision to stop the fixtures.

The break with Lawsie did involve a conscious decision. I had become friendly with another Outwell boy at school. Kevin Rayner was in my form yet did not register at first. No footballer, he was unknown to me from the village since he was one of the Catholics who attended Wisbech Convent as their primary school. I may have coined the nickname 'Fangs'. His incisors all sloped backwards steeply towards his tonsils, making the canines look more prominent. He seemed to take the baptism calmly in his stride, as he did most things.

Fangs lived about as far away from me as Lawsie in the opposite direction, on the way into town. We played football on his lawn at least once, with his younger brother and two blonde Hanslip boys. More often, he would come round to mine, admiring my collection of soldiers as he sought to build up his own. We came to call his house Tangiers.

As we were both in A, I saw more at school of Fangs than I did Lawsie in Alpha. He would sit in the seat on the bus ahead of or behind us, joining eagerly in our conversation. Sometimes I would ask questions about obscure points of Zuni history or mythology. Lawsie pooh-poohed Fangs' attention to these, saying he had no hope of answering them when Lawsie struggled – until one day Fangs got one right.

Fangs soon wanted me to sit with him on the bus. New relationships are often more fun than established ones, as would become clearer, sometimes painfully so, when they started to be with girls. I had not only Cibolan but Beaupré history and ties to Lawsie, with whom Fangs did get on, spending time together without me in which he had admitted nicking men from my house. 'So when you said he's got some the same as you, they probably were yours,' was a dig I did not begrudge Lawsie.

One day Lawsie got on the bus to find Fangs and me sitting together. Nobody said anything. Eyes resolutely ahead of him, he went to a seat further down the bus. We had little or no contact during the rest of our school years, yet never fell out or badmouthed each other. Perhaps he was as happy with the change as Fangs and I were.

Our new seating plan was short-lived. From our fourth year we would be in new premises, no longer with a dedicated pick-up at the grammar school gates. We made our own way to the Horsefair, where several buses waited to take boys, girls and adults home. The latter categories were careless and fearless of occupying whichever vehicle and whatever seats they pleased. Boyish hierarchies were suddenly irrelevant.

'It's going to be bad enough having to teach girls, without you behaving like one, Martin' was probably not our first warning of a merger between the Grammar and Wisbech High School. The speaker was Gerry 'Yokel' Bradley, a Burnley supporter and our new geography teacher. He made a more assertive start than Colin Gough ('Goffy'), who replaced the popular and athletic 'Jimmy' Stewart at divinity. I took Colin initially for a new boy in class; short, plump, bespectacled and fresh-faced, a cherub ripe for bullying. His instructions were not always clear. 'I've stuck the fucking thing in now,' Rick Moden shouted in disgust, after Goffy had changed his mind about some cut-and-pasting exercise. As soon as he could, he grew a thick black beard (that could still not always hide his blushes).

Our form master in third year was Malcolm 'Blocker' Blackwell. A scruffy cord jacket rather than suit, he knew well enough how to keep discipline. He had to, since in his chemistry class quantities of acid were available, as well as Bunsen burners at each workstation (what we called a sink at home). We dipped litmus paper to turn blue in an alkaline, red in an acidic solution. I learned the symbols for the elements without much bother, or any understanding of their properties. The same would soon be true of logarithms, sines, cosines and tangents in maths.

Brian Yates was taking us for English as well as PE. 'It helps the other teachers realise you've got something between the ears if you can do another subject as well as gym,' I heard him remark to an older boy, perhaps a bit of career advice.

Not knowing the term or understanding the concept of plagiarism then, I repeated the sin of *Mr Gregory and the Ghost* in a non-fiction project marked by Yatesie: *Witchcraft*. The source from which I copied or stole most (Gillian Tindall's *A Handbook on Witches*) is mentioned in its bibliography. My introduction may have been the work's only piece of honest personal reflection or invention.

> *On the last Tuesday of the Easter holidays some friends and I were playing football in the local rec'. As they were setting up the goal posts (jackets) two of them noticed, on the ground, the shape of a man, made up of a pullover, sticks (for arms and legs), and three or four bricks in the shape of a head. All very well, some little children playing, no doubt, but then my friends noticed another stick, stuck through the figure's heart. This was more sinister and one of ~~my friends~~ them immediately said, "Hello, somebody's been practising witchcraft," but no one was really very scared. After all it was still day-time and there is safety in numbers (there were at least eight of us).*
>
> *By that night I had forgotten all about the strange representation of a man, but as I was going to bed I saw my friend, who was staying with me during the holidays, looking out of an upstairs window (from which the rec' could be seen). He was looking for a sign of life there but saw nothing. However when I looked I saw what appeared to be a small fire in the rec'. The effigy being burnt? A sacrificial fire with witches dancing naked around it? It was impossible to see anything but the red glow from where we were.*
>
> *We went to bed, of course keeping close together, and read some comics to steady our nerves. I reassured myself with the fact that it was only ten o'clock, not the witching hour, and that, to my very limited knowledge, it was not the Witches' Sabbath or any other such date when sacrifices were performed. (Of course they only sacrifice young girls but it was best to be on the safe side). My mind went back to a film I had seen about witches and, through that, back to the Middle Ages, back to the first witches...*

Seventy pages of my best handwriting later, Yatesie commended the standard of written English as 'excellent', while making it clear he was onto me by adding 'many of the "new" words and phrases will be of value in future work.'

It must have been a time of uncertainty for our teachers. Although the total number of pupils to be taught would not be affected by the upcoming merger, there was a choice to be made for each subject or departmental head between the two incumbents. Taffy Watkeys would not continue at music, despite coming back after our third-form Christmas following a protracted absence. His subject was ungraded for that autumn term, when all we did was listen to records; The Archies' 'Sugar, Sugar' was played over and over in the classroom, which was outside the main school building.

Pop music had become important to us all. Like Spud, Smuzz and others, I would prepare my own weekly hit parade, at first a top ten but for a while a twenty or thirty. I drew some ridicule when 'Rupert the Bear' appeared in my charts, undeniably catchy though the tune was.

My favourite music was Tamla Motown. I came to an awareness of it at about the stage of *Motown Chartbusters IV*, which left me the joy of a substantial back catalogue to discover – not least the splendid Volume III. The Beatles, Rolling Stones, white music generally left me cold, though I would make an exception for individual tracks. I liked Elvis in sentimental or yearning vein, 'Don't Cry Daddy' and 'Kentucky Rain' for instance. That same taste would later bring me to country, then usually called country and western (I like both kinds of music, as the redneck mantra goes). *The Golden Hits from the Legend that was Hank Williams* at home was a record by Tex Williams and the Sundowners. Someone had also given Dad Porter Wagoner's *Confessions of a Broken Man*, which I would occasionally put on for my own pleasure.

Apart from the family radiogram I must have acquired a record player of some sort. As I became keener on music, I shifted camp into the back room downstairs. There was some swapping of records, whether temporarily or for good. In my view singles were a much poorer investment than albums. Not one to save everything I could to buy music, I did get *Ruby, Don't Take Your Love to Town* featuring Kenny Rogers and the First Edition's biggest hit. Labi Siffre I bought as the gentle balladeer of his first self-titled album then *The Singer and the Song*, more than fifteen years before his anthemic '(Something Inside) So Strong'. Chairmen of the Board were my top group, the more so when I learned their leader General Johnson wrote 'Patches', on the back of which I had to get the Clarence Carter album of his only UK single hit. When Johnny Johnson brought his Bandwagon to Wisbech, Hank and I went to see them and 'Blame

It on the Pony Express', as I could not the mud on my height-of-fashion white trousers, Mum's abiding memory when we returned from the gig.

There was no need to buy too much music, as we would try to tape our favourites from TV or radio. *Top of the Pops* on Thursday evenings was the prime source on telly. Radio Luxembourg was unreliable, at least in my house, with reception flickering in and out, while on Radio One the disc jockeys liked the sound of their own voices too much, talking over beginnings and endings. I heard they were trained to do this, precisely to frustrate the likes of me recording rather than buying. *Pick of the Pops*, on Sunday evenings between five and seven, was the safest bet to catch any given tune, as long as it had reached the top twenty, which was played in full from six to seven. It was DJ Alan 'Fluff' Freeman who introduced me during the five to six hour to the genius Isaac Hayes, before he did anything short enough to fit in that chart.

The first use of a tape recorder in our house had been to help me learn French. In the absence of language labs at school, and too young for the student *assistantes*, we otherwise had to rely on Henry or Robbo's accent. The eight-track Grundig was more modern, sleeker, with the capacity for two sets of music on each side, accessed simply by flicking a switch between 1–2 and 3–4. I had no idea of the technology behind it, but it worked fine. I was proud of it. This must have pleased Mum, for whom it had been a substantial investment; substantial enough to stir Dad's jealousy. I forget what purchase of his had been knocked back or questioned, probably something to do with the car. Whatever it was, he shouted down the stairs that she could spend an amount I have forgotten on the new gear for me but not on anything for him. I was surprised at this break in their united front of indulging me, the only such occasion I must say.

As a surprise, the eight-track incident was trivial compared to the reveal from my bridal hag and headless groom narrative, which resulted from a different row altogether. Dad was again upstairs. It was Mum, her face red and contorted with tears, shouting in my face as we stood in the kitchen: 'David, he's got VD.'

Chapter Thirty-Three

The Sunny Side of the House

Wommersom, August 1945
Allen (right) and friend in Belgium

It made several things clearer.

As a small child, when I heard Mum screaming at Dad that things would have been all right 'if you'd kept yourself clean', I assumed a failure to wash his hands had led to germs or lead poisoning, another version of his illness. I now understood why Mum had been so furious at Nana Bailey suggesting it was she who had made him ill. It explained the fund of bitterness, seething resentment, a starting lack of sympathy quite different to an erosion of it, which might have been expected after years of caring for an invalid. She told me she would prick his leg with a needle as he slept, to confirm either a total lack or an excess of feeling he was alleging in it. I forget which.

He came down the stairs to let us know he had heard (he could hardly not have). She may have apologised. She certainly said, 'Perhaps it will be better now that I've been able to tell someone after all these years of keeping it quiet.' What triggered her outburst on that particular day I have no idea, no context to their row. He did not say anything, did not lash out, but retreated to the back room downstairs, then again to bed. Mum was anxious that I should go to him, to reassure him that it didn't change anything. I gave it a go, sitting on the chair at his bedside.

'I can understand how these things happen. I mean, I want to have my fun as well, when the time comes.'

'This isn't much fun,' he answered.

Whether from some long-buried fragment of accusation from Mum or more general reasoning, I assumed Dad had contracted – what? I never asked, was never told beyond the initial initials – his venereal disease during the Allies' liberating advance through Europe. Belgium, I always thought. If there had been any earlier symptoms or diagnosis, he did not share them with Mum before they married. I thought for a long time it was a failure to communicate matched by that around her inability to have children. Only in preparing these memories for publication did I trouble to investigate what his illness might have been. Five minutes on the internet does not make me an expert, but tertiary syphilis looks a close fit, not to be wished on anyone.

Allen could well have been unaware of the development of that illness, the stages of which would also explain how, more happily, he never communicated it to Joyce, as she was quick to let me know. Regretting what she had said in temper, she went on to reflect that their marriage was over anyway, that they had always agreed to stay together only until they had brought me up. She said on another occasion she was proud to have kept him alive already beyond the ten years one doctor had suggested would be a realistic life expectancy for him.

Had this painfully acquired knowledge of Allen's sexual history made Joyce more nervous of his possible involvement with other women? Apart from the bitterness of betrayal, she would have suffered hugely from the social humiliation if he had mysteriously infected someone else. The period of family unity following his parents' death had extended beyond siblings, including a cousin, Margaret, who had moved somewhere up north with her Polish husband Henry. I met her once or twice, a friendly enough woman but not one

I found good-looking. There was some joshing over her and Allen as childhood sweethearts, possibly surfacing in that evening of Grandad's funeral. His sister Olive, Margaret's mother, was not far behind him in death. Dad went to her funeral at Sutton Bridge.

The second or third time I got up, Mum let me stay with her downstairs. It was well after midnight, television closed down. The sound of her sobbing was what had woken me. Dad was still not home. Mum's expressed concern was the three-mile drive along the riverbank from the Bridge to Foul Anchor, where no railings or retaining wall would stop a car veering off into the water. Privately I thought she was more anxious about him enjoying the company of Cousin Margaret.

There were few mourners for Aunt Olive, and of those not all were in grief. Margaret's husband Henry had taken the trouble to equip himself with bottle and glass but not to enter the church. As the coffin left it, he sped his mother-in-law on her way with a whisky toast and the Polish equivalent of 'good riddance to bad rubbish'. This we heard from Dad, though not immediately on his early hours return (Mum had sent me to bed as soon as she was sure it was him, before he came in the house). Not too drunk to realise how drunk he was, he had crawled the car home at twenty miles an hour, nose to the windscreen.

In the end, with drink-driving at that time considered no more a sin than women drinking and smoking while pregnant, she did not have much to reproach him with – we had no phone for him to have let her know he would be late. I would not be so rash as to claim it for certain, but I strongly doubt there was any infidelity during their marriage. Where was the time, the opportunity, the money, never mind the inclination?

Mum's insecurity argued a degree of mistrust, and she clearly liked to be in control of husband and son, knowing where we were and preferring that to be within her sight. Yet I would not overlook the positive side. For all her protestations about the marriage being maintained solely as a life-support system for me, there was much more than habit and history to it. There was passion, a lot of energy between them, most of it positive.

I had few childhood memories of family weddings, unborn or too young for those of Mum and Dad's sisters, while their brothers stayed resolutely single. Mum's architect cousin David, the youngest of Fred and Peggie, married in 1967 at St Clement's then had a do at Upwell village hall, where I trailed dutifully behind Barrie all evening, his constant refrain 'the night is yet young' as the band, or a record player, gave out Engelbert Humperdinck's 'Last Waltz'.

I failed to register Uncle Hugh's attempt to throttle Dad. Ted's wedding in October 1970 would not add to the stock of reminiscences, except in the idealised form I will now grant it, giving the Hills side of my family a final bow and not looking ahead for them except to the good times (and then not too far, to avoid robbing myself of material for future volumes of memories).

Mother of the groom 1970
Nan Dinah with Ted and Iva on their wedding day

Friday Bridge Camp was a base for workers drawn to our area in the summer for fruit picking. It was there Ted met Iva, from Czechoslovakia where the hopes of the Prague Spring in 1968 had fallen under Soviet tanks by autumn of the same year. 'Within a week they were on a caravan holiday together, within a month they were getting married,' was the way Mum put it to me. Allowing for an element of exaggeration in that, Ted and Iva did make their minds up quickly, without worrying what others might think.

Iva was not that much older than me, in her mid-twenties while Ted was nearer forty than thirty. She was a qualified nurse in her own country, a vocation she would resume later in Boston after moving from land to factory work in Wisbech when they first set up home together there. Though physically attractive, Iva had nothing of the siren about her around our family. She was enthusiastically open and constantly friendly, facing an entrenched reserve towards strangers not limited among us to Grandad George.

Bobby Goldsmith was taking bets on it being a pure marriage of convenience, with his cousin Ted receiving three hundred pounds (there was some publicity about these arrangements at the time, including a tariff) against the shelter of British citizenship. Bobby gave it six months at most. He was running the Ex-Servicemen's Club in Wisbech twenty-two years later when Iva took out its back room for Ted's sixtieth birthday party.

The wedding was at Downham Registry Office, Shirley wobbly-legged from drink. Mandy was quick enough to take advantage of her mother's elevation. Asking for something in a shop, she was grandly told, 'You can have whatever you want, my darling.'

Although Doreen and Charlie did not attend the drinks at Tydd – reception is too big a word for the small-scale celebration – I will put them there and take away the chronic back problem Charlie had at the time. They were by now living in the Rowell farmhouse, a warren of small, low-ceilinged rooms where I always felt slightly claustrophobic. He and Doreen were into caravan rallying in a big way and within a few years gave up the farm altogether, taking up jobs with Securicor.

It would not be long before my Rowell cousins embarked on their own round of marriages. Teresa knocked on Madame's door in Arles as part of an extended teenage trip around Europe, and would emigrate to Canada with Barry, whom she married in London in spring 1971, with a party at Parson Drove.

Cousin Barrie, who had graduated from driver's mate in Ted's lorries to designated driver on nights out around town with him, and was about to join the RAF, would not follow our uncle's example of a prolonged bachelorhood, marrying Angela in November 1972.

Graham had just turned seventeen and on his birthday joined the Royal Navy, where he would have an excellent career. He would marry in 1976, and definitively to Linda in 1982.

Vivienne was a table-tennis champion in the making, a tomboy not too brave for me to rescue her from a spider in the bedroom one night when she stayed in Isle Bridge Road. At the wedding party I have her playing happily with Mandy, the cousin she hardly knew because of their mothers' bitter falling-out but who would one day stand bridesmaid for her.

Mandy was a pretty little girl, much indulged as an only child, yet unspoiled, with the Thorpe sweetness of character mellowing the Hills edge. Tom and Shirley were with her now sole occupants of Henson House, his parents fit and well in a nearby bungalow purpose-built on their own land. Tom would be as ever a cheerful and attentive host, ensuring everyone's glass was charged with whisky or whatever their choice might be.

In Bob King's case, it might have been rum. When he got back to Grandad's to spend the night, he went missing for a while. He had come without Grace for the wedding. It is not my imagination but memory that puts him on his hands and knees in the back garden, at the start of the strawberry rows. He may have shared his cousin Bobby's view of the whole affair. He may have been projecting his own experience onto the newlyweds. He may simply have been pissed out of his head. All he could be understood to say is that he was praying for Ted.

Daub would have pursed his lips at Bob's behaviour. I fancy he did not attend the registry office as Saturdays were a busy day at the roadside, leaving Nan Dinah free to do so while he looked after the shop. Although he may not yet have reached the stage of making much conversation with his new daughter-in-law – that was always a stretch for him – it is safe to say he and Nan liked and approved of both Iva and the marriage. Secretively prosperous after his retirement from the buses, he would retire from his roadside business too at the age of seventy. My grandparents had some years to go till their Golden Wedding, but they would make it, never fret.

Dad's briskness with bureaucracy had once again proved invaluable in the steep run-up to Ted and Iva's marriage. He had accompanied her to London, something to do at an embassy or consulate. She spent the night before the wedding in our house. Allen was not capable of holding a grudge like a Hills could; he had resumed his normal, generally affectionate attitude to Joyce. He had work again, pumping petrol at C & B Motors. Somehow he had become friendly with the two transplanted Cockneys who owned it, Colin and Brian. Making himself useful when a car drove over the forecourt cable to ring a bell for service, he was soon trusted to provide it so the boys could stick at their work under a car or elbow-deep in its motor.

Mum was nervous at any formalisation of this arrangement. She expressed concern that an incoming wage would prejudice his entitlement to benefits. Brian made some enquiries for Allen, and it was clarified that he could earn up to a certain amount, above what they would have been paying him anyway (from age sixteen I would also be on their payroll, making 15p an hour for twelve over each weekend). In the face of Dad's enthusiasm, she kept her other worry between herself and me. 'I know the benefit side's all right, David, but it's a matter of his self-respect as well. How do you think he'll feel if it doesn't work out, if he can't stick to it?'

While I heard no further mention of them separating, Mum was disappointed again when she proposed spending money to put a greenhouse in our back garden. The idea was to sell her own produce at Grandad's stall – tomatoes or bedding plants. Dad was against the idea. He never gave a definite reason, but she would not defy him. It was perhaps her last tilt at achieving a degree of financial independence. She would never be free of money worries, though we did not lack for anything. She had seen worse times by far, like those when Allen first became ill. Neither contentment nor idleness sat comfortably with her, but she had her pride, with good reason for it.

Although I have waved it as a convenient chequered flag, Uncle Ted's wedding was not itself a watershed moment in my life. More significant was the beginning of my fourth year at secondary school a month earlier, when we moved across the river to join the girls. It was never the intention in these pages to go beyond boyhood into youth.

Christmas 1970
(L to R) David, Iva, Ted partly obscuring Joyce, Allen, Shirley, Mandy, Grandad and Nana (with Tom taking the picture)

It hardly matters whether I have been the hero of my own narrative and all that David Copperfield guff. After completing an earlier draft, I asked some of those closest to me if they had any questions about my boyhood. I hoped anything they might come up with would be covered, since my goal was to record everything (almost) I could remember, a brain dump or compendium rather than stylish memoir. The only feedback I got was a shorter version of the Irish room-service waiter's famous enquiry to George Best: what went wrong?

Unlike the United legend, I could not point to thousands in readies on my bed and a ready Miss World in it. I could say there was no sign of troubles to come in Blocker's comments as form master on my 3A summer 1970 report. 'He has the determination and ability to succeed and has a bright future.'

But that is ducking the question. You took only three words. So I shall too.

I was outside.

There ended an earlier manuscript. While that close reflects an honest feeling, isn't it a trifle... overblown? And *The Outsider* is already taken. Let me offer a more positive and grateful conclusion, recognising that there has always been someone to watch over me, always people to love me. Although there were some dark corners in my boyhood, I was generally in the place where an official visitor to Princes Street in March 1956, before my adoption had been confirmed, found me 'asleep in pram on the sunny side of the house...'

THE END

Milton Keynes UK
Ingram Content Group UK Ltd.
UKHW030326270724
446123UK00003B/15